The Importance of Cognition in Learning

Dr. Sharon Campbell-Phillips

Dr. Sharon Campbell-Phillips

 pencil

ISBN 978-93-5458-341-4
© Dr. Sharon Campbell-Phillips 2021
Published in India 2021 by Pencil

A brand of

One Point Six Technologies Pvt. Ltd.
123, Building J2, Shram Seva Premises,
Wadala Truck Terminal, Wadala (E)
Mumbai 400037, Maharashtra, INDIA
E connect@thepencilapp.com
W www.thepencilapp.com

Author biography

My name is Dr. Sharon Campbell-Phillips. I am from Trinidad and Tobago. I am very enthusiastic about community work and the development of others. I am also very passionate about conducting research and writing as it allows me the opportunity to share my knowledge with others and educate them as well as enhance and develop myself.

I am currently employed with the local government of Trinidad and Tobago where I work at the Division of Community Development. This Division is dedicated to developing communities so that persons' standard of living can be enhanced.

My writing career began when I was approached by a classmate from Bangladesh to collaborate and write professionally. I accepted the challenge and we began writing together. When I received my first publication, I was very excited and was motivated to continue writing, I am also a Doctor of Health Sciences.

CONTENTS

Preface

Right here we are in the age of the records, relying on an idea of thoughts that is older than the wheel. every other folk's idea, folk physics, folk biology, people economics has needed to yield to greater powerful theories, higher geared up to address the issues of an adventurous civilization. In step with one tale, this has also befallen with theory of thoughts. Something known as 'cognitive technological know-how' arose inside the Nineteen Fifties and advanced rapidly. Its most conspicuous manifestations had been in synthetic intelligence and robotics, but it has had a full-size and every so often innovative impact on all of the behavioral sciences. although it can be real that maximum of the sector's commercial enterprise remains conducted consistent with folk theories of thoughts, this will be best a rely on cultural lag, in an effort to conquer as cognitive technology takes to maintain. The hassle with this story is that for maximum functions the effect of cognitive science has not been to update folk theory but to reinstate it, after its exile with the aid of behaviorism. I do no longer suggest to cut price the accomplishments of cognitive scientists in professional structures, language comprehension, etc. but the cognitive technology that produced these accomplishments has been rooted in the same primary conception of the mind that has been with us as a minimum in view that Plato's time, and that kids within the Western world choose up spontaneously by using the age of six. It's far this folk idea, along with its formalizations in cognitive theories, that has lately commenced being challenged. what's being challenged is the simple idea of the thoughts as a field of gadgets, beliefs, dreams, conjectures, remembered occasions, and so forth, which the thoughts work on in cognition. The challenges had been on diverse theoretical grounds. The plausibility, coherence, and explanatory adequacy of the people concept and its derivatives had been called into query. Critics commonly concede that schooling and thoughts in practical applications people idea do just first-rate. For maximum makes use of, this is authentic and for the exact reason. Our social institutions all embody the folk's principle. We ought to hardly ever make it thru a day indeed, may want to rarely make it across a hectic street without choices based on beliefs and intentions that we attribute to others.

It appears to us that the time has come to weave together the compelling developments affecting the training. Programs that includes the global Baccalaureate, the CCSS Initiative, the STEM schooling Coalition, and the NGSS call for greater rigorous requirements for college kids. The country-wide coaching requirements maintain the call for a brand new and extra rigorous sort of learner-centered, assignment-based totally classroom. Generation is linking people as in no way earlier than and is offering unparalleled get right of entry to records and expertise that spans the world. And neuroscience, cognitive technological know-how, and our collective understanding are joining forces and assisting us to draw close the nature of any learner as a complex, self-directed, dwelling system. The eBook you are holding to your fingers summarizes our passionate commitment to integrating all of the above tendencies as a way of shaping expert improvement and paves the way for a remarkably high-quality view of learning and training. Many humans answer the query in terms of memorizing greater records. However if neuroscience and cognitive science are to be taken critically, then the brain governs a great deal more than reminiscence by myself. The "brain/mind" deals with feelings, movement, creativity, immune responses, language, reasoning, planning, corporation, and dreaming. It permits us to enjoy compassion, interconnectedness, peace, and ambiguity. Upload to that the truth that the environment and stories affect people and their potential to exchange their own brains with the aid of the usage of a selection of processes to exchange their minds, and we're looking at a brand new definition of mastering. So the solution to the query calls for understanding that the body-mind—mind of every student constitutes an interconnected harmony engaged in a dance between their physiology and the environment. It ends in the attention that the brain is biologically designed to examine and that natural twelve mind/mind learning concepts in motion x studying is an issue of constructing wealthy neural networks. Every factor of the technique engages the dual dynamics of notion and action and has an effect on how someone interacts with the actual international. The Caines' at the beginning synthesized a whole lot of the research from many one-of-a-kind disciplines that elucidate those thoughts. For the reason that the functioning of the mind encompasses a lot, what are the implications for educators?

The Caines have cautioned that for schooling to be based on how humans analyze obviously, 3 vital factors want to be a gift: comfy Alertness: inexperienced persons want to be in supportive but tough and empowering social surroundings that elicits their pursuits, purposes, and meanings. They call this environment cozy Alertness.

Theories of all kinds ordinarily work nicely for ordinary purposes, but. Medieval physics lives on in the baseball park, wherein fly balls have "legs" that may or won't be sufficient to carry them over the outfield wall. Professional gardeners get along believing they may be providing food to the flora. however, if the mission is launching a missile into orbit in preference to over the left-discipline fence or doubling the yield of rice paddies, folk theories aren't up to the challenge. Folk theory of mind lives on, I accept as true, because it has in no way been positioned to severe assessments. Till now. How may a kingdom or an agency double its charge of information manufacturing? How do we teach a population to be know-how employees? How does a business enterprise emerge as a getting-to-know agency? Those questions pose novel challenges, which our historical concept of mind has in no way had to wrestle with. Also, they involve queer juxtapositions of terms— expertise manufacturing, understanding work, studying agency—resulting in expressions whose meaning is doubtful. These expressions don't, in truth, make a great deal sense below a idea that has know-how which includes items in people's minds. Yet there is a huge conviction that they consult with very essential matters. This is not a satisfied scenario. To correct it, I consider, we want a brand new concept of mind.

Introduction

The mind begins to mature even earlier than birth. Although it keeps maturing in the course of most of existence, the brain does no longer matures at an equal fee in each individual. This has to no longer be unexpected. In any case, our bodies develop at exceptional fees and we reach puberty at special a while and our emotional adulthood at extraordinary instances as well. Why have our brains been any distinctive? Just because you've got a school room complete of students who're about the identical age doesn't imply they are similarly equipped to learn a particular topic, concept, skill, or concept. It's far crucial for instructors and dad and mom to remember the fact that maturation of the brain affects studying readiness. For instructors, this is mainly critical while designing classes and choosing which strategies to apply. Distinct brain structures mature at extraordinary costs and observe different paths, but maturation starts lengthy before beginning. As a fetus grows, nerve cells (neurons) journey to their eventual places inside the brain. The survival of any individual neuron is not guaranteed. There is opposition among neurons for the restrained area and those that do not find a domestic; place wherein they could live and thrive are pruned again and destroyed. It isn't always yet acknowledged why a few neurons discover a domestic and others do not, but after a neuron settles down it keeps to develop and develop inside its area of the mind. While pruning does no longer happen or is incomplete, disorders in mastering and/or conduct can be the end result. Children research in distinct approaches. And despite the fact that the adulthood of the brain is a crucial aspect on the subject of studying variations, the real tale is extra complex than that. The way kids analyze relies upon age, stage of improvement, and brain adulthood. Mastering variations are also associated with genetics, temperament, and surroundings, however, in this module we are able to focus on how and while the brain matures. As a trainer, all children need to be challenged and nurtured so they can make the most of their education. Instruction that is above or below the adulthood stage of a toddler's brain isn't simplest irrelevant; it could also cause behavior issues to your classroom. Inappropriate behaviours which include avoidance, tough authority, and aggression towards other students can be defined by using a failure to healthy preparation to the mind adulthood of your college students. You ought to also recognize that each one mind features do not mature at an equal price. A young toddler with quite advanced verbal skills may broaden gross and nice motor control greater slowly and feature trouble getting to know to put in writing truly. Every other toddler can be superior bodily but no longer recognize how to manage his/her social abilities. Others may be cognitively superior however display emotional immaturity. For all of these reasons, it's miles crucial to apprehend how our brains mature as well as the differences that may be present at every degree of "ordinary" development. At every level of development, it is vital for teachers to understand the relationship between neurological development and getting to know. This knowledge is, in particular, critical whilst there's a mismatch between improvement and educational expectations. The mismatch can be because of brain maturational differences or it can be due to a developmental disability. Studies have observed variations in brain shape, activation, and improvement in kids with mastering disabilities, interest deficit hyperactivity ailment, and temper problems. In addition, research is needed in all of those regions.

Increasingly more we're getting to know that children with learning disabilities have brains that are extraordinary. With the use of magnetic resonance imaging (MRI), many studies have found that the brain vicinity concerned with matching sounds and letters is compromised in kids with dyslexia. These smaller brain areas correlate with poorer overall performance on checks of analyzing achievement, phrase assault, and speedy naming potential of letters, numbers, and items. The corpus callosum has additionally been determined to differ in children with dyslexia. The differences are observed in regions connecting regions worried in language and analyzing. These differences look like due to reduced costs of pruning for the duration of the 5th and seventh months of gestation. Useful MRI (fMRI) findings are beginning to suggest that youngsters with LDs process information otherwise from those without LDs. Frontal brain areas are extra green in fluent person readers in comparison to children who are starting to examine. As an infant develops, the left frontal region turns into extra active. However, fluent studying appears to be related to this place too. Extra fluent readers prompt this region more than kids with studying difficulties. Furthermore, children with mastering issues display greater activity inside the "wrong" places. As an example, their parietal and occipital areas are livelier, and they display greater pastimes inside the proper hemisphere than the left. In contrast, children without learning problems spark off the frontal regions and the left hemisphere with less activation within the proper hemisphere. Activation of the brain is greater diffuse while youngsters are starting to learn how to read. The activation step by step will become more specialized as analysis improves. Similarly, when asked to study unmarried phrases, ordinary readers show left-hemispheric activation, whereas people with dyslexia display greater right hemispheric activation. Brain regions in the left hemisphere and temporal area had been discovered to be more energetic in precise readers compared to folks who had compensated for their dyslexia and have been able to read accurately. In addition, Gabrieli (2003) determined that improvements were determined in activation following remediation of auditory processing capability. It isn't yet clear whether or not those adjustments maintain through the years; further study is wanted to recognize feasible mind responses to remediation. This locating is crucial due to the fact activation of the left hemisphere, a region specialized for language capabilities, performs a critical role in reading even as the proper hemisphere has commonly been implicated for the processing of novel stimuli. Since children with studying disabilities set off the proper hemisphere once they examine, this appears to signify that they locate studying to be an extra novel venture than a discovered undertaking. Early studying uses visual-perceptual tactics generally placed within the posterior portion of the mind. Because the reading manner turns into greater automatized, the frontal systems come to be greater active. thus, the progression from the simple letter and word calling to real reading comprehension calls for the maturation of neural pathways linking the again of the mind to the front. changes from proper hemispheric processing to left hemispheric processing have additionally been discovered to arise with improvement in analyzing capabilities and improvement in language functioning. Such changes aren't observed for youngsters with dyslexia, and their reading skills do no longer emerge as automatic and easy. Extra research is progressing in getting to know disabilities in older students.

Chapter One Cognition and Social Intelligence Chapter Two The role of Cognition in Learning Chapter Three Cognitive Psychology Chapter Four Academic intelligence Chapter Five Brain Research and Learning Chapter Six Autobiographical Memory Chapter Seven Cognitive Science and Problem Solving Chapter Eight Cognitive Styles and creativity Chapter Nine Cognitive Neuroscience Chapter Ten Learning and Developmental Disabilities

Chapter One

Cognition and Social Intelligence

Have you ever used or pay attention to the phrase cognition? Have you ever marvel what's cognition honestly approximately? What is its purpose, and is it doing anything for us except supplying any other fancy phrase to gloat about? Cognition is set how the thoughts do extremely good matters. It's the overall time period given for mental sports. In cognitive psychology, it is the study of higher intellectual processes; reminiscence, attention, language, reasoning, etc. in assessment to behaviorists; cognitive psychologists are extra prepared to posit mechanisms and techniques that aren't immediately observable, inclusive of reminiscence stores and switches of attention. Cognitive research consists of several extraordinary facets of mental lifestyles, such as using imagery in representation, strategies of decision making, and trouble fixing and reasoning. Cognition is all to do with memory. This involves applying our know-how of the arena around us as well as different cognitive tactics. The notion is a continuous cycle, in which what we anticipate to see affects what we look for and vice versa. Statistics obtained is certainly held in training for some future occasion. As we're storing this fact in our sub aware, it's miles known as long-term memory (LTM). The facts are saved right here prepared to be recalled later. LTM holds a considerable amount of data and may be saved for lengthy periods of time. The data kept in our LTM is diverse and wide-ranging and it includes all of our personal recollections, well-known experts, and our beliefs of the arena. It also holds our plans for the future and it's far the depository for all our understanding of competencies and information. In brief, cognition refers back to the approaches the mind goes approximately perceiving, remembering, and questioning. The technology of cognition is a branch of psychology. As some distance as sciences go, it hasn't been round that complete long. Cognition simply took keep as a critical technology inside the 1950s. It sprung up and began advancing swiftly, right in conjunction with some of its companion sciences, including pc technology, neuroscience, and linguistics. Cognitive psychologists are keen on speaking about a cognitive revolution that came about around that time. One of the leaders of that revolution, George Miller, shared feasible data reflecting again on his revel in and his feelings approximately cognitive revolution in those early years. The revolution commenced because psychologists weren't allowed to apply the phrase "thoughts." at the time, experimental psychologists wanted psychology to be the greater goal. They did this using that specialize in what they might all see. Conduct can be witnessed first-hand. Stuff happening within the thoughts could not. It was out of bounds. The rigid recognition of behavior brought about some thrilling gymnastics of jargon. You couldn't say language in professional circles, for example. Rather, the clinical time period changed into verbal conduct. You couldn't speak approximately reminiscence, because turned into inside the mind, so you needed to restrict yourself to discussing getting to know. Intelligence was interesting, as it positive feels like something on the inner. The manner around this became to outline intelligence as what an IQ check measures. You could see that. Psychologists genuinely learned plenty using stripping down their theories and focusing on what they might objectively measure. One element they discovered became that they honestly did need more than behavior to explain human psychology. Miller stated: As Chomsky remarked, defining psychology because the science of behavior became like defining physics because of the technology of meter reading. It commenced to become clean that to sincerely get everywhere, psychological scientists could need to think about how the thoughts work. They could want to apply a few principles approximately the thoughts to explain the behavioral information. But, they didn't want to head lower back to vintage words that had been used before Behaviorism got here alongside. Cognitive psychologists came into being, who, consistent with Miller, have been "unafraid of words like thoughts and expectation and perception and memory." A flurry of fascinating cognitive studies started to emerge by using the mid-fifties. Quick examples had been:

• George Miller posted what can be the maximum famous result from cognitive psychology, the paranormal range seven, plus or minus. The "magic number" has frequently been taken because of the span of quick-term memory.

• A examination of wondering, through Jerry Bruner, Jackie Goodenough, and George Austin took significantly the notion of cognitive techniques, which brings aim into the combination.

In the 1970s, cognitive psychology becomes prepared to

begin tackling sensible troubles. As an instance, it began to tackle troubles in education. This became a way for the science of cognition to reveal what it can do. It was additionally a manner for cognitive psychologists to check and enhance their theories with extra sensible problems. As Mayer factors out in his theory, troubles in training are regularly addressed through, "well-intended fads, expert reviews, and doctrine-based agendas." This hinders the development of instructional practice. What's wished are educational techniques based totally on studies evidence and examined theory. Cognitive psychology enables this. Mayer describes popular areas wherein cognition has contributed to training:

- Cognition of middle subjects
- Teaching of Cognitive techniques and Cognitive capabilities

Cognition and its techniques

Cognitive psychologists have helped pick out particular principles and skills needed for challenging areas. These include studying, math, technology, and history. A brief example for math is figuring out an appropriate knowledge had to learn how to upload and subtract two numbers. One factor that cognitive psychologists have tested is "variety sense." quantity sense approach that someone has the concept of several lines and skills to apply it. It can be tested by way of asking questions like "Is six or two toward five?" Mayer describes proof that having the intellectual wide variety line down is associated with mastering arithmetic. Cognitive studies with six-year vintage kids first showed that folks that knew the range line should analyze simple arithmetic fairly without difficulty. Those without variety experience had lots greater trouble. It's been estimated that half the coming into college students don't have it. In the next step, cognitive researchers tried educating youngsters on the intellectual variety line. They used numerous games, along with evaluating dice to see which range is higher. They examined their thoughts with the aid of evaluating a control organization that did not get hold of the education. Using the end of the year, twice as many educated students mastered basic arithmetic as did college students in the manipulation. The evidence confirmed the education to improve number feel turned into effective. This is however one example. Cognitive psychologists have carried out myriad studies that make contributions to mastering unique subjects in faculty.

Cognitive strategies are approaches the learner deliberately impacts getting to know and cognition. Examples encompass take a look at capabilities, such as techniques to enhance studying comprehension. They also consist of wondering talents, which include techniques for evaluating assets at the net. Masses of research have yielded evidence attesting to the effectiveness of some cognitive strategies. Mayer points out that work on cognitive skills and strategies represents a paramount contribution of cognition applied to education. With a stable research base constructed over the last numerous decades, we can now improve how college students examine and think by using assisting them in domesticate and use cognitive techniques. enhancing our information of the cognition underlying particular subjects, and of the cognitive strategies human beings use to tackle challenging intellectual work are just approaches cognition has aided education up to now.

Other areas of development encompass new methods of assessing getting to know consequences, new methods of considering intellectual capability (properly beyond what IQ checks measure), and new approaches of using computer systems for practice. At international Cognition, we've been exploring cognition "within the wild" to aid the development of complicated capabilities that are nevertheless poorly understood. For instance, we are operating to apprehend and improve the cognitive techniques people use to adapt to new cultures. Cognition has additionally made contributions in several other fields, along with clinical exercise, jury decision-making in regulation, advertising, and marketing, voter behavior in politics, the layout of airplane cockpits and the dashboard in your automobile, making computers that absolutely everyone can use (and ones which could suppose for themselves). And the listing is going on. There's a very good bet that's why the phrase is turning into increasingly famous and extensively used. The science of psychology has advanced dramatically within the last several a long time, propelled ahead by using the cognitive revolution. Now is the time to put extra of that top idea into exercise.

Intelligence, as described in general dictionaries, has instead distinctive meanings. In its most familiar which means, intelligence has to do with the individual's potential to study and purpose. It's this meaning which underlies common psychometric notions which include intelligence checking out, the intelligence quotient, and so forth. It's less common which means, intelligence has to do a body of data and know-how. This second means is implicated within the titles of sure government organizations, including the primary Intelligence organization inside the

US, and its British counterparts MI-5 and MI-6. Further, each meaning is invoked using the idea of social intelligence. As at the beginning coined with the aid of E.L. Thorndike (1920), the term referred to the individual's potential to apprehend and manipulate other humans, and to have interaction in adaptive social interactions. Greater lately, however, Cantor and Kihlstrom (1987) redefined social intelligence to consult the man or woman's fund of understanding about the social global. Human intelligence includes several interwoven abilities or wonderful forms of intelligence inclusive of abstract, practical, Emotional, Aesthetic, Kinesthetic, and Social. Initially, one of the most critical is social intelligence. Social intelligence can be defined as a combination of capabilities; knowledge, and interaction. Social intelligence is visible as attractive to many human beings and it is clear that there are numerous benefits. One of the blessings of social intelligence is readability. Clarity provides a hazard for humans to specific themselves clearly, explain concepts surely, and use their language efficiently. it's miles apparent that talents of this kind are vitally critical for human beings' everyday and commercial enterprise lifestyles due to the fact humans' everyday and enterprise lifestyles are already complicated and people want folks who can solve issues, make life easier, and explicit themselves actually. It's miles an undeniable fact that people who've social intelligence are typically a hit inside the business sector and they're visible as idols in society. Consequently, their social intelligence helps them to capture a golden opportunity. Some comedians together with Cem Yilmaz can be shown because of the pleasant example of this due to the truth that he is a success in his area and he's well-preferred by people. On the subject of the second point, another gain of social intelligence is the focus. Focus may be defined as understanding the social contexts which have an impact on discovered human behaviors and selecting the behavioral techniques most probable to be successful. In other phrases, to put it differently, it can be described as "reading situations". Consequently, it could be said that humans who have social intelligence can make higher decisions and determine higher strategies with the aid of the use of their social intelligence. There are plenty of benefits of social intelligence. Social intelligence is a crucial component for people to specific themselves truly, deliver clean clarification, and make informed decisions and judgments. Social intelligence is regularly greater approximately the future so it is clear that it's far a fundamental aspect to survive and succeed. It's far carefully related to cognition and emotional intelligence. Goleman's research suggests that our social relationships have a right away impact on our physical fitness, and the deeper the connection, the deeper the impact.

Cognitive intelligence

Then again, Cognitive intelligence is defined as the highbrow talents together with writing, studying, common sense, reading, cause, and prioritizing. Assessments conducted to degree cognitive capacity are used in performance evaluation. Such tests are used to degree and person's capacity to remedy troubles in diverse cognitive spheres. The distinction between emotional intelligence and cognitive intelligence is evidenced inside the psychometric checks of assessing cognitive ability and psychometric checks of intelligence. Cognitive intelligence as a latent trait is classified using psychometric checks. The cognitive potential is also assessed by using tests that alternate through the years; varying at age as well as intelligence. Almost about activity performance, cognitive intelligence has been diagnosed to relate to such activity performance dimensions as organizational citizenship conduct (OCB) and project overall performance. Even as OCB involves activities that might be crucial in attaining the organization's goals, even though not formally considered as part of a process, assignment performance concerns the number one noticeable duty which can be formally taken into consideration as a part of the job. Theoretically, cognitive intelligence fosters venture overall performance thru the know-how of guidelines, tactics, and facts applicable to the technical middle of the process. It further complements OCB thru such components as regulations, tactics, and information critical for powerful cooperating, supporting, and endorsement for the organization. Personnel taken into consideration restricted through their cognitive abilities may additionally reconsider focusing on the blessings of excessive emotional intelligence as they frequently document low job overall performance in most jobs. With low job performance, there may be a highly larger room for correction and improvement. As an instance, a sales clerk who fails to keep the hobby of viable clients is in all likelihood to decrease the possibility of mistakes in destiny. As such, failure to reap task overall performance through cognitive intelligence can be compensated for via complementary mechanisms underneath emotional intelligence. a number of the strengths of emotional intelligence are as follows: First, additional mechanisms include scalability at identifying and expertise the emotions of different individuals. That is possible within the working environment whereby organization individuals interact with coworkers, supervisors, guide group of workers, and with outsiders inclusive of sufferers, clients, and customers. Inside the technique of interacting, feelings are publicly displayed thru vocal, facial, and bodily indicators that relay vital messages about their intentions, attitudes, and dreams. For people with low cognitive intelligence and excessive emotional intelligence, such pertinent information may be transformed to excessive-danger overall performance. On the contrary, a character with excessive cognitive intelligence and occasional emotional intelligence can correctly discover the publicly displayed feelings to facilitate interpersonal functioning and coordination necessary for reinforcing venture performance. Additionally, statistics about other human beings' intentions, attitudes, and desires can be transformed into frequent OCB through individuals exhibiting low cognitive intelligence and excessive emotional intelligence. Such people can, for example, depict the want for assistance for individuals displaying anxiety and disappointment. Secondly, emotional intelligence can enhance the task performance of low-cognitive-intelligence people' thru regulating emotional effects to cater to social relationships. If a worker generates and displays actual emotions, in preference to fake ones, he/she is probable to obtain favorable reactions. Showing actual concern for coworkers' issues allows employees to expand stronger relationships than personnel showing less concern.

To broaden appropriate social relationships, individuals

with high emotional intelligence and low cognitive intelligence can also use their abilities to control emotions. With nicely hooked up and sturdy social relationships, there are better chances of enhancing task performance thru advice and social support. Further, beneficial running relationships will pretty prompt personnel to participate in OCB greater often to the gain of fellow workers. Thirdly, activity overall performance individuals with low cognitive intelligence may be more suitable with the aid of emotional intelligence thru the results of feelings at the people's mind and moves. people with low cognitive intelligence but wise emotionally can obtain high levels of undertaking overall performance and OCB in maximum jobs, by way of managing their emotions towards strengthening their motivation and exceptional in their decisions. as an example, the knowledge that anger leads people to undermine the level of chance in conditions activates managers to suppress anger whilst within the procedure of creating an important monetary selection; accordingly portraying superb task performance. Further, an employee that is aware of the significance of high-quality feelings in enhancing motivation will enhance advantageous feelings in the direction of accomplishing OCB. Even though open for discussion, it's been proven that emotional intelligence will often relate to the process performance of a person within the agency with low cognitive intelligence, and in turn, atone for the low cognitive intelligence. However, as cognitive intelligence increases, emotional intelligence needs to be less definitely associated with task performance. Emotional intelligence is associated with certain blessings. not like in 1918, the Intelligence quotient (IQ) is now rated twenty-four points better; a right away outcome of greater education, better nutrition, and smaller family sizes. However, the emotional quotient (EQ) is lower among the two intervals. The low EQ is evidenced with the aid of the behaviors common with kids in contemporary times; extra competitive, greater angry and unruly, more lonely and depressed, anxious, and susceptible to fear. Cases of crime and violence are at the upward thrust; drug abuse is persisting, cases of alienation and despair rising, undesirable pregnancies, faculty dropouts, consumption problems, or even bullying. In commercial enterprise and psychology, it has ended up a skip time to expect job overall performance. Whilst the overall performance evaluation is done comprehensively by the usage of facts from subordinates, peers, and superiors, EQ predicts a better performance three times as proper as IQ. Emotional intelligence contributes up to ninety percent for management via affect, group skills, self-assurance, political attention, and achievement drive. But, unsuccessful leaders, we depicted as being irritated, missing empathy, moody, protective and essential.

Incorporate setting and blue-collar occupations, emotional intelligence assessments had been hired in predicting fulfillment and failure. Furthermore, the tests had been instrumental in predicting aggression inside the place of business, academic dropout, capacity to recover from intense intellectual conditions, and potential to address severe clinical conditions.

Boundaries of emotional and cognitive intelligence

Even though many writers and scholars of intelligence have denoted the want for emotional intelligence as an important situation for effective leadership or effective leader-individuals family members, an empirical take looks at to scrutinize this link indicates otherwise. Contention and problems of controversy contact on the definition and methods of measurement or predicting emotional intelligence; and what EI is meant to degree or predict. Although it permits us to hold relationships and hold our movements beneath manage, emotional intelligence is variously dismissed as being just another control idea. More often than now not, organizations encourage their personnel to include emotional intelligence both for the duration of the hiring and development degrees of their careers on the company. Individuals with low emotional intelligence view the circulation with the aid of HR as an intrusion or problem into their non-public lives. Therefore, emotional intelligence cannot be found out overnight but requires time and effort to examine and exercise it efficaciously. Not like cognitive intelligence, this is measurable the use of psychometric exams, emotional intelligence is people capacity, and the dimension of the social skills among people is a frightening project. Numerous evaluations and attempts are required so as for a hit evaluation to be conclusive.

Cognitive potential and emotional intelligence

Businesses instituting leadership development programs depend on the comments of coworkers to have a clue of the way their leaders behavior themselves inside the place of work. Versions exist within the outcomes of employees' self-ratings compared to the scores by way of their supervisors, coworkers, and subordinates. Management improvement often specializes in number one abilities, abilities, and know-how that are taken into consideration essential to excessive-appearing people or effective leadership behaviors.

The crucial chief behaviors are defined and recounted in a manner that permits for his or her assessment and feeding again to the person. Once an analysis of the key tendencies is finished, the worried man or woman is inspired to grow their understanding of areas of strength and weak point, in flip driving the improvement of progressed management behaviors. As a way to improve the organization as well as the man or woman's performance, corporations make investments widespread resources into talent development the people at the management stage and above. As expected, increase inside the go back on investment factors to the innovative worker improvement strategies. Further to the management of talent improvement at some stage in a control-development initiative, it is critical to take into account the skills a company phrases important for development. Agencies are assured of better acting leaders championing higher returns on funding if investment within the right skills is a hit. In a similar tone, the lines of intelligence trying out motion are adhered to by roots of emotional intelligence. Numerous kinds of intelligence, which include social intelligence or the ability to act accurately in the direction of different individuals exist. This issue of intelligence has because its concept has been a frightening undertaking to measure, in comparison to measuring an individual's cognitive abilities. Despite the demanding situations, attempts to degree social intelligence have mounted that it's far composed of three factors: social information, mindset toward society, and degree of social justice. In addition, research changed into instrumental in coining of the concept of emotional intelligence, because of the presence of cognitive ability. It changed into some years later that emotional intelligence turned into brought to the mainstream public and turned into quickly embraced by using the management improvement community. Enterprise fee emotional intelligence as it provides a framework for the measuring and designing of emotionally-primarily based tender talents. Emotional intelligence is designed for use in organizational concepts, research, and exercise to expand the effectiveness of individuals both in management positions and places of business. Emotional intelligence in organizational outcomes has additionally been correlated with overall performance, and in particular with linkage to management performance. Research conducted by using Sosik and Megerian (1999) set up leaders with excessive emotional intelligence achieved higher than their low emotional intelligence colleagues. Overall performance on task-associated cognitive capacity responsibilities has also been related to emotional intelligence. A survey performed in 1997 on benchmark become performed on diverse groups. From the survey, Goleman (1998) determined eighty percentage of companies focused on looking to promote emotional intelligence in their employees via education and improvement. Whilst it was carried out in the course of the recruiting and assessment strategies, nearly 90 percent of preferred trends for entry-stage workers but had been correlated with emotional intelligence. Following the effects of various research conducted throughout groups across the world; it turned into conclusive that proof pointed to the significance of emotional intelligence for access and fulfillment in the place of business nowadays. Further, the inclusion of emotional intelligence abilities is critical as concluded with the aid of rural education research. Goleman (1998) in addition argues that as a way to practice emotional intelligence inside the workplace, a set of abilities have to exist: personal and social. In addition, a divergent view postulates that eight factors ought to be considered at the same time as imposing emotional intelligence in an organization. Those reservations get up because individuals differ in their abilities to deal with feelings; at the same time as others may additionally manage personal emotions and anxieties nicely, handling different human beings' feelings might show not possible. As such, researchers have concluded that individuals' underlying basis for their degrees of potential is neutral. Moreover, the human brain is taken into consideration plastic; ready to research at every given possibility. Variations in emotional abilities may be compensated, especially if the concerned events are willing to take in the venture.

The Psychometric View

The psychometric view of social intelligence has its origins in E.L. Thorndike's (1920) department of intelligence into 3 sides, relating the capability to apprehend and manage ideas (summary intelligence), concrete objects (mechanical intelligence), and people (social intelligence). In his classic method: "by social intelligence is meant the capability to recognize and control men and women, boys and ladies -- to act accurately in human members of the family". in addition, Moss and Hunt (1927) defined social intelligence as the "capability to get at the side of others", provided the most wide-ranging definition of social intelligence because the man or woman's "potential to get alongside people in well-known, social approach or ease in society, the know-how of social topics, and susceptibility to stimuli from other contributors of a group, in addition to insight into the temporary moods or underlying character traits of strangers". Using contrast, Wechsler (1939, 1958) gave scant attention to the idea. Wechsler did renowned that the image association subtest of the WAIS would possibly serve as a degree of social intelligence because it assesses the individual's capacity to recognize social situations. In his view, but, "social intelligence is just fashionable intelligence implemented to social conditions". This dismissal is repeated in Matarazzo's fifth edition of Wechsler's monograph, wherein "social intelligence" dropped out as an index time period. Defining social intelligence seems smooth enough, mainly by analogy to summary intelligence. While it came to measuring social intelligence, but, E.L. Thorndike (1920) mentioned truly ruefully that "convenient assessments of social intelligence are tough to plot. Social intelligence indicates itself abundantly in the nursery, on the playground, in barracks and factories and salesroom, but it eludes the formal standardized conditions of the testing laboratory and it requires humans to respond to, time to conform its responses, and face, voice, gesture, and mien as tools". though, true to the dreams of the psychometric culture, the abstract definitions of social intelligence have been quickly translated into standardized laboratory devices for measuring person differences in social intelligence (for additional reviews.

Social Intelligence test

The first of those was the George Washington Social Intelligence test which turned into composed of several subtests, which may be blended to yield a mixture rating. The subtests are:

- Judgment in Social situations;
- Reminiscence for Names and Faces;
- Commentary of Human conduct;
- Reputation of the intellectual States in the back of phrases;
- Recognition of intellectual States from facial expression;
- Social facts; and
- Sense of humor:

The first four subtests were employed in all editions of the GWSIT. The facial features and Social statistics subtests have been dropped, and the Humor subtest added, in later versions. Hunt (1928) initially verified the GWSIT thru its correlations with person occupational status, the number of extracurricular activities pursued via university college students, and supervisor scores of employees' potential to get at the side of people. But, a few controversies ensued approximately whether social intelligence should be correlated with persona measures of sociability or extraversion. Most vital, but, the GWSIT got here below instant complaint about its highly excessive correlation with abstract intelligence. For that reason, Hunt (1928) determined that aggregate GWSIT score correlated r = .fifty four with combination rating on the George Washington University intellectual Alertness check (GWMAT), an early IQ scale. A component evaluation through R.L. Thorndike (1936) indicated that the subtests of the GWSIT loaded tremendously on the same standard element because of the subtests of the GMAT. Woodrow (1939), studying the GWSIT with a far larger battery of cognitive assessments, located no proof for a unique issue of social intelligence. R.L. Thorndike and Stein (1937) concluded that the GWSIT "is so heavily loaded with the capability to work with words and ideas, that differences in social intelligence tend to be swamped with the aid of differences in abstract intelligence". The lack of ability to discriminate between the social intelligence and IQ, coupled with difficulties in choosing external criteria towards which the size will be proven, caused declining interest in the GWSI, and indeed within the complete concept of social intelligence as an awesome highbrow entity. Spearman's (1927) model of g afforded no unique location for social intelligence or path. Neither is social intelligence protected or may be implied, in Thurstone's (1938) list of number one mental abilities.

After a preliminary burst of hobby within the GWSIT work on the evaluation and correlates of social intelligence fell off sharply until the Sixties while this line of studies become revived in the context of Guilford's (1967) shape of intellect version. Guilford postulated a gadget of at least one hundred twenty separate intellectual abilities, primarily based on all possible mixtures of five classes of operations (cognition, memory, divergent production, convergent manufacturing, and assessment), with four classes of content (figural, symbolic, semantic, and behavioral) and 6 categories of products (gadgets, lessons, family members, systems, modifications, and implications). Curiously, Guilford considers his system to be a diffusion of the tripartite class of intelligence at the start proposed using E.L. Thorndike. As a result, the symbolic and semantic content domains correspond to abstract intelligence, the figural domain to practical intelligence, and the behavioral area to social intelligence. The greater differentiated system, social intelligence is represented because the thirty (five operations x six products) skills lying inside the area of behavioral operations. In assessment to its big work on semantic and figural content, Guilford's institution addressed troubles of behavioral content material best very past due of their software of studies. though, of the thirty sides of social intelligence predicted by using the shape-of-mind model, real tests had been devised for six cognitive abilities and six divergent manufacturing which described the category of behavioral cognition as representing the "capability to judge humans" with appreciate to "feelings, motives, thoughts, intentions, attitudes, or other psychological tendencies which may affect a person's social behavior". They made it clear that one's capacity to choose man or woman humans was not similar to his or her comprehension of people in popular, or "stereotypic understanding" (p. 5), and bore no a priori relation to one's potential to apprehend oneself. Reputedly, those factors of social cognition lie outside the same old shape-of-mind version. In building their exams of behavioral cognition, and it is assumed that "expressive behavior, greater mainly facial expressions, vocal inflections, postures, and gestures, are the cues from which intentional states are inferred". even as spotting the fee of assessing the potential to decode those cues in actual-lifestyles contexts with real humans serving as objectives, economic constraints pressured the investigators to rely on pics, cartoons, drawings, and tape recordings (the fee of the film became prohibitive); verbal substances were avoided anyplace viable, possibly to keep away from contamination of social intelligence using verbal skills. Within the very last analysis, O'Sullivan et. al advanced at least 3 extraordinary tests inside each product domain, which everyone takes a look at which includes 30 or more separate items by way of any widespread, a huge effort at principle-guided test creation. The six cognitive skills defined through O'Sullivan et al. have been:

- Cognition of behavioral gadgets: the capability to become aware of the inner mental states of people;
- Cognition of behavioral instructions: the potential to group with other humans' mental states on the premise of similarity;
- Cognition of behavioral members of the family: the ability to interpret significant connections amongst behavioral acts;
- Cognition of behavioral structures: the potential to interpret sequences of social conduct;
- Cognition of behavioral ameliorations: the capacity to reply flexibly in deciphering changes in social conduct; and
- Cognition of behavioral implications: the capability to expect what is going to manifest in an interpersonal situation.

After devising those checks, O'Sullivan et al. (1965) conducted a normative study wherein three hundred and six excessive-school students acquired twenty-three one-of-a-kind social intelligence checks representing the six hypothesized factors, together with twenty-four measures of twelve non-social capacity elements. A most important aspect evaluation with orthogonal rotation yielded twenty-two elements, inclusive of the twelve non-social reference elements and six factors truly interpretable as cognition of conduct. In trendy, the six behavioral factors have been now not contaminated through non-social semantic and spatial abilities. As a result, O'Sullivan et al. seemingly succeeded in measuring expressly social talents which were essentially independent of summary cognitive capability. However, echoing in advance findings with the GWSIT later studies determined widespread correlations between IQ and rankings at the man or woman Guilford subtests, in addition to numerous composite social intelligence ratings. Nonetheless, Shanley et al. conceded that the correlations received have been now not robust sufficient to warrant the belief that social intelligence is not anything extra than well-known intelligence carried out in the social domain. In one of the ultimate check-creation efforts by way of Guilford's group, Hendricks attempted to broaden exams for handling other human beings, no longer simply information them through their behavior -- what they knew as "fundamental solution-locating abilities in interpersonal members of the family". Because a hit coping entails the innovative generation of many and diverse behavioral ideas, these investigators labeled those divergent-questioning capabilities creative social intelligence. The six divergent production skills described by Hendricks et al. were:

• Divergent production of behavioral devices: the ability to have interaction in behavioral acts which talk internal mental states;

- Divergent production of behavioral lessons: the ability to create recognizable categories of behavioral acts;
- Divergent production of behavioral relations: the capability to carry out an act which has to touch on what any other individual is doing;
- Divergent manufacturing of behavioral systems: the capacity to keep a chain of interactions with any other person;
- Divergent production of behavioral alterations: the ability to adjust an expression or a series of expressions; and
- Divergent manufacturing of behavioral implications: the capacity to are expecting many feasible consequences of a putting.

As with the behavioral cognition abilities studied by using O'Sullivan et al. (1965), the very nature of the behavioral area raised critical technical issues for taking a look at development in the behavioral domain, mainly concerning contamination by using verbal (semantic) skills. Preferably, of direction, divergent production would be measured in actual-world settings, in phrases of real behavioral responses to actual people. Failing that, testing should rely on nonverbal behaviors such as drawings, gestures, and vocalizations, however, such checks should properly be contaminated with the aid of person variations in drawing, performing, or public-talking ability that doesn't have anything to do with social intelligence in keeping with se. still, following the pattern of O'Sullivan et al., (1965), a battery of creative social intelligence exams, twenty-two for divergent production of behavioral merchandise and another sixteen representing eight categories of cognition of conduct and divergent manufacturing within the semantic domain, turned into administered to two hundred and fifty-two high-faculty students. As is probably anticipated, scoring divergent productions proved appreciably more difficult than scoring cognitions, as within the former case there is nobody best solution and the difficulty's responses have to be evaluated through independent judges for best as well as the amount. The important components analysis yielded 15 factors, with six elements genuinely interpretable as divergent production within the behavioral area. Again, the divergent-manufacturing abilities inside the behavioral domain had been essentially unbiased of each divergent semantic production and (convergent) cognition in the behavioral area. A later look at with the aid of Chen and Michael (1993), using extra present-day factor-analytic strategies, essentially showed these findings. In addition, Chen and Michael extracted a hard and fast of better-order factors which in large part conformed to the theoretical predictions of Guilford's (1981) revised shape-of-intellect model. A similar re-evaluation of the O'Sullivan et al. (1965) has yet to be pronounced. In summary, Guilford and his colleagues were a success in devising measures for two as substitute exceptional domain names of social intelligence: knowledge of the behavior of other humans (cognition of behavioral content), and managing the conduct of other human beings (divergent manufacturing of behavioral content material). Those aspect capabilities have been notably impartial of each other within the behavioral area, and every change into also incredibly impartial of the non-behavioral abilities, as predicted (and required) by the structure-of-intellect model. despite the huge amount of effort that the Guilford group invested inside the dimension of social intelligence, it has to be understood that the studies of O'Sullivan et al. (1965) and Hendricks et al. (1969) went handiest a part of the manner in the direction of setting up the assemble validity of social intelligence. Their research described basically established convergent and discriminant validity, via displaying that ostensible exam of the numerous behavioral abilities hung together as predicted by way of the idea, and had been not contaminated through other abilities outside the behavioral area. As yet, there is little evidence for the ability of any of those checks to expect outside standards of social intelligence. assessments of the remaining 3 structure-of-mind domain names (memory, convergent production, and assessment) had no longer evolved by the point the Guilford application got here to a near. Hendricks et al. (1969) referred to that "these constitute by using far the finest variety of unknowns within the [shape of the intellect] model". However, O'Sullivan et al. (1965) did a comic strip out how those skills had been described. Convergent production in the behavioral area was described as "doing the proper thing at the right time", and presumably is probably tested through knowledge of etiquette. Behavioral reminiscence changed into defined because of the capacity to bear in mind the social characteristics of humans (e.g., names, faces, and personality trends), while behavioral evaluation becomes defined because of the capability to choose the appropriateness of conduct.

Convergent and Discriminant in Social Intelligence

Following the Guilford studies, several investigators

persisted the try to define social intelligence and determine its relation to preferred summary intelligence. Most of those studies explicitly rent the good judgment of the multitrait-multimethod matrix, using multiple measures of social and nonsocial intelligence, and analyzing the convergent validity of opportunity measures inside every area, and their discriminant validity throughout domain names. for example, Keating (1978) measured social intelligence with a battery of units such as relaxation's (1975) Defining problems take a look at, derived from Kohlberg's (1963) theory of ethical development; Chapin's (1942) Social insight test, which asks the subject to remedy diverse social dilemmas; and Gough's (1966) Social adulthood Index, a self-document scale derived from the California psychological stock measuring effective social functioning. Applying a multitrait-multimethod analysis, Keating found no proof that social intelligence, so defined, became discriminable from instructional intelligence. As a result, the average correlation among tests inside each area became truly lower than the corresponding average across domain names. at the same time as an issue evaluation produced two factors, each of those elements consisted of a mix of the two forms of intelligence take a look at. Eventually, Keating located that the three measures of summary intelligence were certainly higher predictors of Gough's (1966) Social maturity Index than have been the remaining two measures of social intelligence. However, it must be referred to that Keating's putative measures of social intelligence are particularly verbal in nature, so a few contaminations by using abstract verbal and reasoning capability are probably predicted. In reaction to Keating's (1978) look, Ford and Tisak (1983) conducted a good more tremendous examination related to over six hundred high-faculty students. 4 measures of verbal and mathematical capacity were derived from faculty information of grades and standardized test ratings. Social intelligence was measured with the aid of self-, peer-, and teacher-ratings of social competence, Hogan's (1969) empathy check, self-reports of social competence, and a judgment based on an individual interview. In comparison to Keating's (1968) effects, Ford and Tisak found that the measures of academic and social intelligence loaded on various factors. Moreover, the three ratings of social competence and Hogan's empathy scale have been greater especially predictive of the interview ratings of social competence than were the educational measures. Ford and Tisak attributed those effects to the choice of social intelligence measures in step with a criterion of behavioral effectiveness in social conditions, in preference to a cognitive knowledge of them. Put another way: measures of verbal ability, together with fashionable measures of IQ, are possibly to correlate particularly with verbal measures, however not nonverbal measures, of social intelligence. Similar findings have been obtained through several different investigators who assembled a big battery of personality measures ostensibly tapping diverse factors of social intelligence. Element analysis of those contraptions yielded five dimensions of social intelligence: hobby and issue for other people, social performance capabilities, empathic capability, emotional expressiveness and sensitivity to others' emotional expressions, and social tension and lack of social self-efficacy and self-esteem. Issue rankings on these dimensions of social intelligence had been essentially unrelated to measures of verbal and summary intelligence. In comparing studies, however, it has to be referred to that the apparent independence of social and fashionable intelligence may be at least partially an artifact of method variance. Unlike the GWSIT, and the batteries of cognitive and divergent-production measures devised via the Guilford institution, Marlowe's ostensible measures of social intelligence are all self-record scales, whereas his measures of verbal and abstract intelligence were the usual types of objective overall performance exams. The distinction in facts series strategies alone might also give an explanation for why the social and verbal/summary dimensions covered upon different factors. In any event, the measurement of man or woman differences in social intelligence via self-record scales is a prime departure from the tradition of intelligence testing, and it appears essential to verify Marlowe's findings the use of objective performance measures of the diverse sides of social intelligence. For instance, Frederickson, Carlson, & Ward (1984) employed an extensive behavioral evaluation process, on the side of a battery of overall performance exams of scholastic aptitude and success and clinical and non-clinical hassle solving. Further, every challenge performed ten interviews with simulated medical patients and nonmedical customers. Based totally on coding in their interview conduct, each subject obtained ratings of enterprise, warmth, and management. None of the measures of flair, fulfillment, or hassle-fixing conduct correlated appreciably with any of the interview-based ratings of social intelligence. Lowman and Leeman (1988), employing some of the overall performance measures, acquired proof for 3 dimensions of social intelligence: social wishes and pursuits, social expertise, and social capability. Interestingly, the correlations of all 3 dimensions with grade factor average, a proxy for educational intelligence, have been both null and poor. On the other hand, Stricker and Rock (1990) administered a battery of performance measures of social intelligence and discovered that subjects' accuracy in judging a person and a scenario portrayed in a videotaped interview was correlated with verbal capability. Wong, Day, Maxwell, and Meara (1995) constructed measures of social perception (accuracy in decoding verbal and nonverbal behavior), social perception (accuracy in interpreting social conduct), and social know-how (cognizance of the guidelines of etiquette). Thing analysis showed that social perception and perception were intently associated, neither of those dimensions became carefully related to social expertise, and not one of the social abilities was associated with a conventional educational capability. Expanding at the take a look at using Wong et al., Jones and Day (1997) primarily based their analysis on Cattell's (1971) distinction between fluid and crystallized intelligence. Within the social area, crystallized intelligence reflects the person's gathered fund of knowledge approximately the social global, which includes his or her vocabulary for representing social behaviors and situations; fluid intelligence, by comparison, reflects the man or woman's potential to quickly and as it should be remedy problems posed via novel social conditions. Jones and Day assembled four measures of every form of capacity, inclusive of verbal and pictorial overall performance measures, self-scores, and instructor rankings. Additionally, they had more than one measure of instructional potential. Confirmatory issue analyses checking out numerous precise fashions of the relations between social and academic intelligence indicated that crystallized social intelligence changed into discriminable from fluid social intelligence, however now not from instructional intelligence. definitely, more research using performance-based total measures is wanted before any definitive conclusions can be drawn about the family members among numerous components of social intelligence (convergent validity) and the members of the family among social intelligence and different intellectual talents (discriminant validity).

Social Intelligence as a Cognitive Module

An exception to the overall rule that social intelligence plays little position in clinical theories of intelligence is the principle of more than one intelligence proposed with the aid of Gardner. Unlike Spearman (1927), and other advocates of widespread intelligence. Gardner has proposed that intelligence is not a unitary cognitive capacity, however that there are seven (and perhaps greater) quite exclusive types of intelligence, every hypothetically dissociable from the others, and every hypothetically associated with a distinct brain system. Even as most of this proposed intelligence (linguistic, logical-mathematical, spatial, musical, and physical-kinesthetic) are "cognitive" abilities rather than harking back to Thurstone's number one mental talent, two are explicitly personal and social in nature. Gardner defines intrapersonal intelligence as the person's capacity to advantage get admission to his or her own inner emotional life, and interpersonal intelligence as the character's potential to note and make differences among other individuals. although Gardner's (1983) couple of intelligence is individual-variations constructs, wherein some human beings, or some agencies, are assumed to have extra of those capabilities than others, Gardner does no longer rely on the traditional psychometric approaches -- scale creation, issue analysis, multitrait-multimethod matrices, outside validity coefficients, and so forth. For documenting man or woman variations. As a substitute, his favored method is a really impressionistic analysis based on a convergence of symptoms supplied using eight different lines of evidence. chief amongst those symptoms are isolation by way of brain harm, such that one form of intelligence may be selectively impaired, leaving different kinds exceedingly unimpaired; and top-notch instances, individuals who possess tremendous tiers of ability in a single domain, in opposition to a history of regular or even impaired abilities in different domain names (as an alternative, a person can also show surprisingly low ranges of capacity in one area, towards a heritage of regular or particularly excessive levels of ability in others). So, for instance, Gardner (1983) argues from neurological case research that harm to the prefrontal lobes of the cerebral cortex can selectively impair non-public and social intelligence, leaving other skills intact. The conventional case of Phineas Gage may serve as an instance. However, "the man with a shattered world", sustained harm in the occipital and parietal lobes which significantly impaired the maximum of his highbrow capacities, but left his personal and social competencies enormously intact. Gardner also notes that while each Down syndrome and Alzheimer's disease have extreme cognitive effects but little impact on the man or woman's capability to get in conjunction with other human beings, pick out's sickness spares at least some cognitive capabilities even as seriously impairing the individual's capacity to interact with others. In related work, Taylor and Cadet (1989) have proposed that three distinct mind systems offer the neurological substrate of social intelligence: a balanced or integrated cortical subsystem which is predicated on long-time period memory to make complex social judgments; a frontal-dominant subsystem which organizes and generates social behaviors; and a limbic-dominant subsystem which rapidly produces emotional responses to activities. However, it should be noted that, aside from emotion (for an authoritative summary, studies at the neurological underpinnings of social cognition and behavior are tremendously impressionistic and speculative (for an evaluation of neuropsychological tactics to social cognition and social intelligence). With recognition to first-rate individuals, Gardner offers Sigmund Freud and Marcel Proust as "prodigies" inside the domain of intrapersonal intelligence, and Mahatma Gandhi and Lyndon Johnson as their counterparts inside the domain of interpersonal intelligence. Each of those people; Gardner claims, displayed high stages of personal and social intelligence towards a background of greater "normal" talents in different domain names. On the terrible side, Gardner notes that infantile autism significantly impairs the person's ability to apprehend different humans and navigate the social world. Similarly, Gardner postulates numerous other signs and symptoms suggesting unique kinds of intelligence. Among these are identifiable center operations, coupled with experimental tasks which allow an analysis of these core operations and psychometric assessments which monitor individual variations' incapability to perform them. With admiration to social intelligence, of the route, the core operations are those which shape the center of studies on social cognition: character notion and impression formation, causal attribution, man or woman memory, social categorization, affect control, etc. The social cognition literature gives numerous paradigms for analyzing those operations, of the route, and every so often these experimental approaches had been translated into strategies for the analysis of character differences. For instance, Kaess and Witryol (1955) studied memory for names and faces; Sechrest and Jackson (1961) tested character variations within the capacity to expect other people's conduct in various types of conditions, and Sternberg and his colleagues have assessed man or woman differences inside the capability to decode nonverbal communications. Whether the core operations concerned in social cognition vary qualitatively from that concerned nonsocial cognition is, but, an open query. Whilst perceiving emotion in a face may additionally appear to vary qualitatively from mentally rotating a photograph of the letter R, an operating assumption in maximum social cognition studies is that the underlying mental techniques are similar to the ones deployed in nonsocial cognition. Therefore, for example, studies on prototypes in character perception become meant as a reasonably direct translation of Rosch's (1978) pioneering work on fuzzy-set procedures to nonsocial classes. And at the same time, as it's miles pretty viable to indicate that the perception of faces, the ones most social of stimuli, follows unique guidelines and is mediated by a special mind location, latest experimental and neuroimaging evidence suggests that face popularity is certainly an example of broader expertise for figuring out objects at subordinate stages of categorization. One probably vital difference among the social and nonsocial domain names, of course, is that in social cognition the object (i.e., the individual) represented in the observer's thoughts is shrewd and conscious. As a result, the character being perceived might also try to manage the impression shaped by way of the perceiver through a variety of affect-management techniques. To complicate matters in addition, the perceiver can be aware of the opportunity of strategic self-presentation, and hence modify his or her perceptions for this reason, even as the man or woman being perceived may additionally modulate his or her influence-management sports to be able to decrease those corrections. Such interplay rituals are not probable to occur in nonsocial perception and cognition. Further to experimental and psychometric evidence, Gardner (1983) additionally assumes that qualitatively distinct varieties of intelligence will display unique developmental histories. From an ontogenetic factor of view, then, the hypothesis is that the acquisition and mastery of talents in the social domain follows an exclusive developmental trajectory, from infancy through formative years and adulthood to old age than different capabilities. in addition, from a phylogenetic point of view, the hypothesis would be that personal and interpersonal abilities hint at distinct evolutionary pathways as well. Therefore, Gardner locating that humans and chimpanzees, however now no other primates (and no longer different mammals) skip the reflect-photos at of self-reputation. Finally, Gardner argues that each form of intelligence is encoded in a unique symbol device by way of which the potential in question may be manipulated and transmitted by way of a subculture. For a number of his proposed intelligence, the existence of the image gadget is reasonably obvious: written language, mathematical symbols, and musical notation are clear examples. As evidence suggestive of special non-public symbol systems, Gardner cites Geertz's (1975) ethnographic work in Java, Bali, and Morocco, which revealed vast cultural variety inside the approach with the aid of which humans keep a feeling of self and the policies which govern their social relations -- non-public and social intelligence that's obtained via socialization. Truly, the English language includes a huge vocabulary of words -- 17,953 by way of one rely on that may represent humans' cognitive, emotional, and motivational states, behavioral inclinations, and different psychosocial characteristics. And within Western culture, systems like the traditional fourfold classification of temperament (melancholic, phlegmatic, choleric, and sanguine; Kant, 1798/1978) and the big five persona dimensions (neuroticism, extraversion, agreeableness, conscientiousness, and openness to experience; John, 1990) are normally employed to capture and speak the gist of another person's character.

The Prototype of Social Intelligence

Although social intelligence has proved tough for psychometricians to operationalize, it does seem to play a major role in humans' naive, intuitive ideas of intelligence. Following up on earlier work, Sternberg and his colleagues requested subjects to list the behaviors which they considered a function of intelligence, educational intelligence, regular intelligence, and unintelligence; extra companies of topics rated every of two hundred and fifty behaviors from the primary listing in terms of how "function" each became of the best individual possessing each of the three varieties of intelligence. Component evaluation of scores provided using laypeople yielded an aspect of "social competence" in each context. Prototypical behaviors reflecting social competence were:

- Accepts others for what they may be;
- Admits errors;
- Presentations interest inside the international at huge;
- Is on time for appointments;
- Has a social sense of right and wrong;
- Thinks before speaking and doing;
- Shows interest;
- Does now not make snap judgments;
- Makes honest judgments;
- Assesses nicely the relevance of records to a hassle to hand;
- Is touchy to different humans' needs and goals;
- Is frank with self and others; and

Presentations hobby within the immediate environment

Apparently, a separate dimension of social competence did not continuously emerge in rankings made by way of a collection of intelligence experts. As an alternative, the specialists' dimensions focused on verbal intelligence and problem-fixing capability, with social competence expressly emerging only in the ratings of an appropriate "almost smart" person. Possibly these specialists shared

Wechsler's (1939) dismissive view of social intelligence. A comparable study turned into executed and primarily based largely on earlier studies by using Orlik (1978), those investigators assembled a list of 18 capabilities that make up human beings' implicit idea of social intelligence. When subjects have been asked to fee how vital every characteristic became to their own personal understanding of social intelligence, the following dimensions emerged as most important to the prototype:

- Knows human beings' thoughts, emotions, and intentions well;
- Is ideal at managing people;
- Has large expertise of policies and norms in human relations;
- Is right at taking the perspective of other humans;
- Adapts nicely in social situations;
- Is heat and worrying; and
- Is open to new studies, thoughts, and values.

In any other part of the observation, subjects have been asked to rate a person they preferred on every one of these attributes. After statistically controlling for differential likability of the traits, an element analysis yielded a clear size of social intelligence, defined through the attributes listed above. The ultimate two factors have been named social affect and social memory. A current psychometric have look at social intelligence used a methodology similar to that of Sternberg et al. (1981) and Kosmitzki & John (1993). Schneider, Ackerman, and Kanfer (1996) requested topics to generate descriptions of socially equipped behavior. Those descriptors were then collated and reduced to form a Social Competence Questionnaire, in which subjects are asked to fee the quantity to which each object defined their standard social conduct. An aspect evaluation found out seven dimensions of social competence: extraversion, warmth, social influence, social perception, social openness, social appropriateness, and social maladjustment. Composite rankings on these dimensions have been basically uncorrelated with measures of quantitative and verbal/reasoning potential. On the premise of these findings, Schneider et al. concluded that "it's time to put to relaxation any residual notions that social competence is a monolithic entity, or that it is simply popular intelligence implemented to social situations". As with Marlowe's (1986) have a look, however, the reliance on self-report measures of social intelligence compromises this conclusion, which stays to be showed the use of goal performance measures of the diverse dimensions inside the social area. Sternberg et al. (1981) has noted that during comparison to specific theories of intelligence, which try to explain what intelligence is, implicit theories try to capture human beings' views of what the word intelligence means. Social intelligence performed a little function in Sternberg's early componential view of human intelligence (however see Sternberg, 1984), which changed into supposed consciousness on reasoning and hassle-solving skills as represented by conventional intelligence exams. However, social intelligence is explicitly represented in Sternberg's extra latest triarchic view of intelligence. Consistent with the triarchic concept, intelligence is composed of analytical, innovative, and practical abilities. Realistic intelligence is described in terms of problem-solving in regular contexts and explicitly includes social intelligence. According to Sternberg, every form of intelligence reflects the operation of three specific sorts of component procedures: overall performance additives, which clear up troubles in various domains; government meta-components, which plan and compare problem-fixing; and expertise-acquisition components, by which the first two components are learned. To complicate things similarly, Sternberg (1985, 1988) argues that the measurement of all types of intelligence is sensitive to the context in which it is assessed. This may be particularly the case for practical and social intelligence: for instance, the correct solution to a question of social justice may well be distinctive if it's far posed in a corporate or navy context. For Sternberg, those abilities, and therefore their underlying additives, can be really impartial of each different. There is no implication, as an instance, that a person who is sturdy on analytical intelligence may also be sturdy in creative and sensible intelligence. In any event, the relation among numerous highbrow competencies is an empirical question. Answering this query, of the path, calls for that we've got ok gadgets for assessing social intelligence -- exams which adequately sample the domain in query, similarly to being dependable and valid. At gift, these instruments do not seem to exist. However, future investigators who want to make the striving probably properly suggested to start with the intuitive idea of social intelligence held in the thoughts of the layperson. In any case, social intelligence is a social construct, now not simply an educational one.

Personality as Social Intelligence and Cognitive views of personality

In assessment to the psychometric procedures reviewed

above, the social intelligence view of persona does no longer conceptualize social intelligence as a trait, or institution of trends, on which individuals can be compared and ranked on a size from low to excessive. Instead, the social-intelligence view of personality begins with the idea that social conduct is clever -- that it's mediated by way of cognitive strategies of belief, reminiscence, reasoning, and hassle-fixing, in place of being mediated with the aid of innate reflexes, conditioned responses, evolved genetic packages, and the like. For that reason, the social intelligence view construes man or woman variations in social conduct -- the general public manifestations of persona -- to be fabricated from individual variations in the expertise which individuals deliver to undergo on their social interactions. Variations in social understanding cause variations in social behavior, however, it does not make experience assemble measures of social IQ. The important variable isn't always how a lot of social intelligence the person has, however as a substitute what social intelligence she or he possesses. The social intelligence view of persona has its origins in the social-cognitive culture of personality concept, in which construal and reasoning strategies are relevant to troubles of social version. for this reason, Kelly (1955) characterized human beings as naive scientists producing hypotheses about future interpersonal events primarily based on a set of personal constructs regarding self, others, and the world at big. These constructs had been idiographic with recognition to both content material and enterprise. people have probably ranked in phrases of the complexity in their private assemble structures, however, the essential trouble for Kelly changed into knowing what the man or woman's personal constructs were. Past complexity, the idiosyncratic nature of private construct systems precluded lots of nomothetic contrast.

Whilst Kelly's idea becomes extremely iconoclastic, comparable developments befell in the evolution of social getting to know theories of persona. The preliminary formulation of the social getting to know the idea, an aggregate of Freudian psychoanalysis and Hullian mastering concept, held that personality became in large part found out the conduct, and that understanding personality required information the social situations underneath which it turned into received. but, the sluggish upward push of cognitive theories of gaining knowledge quickly lent a cognitive taste to social mastering idea itself. as a consequence, addiction and power performed the little role in Rotter's (1954) cognitive social learning theory. In contrast to advance behaviorist conceptions of organismal responses to environmental stimuli controlled with the aid of objective contingencies of reinforcement. Rotter argued that the individual's behavior contemplated selections that followed from their goals in a particular state of affairs and their expectancies of the results in their behavior. in addition, Bandura argued for the purchase of social information via principle and instance rather than the direct enjoy of rewards and punishment, and later (1986) distinguished among the expectations of the final result emphasized by using Rotter (1954) and expectancies of self-efficacy - the person's judgment of belief concerning his or her potential to carry out the movements required to acquire manage over the activities in a situation. Self-efficacy affords the cognitive foundation for motivation, however, it has to be understood that judgments of self-efficacy are noticeably context-specific. Although Rotter (1966) proposed a character-difference measure of inner vs. external locus of control, it would by no means arise to Bandura to propose a nomothetic instrument for measuring person variations in generalized self-efficacy expectancies. The essential consideration is not whether or not an individual is notably excessive or low in self-perceptions of competence, but alternatively whether or not the character feels capable to perform a selected behavior in some unique state of affairs. The instantaneous predecessor to the social-intelligence view of character is cognitive social-gaining knowledge of reconceptualization of persona. Even though now and again couched in behaviorist language, provocative critique of the trait method to personality was explicitly cognitive in nature: "One must realize the... that means that the stimulus has acquired for the situation. The assessment of the obtained meaning of stimuli is called the core of social behavior evaluation. For this reason, know-how character variations in social conduct call for information on individual differences inside the meaning given to conduct, its final results, and the state of affairs in which it takes place.

This emphasis on the subjective which means of the state of affairs marked Mischel's early concept as cognitive in nature. because that time, Mischel (1973) has broadened his conceptualization of character to include an extensive range of different constructs, a few derived from the sooner work of Kelly, Rotter, and Bandura, and others reflecting the importation into character theory of concepts originating within the laboratory study of human cognitive processes. All are construed as modifiable personal differences, merchandise of cognitive improvement, and social learning that decide how functions of the scenario can be perceived and interpreted. Accordingly, they contribute to the development of the means of the stimulus scenario -- in other words, to the cognitive production of the situation itself -- to which the man or woman in the long run responds. From Mischel's (1973) point of view, the most critical made of cognitive development and social mastering is the man or woman's repertoire of cognitive and behavioral creation capabilities- the capability to interact in a huge type of skilled, adaptive behaviors, including both overt movement and covert intellectual activities. These creation abilities are as close as Mischel receives to the psychometric belief of social (or, for that count, nonsocial) perception of intelligence. The significance of belief and interpretation of occasions in Mischel's machine requires a second set of man or woman variables, having to do with encoding strategies governing selective interest and private constructs -- Kelly-like categories which filter human beings' perceptions, memories, and expectations. Then, of the path, following Rotter and Bandura, Mischel additionally stresses the role of stimulus-final results, conduct-outcome, and self-efficacy expectations concerning the consequences of environmental activities and personal behaviors, in addition to self-efficacy expectations. Additionally, in step with Rotter's theory, Mischel notes that conduct might be ruled by way of the subjective values associated with various outcomes. A very last set of relevant variables consists of self-regulatory structures and plans, self-imposed dreams, and results that govern behavior in the absence (or in spite) of social video display units and outside constraints.

The development of Social Intelligence

Even though the psychometric and personality views of social intelligence are opposed to many important factors, inclusive of the matter of comparative assessment of people, they arrive together nicely in recent work on the improvement of social intelligence. Of path, social intelligence has usually performed a position in the concept of intellectual retardation. This psychiatric analysis calls for now not only proof of subnormal highbrow functioning but additionally demonstrated evidence of impairments in "conversation, self-care, home dwelling, social and interpersonal talents, use of community assets, self-path, useful educational talents, work, leisure, health, and protection" (American Psychiatric affiliation, 1994, p. 46). In different words, the prognosis of intellectual retardation involves deficits in social in addition to academic intelligence. Moreover, the wording of the diagnostic standards means that social and academic intelligence isn't noticeably correlated -- it calls for fantastic evidence of both kinds of impairment, which means that the presence of one cannot be inferred from the presence of the other. While the traditional diagnostic criterion for mental retardation places primary emphasis on IQ and highbrow functioning Greenspan (1979) has argued that it needs to emphasize social and practical intelligence as a substitute. To this give up, Greenspan proposed a hierarchical version of social intelligence. In this model, social intelligence consists of three additives: social sensitivity, meditated in function-taking and social inference; social insight, including social comprehension, psychological insight, and moral judgment; and social verbal exchange subsuming referential conversation and social trouble solving. Social intelligence, in turn, is best one issue of adaptive intelligence (the others being conceptual intelligence and practical intelligence), which in flip joins bodily competence and socioemotional adaptation (temperament and person) because the essential dimensions of personal competence extensively construed. Greenspan did no longer suggest particular checks for any of those components of social intelligence, however, implied that they will be derived from experimental tactics used to look at social cognition in preferred.

All that is nice and correct, however whilst the criterion for impaired intellectual functioning is in reality operationalized using an IQ threshold, there's as yet no fashionable with the aid of which impaired social functioning -- impaired social intelligence can be decided. The Vineland Social maturity Scale became an important step in this direction: this tool, which yields mixture rankings of social age (analogous to mental age) and social quotient (by using analogy to the intelligence quotient, calculated as social age divided through chronological age). but, it is a telling point that this instrument for comparing social intelligence and different aspects of adaptive conduct became delivered almost a half-century after the primary but its adequacy as a measure of social intelligence is compromised by using the truth that linguistic capabilities, motor capabilities, occupational capabilities, and self-care and self-route are assessed in addition to social relations. As an alternative, Taylor (1990) has proposed a semi-established Social Intelligence Interview masking such domains as social reminiscence, moral development, the popularity of and reaction to social cues, and social judgment. However, Taylor concedes that such an interview, being ideographically constructed to take account of the character's unique social environment, cannot easily yield numerical ratings by way of which individuals may be as compared and ranked. extra essential than ranking people, from Taylor's factor of view, is pick out areas of high and low functioning inside numerous environments skilled by using the person, and to determine the goodness of match among the man or woman and the environments wherein she or he lives. This latter intention, of the route, is a primary thrust of the social intelligence view of personality espoused with the aid of Cantor and Kihlstrom (1987). A further step far away from the psychometric emphasis on ranking in the direction of the social-cognitive emphasis on widespread strategies is illustrated using the latest developments in studies on autism. particularly, it's been proposed by using Leslie (1987) and Baron-Cohen (1995), among others, that autistic children and adults lack an "idea of thoughts" using which they can attribute mental states to different human beings and replicate on their personal intellectual lifestyles. For example, Baron-Cohen, Leslie, and Frith (1985) cautioned that the core deficit in autism is that the affected kids are unable to appreciate that other people's ideas, attitudes, and reports might differ from their own. This speculation brought the problem of assessing social intelligence in disabled populations (including intellectual retardation and getting to know incapacity as well as autism; directly in touch with literature at the improvement of social cognition in everyday children which were rising since the Nineteen Seventies. on this manner, the medical information of social cognition in widespread started to persuade research and concept on individual variations in social cognition.

Nevertheless, the hassle remains. Is the core deficit in autism one among social intelligence, as Baron-Cohen (1995) claims? on this appreciate, it is exciting to word, together with Gardner (1983), that autistic people can show an impaired capacity to understand others' intellectual states, but spared abilities to deal cognitively with nonsocial objects and occasions, as well as to recognize social conditions where they are now not required to understand another man or woman's know-how, perception, feelings, and dreams. On the other hand, Bruner and Feldman (1993) have proposed that these deficits in social cognition are secondary to deficits in widespread cognitive functioning. As a result, although research on regular and odd development is extra closely in contact with widespread social-cognitive theory than before, the fundamental questions undergo: Is social cognition a separate college from nonsocial cognition? Is social intelligence something one of a kind from fashionable intelligence implemented to the social area? As psychologists are keen on saying, in addition, studies are wanted to answer those questions. But, we can hope that future research on social intelligence will have a unique individual than it has had inside beyond. one of the maximum salient, and distressing, capabilities of the history of intelligence is how little contact there has been between the contraptions through which we examine person differences in highbrow potential and our knowledge of the techniques which deliver the cognitive substrate of intellectual capacity. The IQ check, as soon as touted as "psychology's maximum telling accomplishment up to now" is nearly entirely theoretical, having been pragmatically built to version the sorts of matters which youngsters do in college. So too with social intelligence, which all too regularly has been conceptualized informally, and assessed by using a jury-rigged assortment of assessments. perhaps new theoretical tactics, together with the social-intelligence view of the character and the "principle of thoughts" view of development, will exchange this example, so that destiny opinions of this kind could be capable of describing checks of social intelligence which are grounded in an understanding of the overall social-cognitive strategies out of which man or woman variations in social behavior emerge. From a cognitive point of view, Mischel's "cognitive-social gaining knowledge of character variables" all constitute the person's expertise and expertise -- intelligence -- concerning him- or herself and the encircling social world. This social intelligence is classed into two broad categories: declarative know-how, along with abstract standards and particular memories, and procedural knowledge, which includes the guidelines, abilities, and strategies by way of which the character manipulates and transforms declarative knowledge, and interprets information into motion. The individual's fund of declarative knowledge, in turn, may be broken down further into context-free semantic memory about the arena in standard and episodic reminiscence for the occasions and stories, every related to a unique spatiotemporal context, which makes up the individual's autobiographical document. Similarly, procedural information can be sub-categorized in terms of cognitive and motor talents. Those principles, personal memories, interpretive rules, and motion plans are the cognitive systems of personality. Collectively, they constitute the knowledge that publications a person's approach to fixing the issues of social life.

Chapter Two

The Role of Cognition in Learning

What is Cognition, and what is its courting to learning? We've got all visible a schoolroom of students sitting and looking their trainer impart upon them the historic know-how in their elders (or teaching them nation capitals; each is vital). Did you ever wonder what turned into going on internal their heads? Just how do the records they may be taking a turn out to be actual understanding? Nicely, wonder no greater, because nowadays we're going to walk thru the manner of how we learn through cognition. The first aspect we need to do is define keywords: cognition and learning. Cognition is the manner of acquiring and knowledge understanding through our mind, studies, and senses. Gaining knowledge includes obtaining understanding via enjoying, look at, or being taught. In case you assume that these two principles are awfully similar, you're right. Each is inexorably linked - getting to know requires cognition and cognition entails studying. Each time you notice or listen to something new, you undergo a series of cognitive processes, which can be the procedures that result in gaining knowledge. Cognition refers to mental interest such as wondering, remembering, gaining knowledge of, and the use of language. While we apply a cognitive technique to learning and teaching, we awareness at the information of statistics and ideas. If we're capable of recognizing the connections among principles ruin down data and rebuild with logical connections, then our retention of cloth and information will grow. While we are privy to these mental movements, monitor them, and control our learning techniques it's far called metacognition, which varies from scenario to scenario, will significantly affect how individuals behave in a given situation. The expertise of language, or psycholinguistics, is critical to our knowledge of print and oral acquisition of know-how. Comprehension and belief will permit people to interpret facts. Step one inside the cognitive gaining knowledge of manner is attention. Which will start studying, a student should be paying attention to what they are experiencing. As anyone who has been in a class full of youngsters knows, attention isn't unlimited and may be quite fleeting. Academic psychologists have come to the belief that the common man or woman can keep approximately two or three found out duties in their attention at the equal time. This means if you are attempting to dirt and vacuum concurrently you will be capable to drag it off but throw in consuming a sandwich and odds are exact you may take a chunk from your duster and smear lunch meat at the walls. We additionally recognize the common person can best attend to at least one complicated assignment at a time. Trying to drive and do long department? Not going to show up. Talk on the cellphone at the same time as waltzing? Unlikely, in case you're questioning, that is additionally a compelling reason to now not speak on the phone and force - you simply do not have enough interest to do every challenge absolutely. Subsequently, the facts to which you are being attentive have to be placed into reminiscence in a method known as the garage. There are three levels of reminiscence thru which statistics should tour to be truly discovered. Shall we say that for the first time you pay attention that the capital of the country of Oregon is Salem? This information is now to your sensory sign-up, which holds the entirety you are uncovered to for just a second or. By the cease of this sentence, you could have already forgotten the capital of Oregon. In case you pay interest and reread the sentence, but, that statistics will move from the sensory sign up into brief-term memory. This vicinity of your memory will keep information everywhere from twenty seconds to as much as a minute. In case you rehearse the statistics, which include repeating it to yourself, taking notes, or studying it, it has the chance to move for your lengthy-time period reminiscence. This location will preserve facts indefinitely and has an infinite capacity. The task, as we shall see, can be in finding things in there. Now which you've paid attention and moved the information into reminiscence, your brain must arrange this fact so it can be retrieved later. Encoding can work via several methods, together with growing verbal mnemonics or the delightfully named method of loci, but the ultimate goal is to assign a selected that means to something you've got discovered. The mnemonic for remembering the planet's order involves thoughts: 'My Very educated mother just Served Us Nachos.' consider this and you could speedy don't forget the names and order of all of the planets. Retrieval is going hand-in-hand with encoding by using actually reversing the method of encoding. If you want to remember which planet is fourth from the sun, just run thru your mnemonic and you have your answer. Since the fourth phrase is mother, the fourth planet is Mars!

Studying is also described because of the everlasting trade in people's thoughts, voluntary or involuntary. It occurs through a revel in that can bring about a rather permanent trade in an individual's knowledge or conduct. Behaviorist defines getting to know as the adjustments in an individual's mind resulting in permanent exchange. it is studying that takes region intentional or unwillingly in individuals. Cognitive psychologist defines mastering as the adjustments in the information that can be an inner mental interest that cannot be discovered at once. Learning involves acquiring and modifying information, abilities, strategies, beliefs, attitudes, and behaviors to apprehend old or new statistics. People learn capabilities from studies that tend to take the form of social interactions, linguistic or motor capabilities. Academic professionals define gaining knowledge as an 'enduring exchange in behavior or inside the ability to act in a given style which ends from exercise or other varieties of experience'. One may additionally ask how getting to know occurs. Learning occurs every day to each character, it doesn't simplest occur in the lecture rooms, schools, or universities homes however it can show up anywhere and every day. Studying can occur through interacting with others, gazing, or genuinely simply paying attention to communication. Mastering takes place via reports precise and horrific, or ones that can provoke an emotional reaction or virtually offer a second of revelation. Behaviorist and cognitive theorist believed that gaining knowledge may be affected by the environment a man or woman resides however behaviorist targeted greater on the position of the surroundings and the way the stimuli is supplied and set up and the responses reinforced. Cognitive theorist then again agrees with behaviorist but tend to cognizance greater on the learner's competencies, beliefs, values, and attitudes. They accept as true that learning occurs by way of consolidation that is the forming and strengthening of neural connections which encompass the factors organization, rehearsal, elaboration, and emotion. studying takes place in lots of approaches, psychologists accept as true with that getting to know is the important thing concept of dwelling whether or not it's intentional or accidental that is why they got here up with the studying theories.

Studying theories are taken into consideration theoretical frameworks in describing how facts are included, refined, and maintain during learning. Getting to know is an important pastime inside the lives of individuals; it's far the core of our instructional procedure, even though learning starts in the study room. For many years psychologists sought to recognize what's learning, the nature of it, how is it transpired, and how individuals impact studying in others through teaching and similar endeavors. Gaining knowledge of theories tend to be based on scientific evidence and more valid than private critiques or stories. There are five basic sorts of theories used in instructional psychology which are: Behavioral, Cognitive, Social & Cultural, and Constructivism.

Behavioral concept: The behavioral method is the behavior view that usually assumes that the outcome of mastering is the trade-in conduct and emphasizes the effects of inner events on an individual. in the behaviorist approach, they believed that people haven't any loose will and that the surroundings and character is an area in determines their behavior. They accept as true that people are born with a clean slate and that behaviors can be discovered from the environment. The getting to know theories from the behaviorists Pavlov, Guthrie, and Thorndike have historical importance on mastering. Although they'll vary each concept has its very own technique of forming associations among stimuli and responses. Thorndike believed that responses to stimuli are strengthening whilst it's accompanied via a fulfilling consequence. Guthrie reasoned that the relation between stimulus and responses is installed via pairing. Pavlov, who evolved classical conditioning, established how stimuli can be conditioned to obtain positive responses whilst being paired with any other stimulus. The behavior theory is expressed in conditioning theories that explain gaining knowledge of within the phrases of environmental occasions but are not the only conditioning concept. B. F. Skinner developed the Operant conditioning; this shape of conditioning is based totally on the assumptions that the features of the environment serve as cues for responding. He believed that we learn how to behave in sure approaches as we function in the environment. In operant conditioning, reinforcement strengthens the responses and will increase the probability of occurring whilst the stimuli are present. Operant conditioning is a 3-term contingency that includes the antecedent (stimulus), the behavior (response), and the outcomes. Operant conditioning involves consequences that can decide how people respond to environmental cues. Results can be either precise or terrible for people; it may reinforce conduct that increases it or a reinforcement that decreases conduct. There are other operant conditioners which include generalization, discrimination, primary and secondary reinforcements, reinforcement schedules, and the Premack principle. Shaping is any other shape of operant conditioning, it is the manner used to alter behavior in individuals. Shaping is the successive approximations that involve reinforcing development. It's the complex behaviors that might be shaped by the linking of simple behaviors within the three-term contingencies. This operant conditioning entails self-law which's the system of obtaining a man or woman stimulus and reinforcement manipulate of themselves.

Cognitive idea: The cognitive concept specializes in the internal sports of the mind. The cognitive theory states that expertise is discovered and the adjustments in knowledge make the modifications in conduct viable. Both the behavioral and cognitive ideas trust that reinforcement is important in studying however for special motives. The behaviorist shows that reinforcement strengthens responses however cognitive propose that reinforcement is a supply of feedback approximately what is possible to show up if behaviors are repeated or changed. The cognitive technique shows an essential element inside the studying procedure is the knowledge a character has closer to a scenario. Cognitive theorists accept as true that the statistics we already realize determine what we will understand, study, remember, and neglect. There are three important theorists of cognitive development Gestalt, Kohler, and Koffka. Gestalt gaining knowledge of principle technique proposes that gaining knowledge of consists of grasping of a structural whole and not just a mechanistic response to a stimulus. The principle concept of his idea becomes that once we procedure sensory stimuli we're privy to the configuration or the overall pattern that is complete. Kohler's idea said that studying can occur via a 'surprising comprehension' as to gradually information. This concept may want to take place with no reinforcement and there will be no need for an overview, education, or investigations. Koffka's idea recommended that he supported the fact that animals are can be members in studying because they are much like human beings in lots of methods. He believed that there has been no such element as meaningless learning and that the concept of interdependent of facts changed into more vital than knowing many person facts.

Social & Cultural principle: The social and cultural principle is based on how individuals functioning are associated with cultural, institutional, and historic context. Vygotsky was a psychologist in Russia who identified the Social & Cultural idea additionally called sociocultural principle. The Sociocultural principle is known as the combining principle in psychology as it mentioned the crucial contributions society makes on a man or woman's development and cognitive views of Piaget. The principal cautioned that gaining knowledge occurs between the interactions of humans. Lev. Vygotsky believed that mother and father, Caregivers, friends, and subculture played a vital in the improvement of an excessive order characteristic. In keeping with Vygotsky, each characteristic is the kids' cultural improvement that appears twice: first off on the social stage, secondly on a man or woman stage. The social-cultural theory tends to consciousness no longer handiest on how adults or peers influence gaining knowledge of but how a person culture can impact how studying takes place. In line with Vygotsky, kids are born with fundamental constraints on their thoughts. He believed that each tradition affords 'tools of highbrow version' for every man or woman. Theses variation permits children to apply their fundamental intellectual capacity to conform to their culture as an example a way of life may also apply tools to emphasize on memorization strategies. Vygotsky becomes a top-notch man, he worked alongside Piaget in growing the cognitive concept their theories range in positive ways. Firstly Piaget's idea becomes basically based totally on how children's interactions and explorations encouraged development; Vygotsky positioned extra emphasis on the social factors that influence improvement. any other distinction is the Vygotsky advised that cognitive improvement may be one-of-a-kind between cultures at the same time as Piaget's idea recommended the development is prevalent. There may be one essential concept in the sociocultural theory referred to as the sector of proximal. The quarter of proximal is considered to be the extent of impartial problem solving and a stage of ability development, thru hassle solving under the steerage of an adult or with friends. It consists of the skills that someone can not recognize or perform on their personal but, but is capable of getting to know with guidance.

Constructivism theory: The constructivism mastering idea is described as how novices or individuals assemble knowledge from previous stories. Constructivism is frequently related to a pedagogic approach that regularly promotes studying or learning by using doing. The building is known as the means for studying because constructivism makes a specialty of the person considering getting to know. The constructivist concept argues that people can generate expertise from interactions between studies and thoughts. Constructivism examined the interactions among people from infancy to maturity to attempt to understand how gaining knowledge is completed from studies and behavior styles. The constructivist concept is attributed to Jean Piaget who articulated the mechanisms via pointing out that information is internalized via rookies. Piaget stated that thru the techniques of model the accommodation and assimilation, individuals can construct new information from beyond studies. By Piaget's principle of constructivism, lodging is the method of a character reframing one's mental view of the world and tries to match in new stories. Accommodation may be understood while failure results in gaining knowledge of, as humans if we have a concept that the arena works simplest one manner and that way fails us then we can fail. In lodging, we examine our failure or the screw-ups of others. The constructivism principle describes how getting to know takes place whether or not the people learn from the use of their reviews to apprehend facts or by way of simply following instructions to assemble something. In both cases, constructivism proposes that learners construct know-how from reviews. The constructivism theory has a tendency to be associated with active mastering because5 individuals learn from reviews, something that becomes already did. Several cognitive psychologists argued that constructivist theories are deceptive or can contradict findings. As an educator you can facilitate studying by encouraging my college students, assisting them to increase to their fullest capacity. As an educator, you are forced to vie and asses learning patterns so that you can meet each pupil's needs in the study room. As an educator, I want to intend to permit students to research steadily. You would you're your students to thrive academically and socially inside and outside of the study room. From the know-how, the four gaining knowledge of theories mentioned would all make contributions to my understanding of studying. Despite all the specific theories, every principle gave me a brand new insight on gaining knowledge of what occurs inside and out of a category, university, or college. From the Behaviorist angle view of getting to know is the trade-in conduct and emphasis of outside events on an individual. For instance, Pavlov test in classical conditioning, in which he taught dogs to salivate once they pay attention to the tuning of a fork. If we used each conditioning theory with the school rooms can educate college students to act and operant within the way they would need them to. The idea that may be utilized in tune is the Behaviorist idea, I say this because the track is the incorporating information and feeling. song units the ecosystem for an environment as an instance if a calming song is being played at domestic, that track puts the man or woman in a chilled temper, in the behaviorist theory the environment influences the reaction of an individual so the enjoyable track will evoke a relaxed reaction as finished in Pavlov test of classical conditioning with the dogs that initiate salivating while hearing the tuning of a fork. In tune classical conditioning is where college students may be conditioned to love or experience a chunk of the song. as an instance, if a classical tune is being played that the scholars don't recognize or like the instructor can play it time and again as a way to get a knowledge of it, and eventually, the students will experience the tune because of the repetition of the tune being played.

Gaining knowledge of and Cognition

Learning begins from the first actual days of human lifestyles. Humans discover ways to walk, the way to carry out complicated obligations, and how to cooperate with different people. People have tried to recognize what mastering is in the course of centuries. There are numerous techniques to this issue. However, all researchers agree that gaining knowledge is intently connected to such concepts as cognition. Although, there are researchers who challenge this assumption pointing out that there are cases while gaining knowledge is viable without cognition. To recognize the connection between cognition and getting to know, it is vital to take a better have a look at the concept of learning. Firstly, it is important to provide a proper definition for the idea of learning. A few humans see mastering as "an outcome of the social reviews inside and outside of schools to which young humans are exposed". However, it's far clear that getting to know is going past lecture room surroundings. Humans collect expertise and benefit from new abilities in a variety of settings. Ellstrom (2011) affords a greater comprehensive definition of studying, "studying is a system of information acquisition thru skilled-based totally changes in cognition or movement". Consequently, gaining knowledge happens in diverse settings, but it's far related to positive changes, i.e. acquisition of knowledge and abilities that's, in its flip, related to cognition. It's important to be aware that behaviors perform an essential function in studying. For instance, lively humans can be uncovered to an exceptional amount of records that can be learned easily. At the same time, a few human beings find it rather tough to concentrate as they're regularly distracted via several matters. Loss of attention can cause problems at the same time as mastering. Appreciably, those who are much less active aren't exposed to new information as they tend to be in settings they recognize perfectly properly, i.e. they stay at the secure facet. Curiously, behavior and learning are regarded in terms of the evolutionary technique. Capability to collect know-how and actively use it is associated with the potential to live on inside the animal international. this will additionally be implemented to the current global as those who gather greater expertise have masses of opportunities, e.g. they get better jobs and get greater assets, and many others. Other than distinctive types of conduct, there are styles of studying. Accordingly, mastering may be specific and implicit. Explicit studying is frequently related to training. Human beings are explicitly exposed to sure information. They are trying to apply a ramification of techniques to facilitate gaining knowledge. For instance, college students attempt to memorize statistics, and that they train the capabilities they have obtained. Adult humans additionally must analyze new competencies, e.g. expert, communicative, management skills, and so forth. As a way as implicit studying is involved, it happens without education or more attempt. As has been stated above, human beings are frequently exposed to a lot of data. They memorize information, faces, and locations without greater effort. That is a function of the human cognitive capacity to perceive and procedure statistics. Therefore, the two sorts of getting to know to assist humans to gain information and broaden cognitive abilities. Sincerely, learning and cognition are interrelated. Researchers claim that there may be no mastering without cognition. Admittedly, people learn matters after they have processed facts cognitively. It is easy to offer an instance to this concept. A five-year-antique child may be given a mission to build a toy residence. The kid will be given major elements of the residence, i.e. four partitions and the roof. There can be no problems and the child may be able to build the toy house as he has the vital experience, i.e. he/she has visible plenty of houses. but, if the kid may be proven (and given commands on) how to construct the toy house fast, he/she will be able to spend much less time constructing the residence as the child has visible the way to do it, i.e. have received revel in. consequently, the kid looks at and touches the components of the residence and gets information about the cloth and form. The child pics homes he/she has visible in his/her life. This allows the kid to place the components of the house collectively. Next time, the child will be able to complete the same mission much quicker. Admittedly, if the child had no longer had the instructions and positively enjoy, he/she would no longer be capable of carrying out the challenge. Even though a few researchers claim that cognition isn't an integral part of learning as studying without cognition is also feasible. But, those theories are but to be researched and level-headed. To sum up, it is feasible to word that mastering and cognition are interrelated. People get the sizeable majority of information because of their cognitive skills. Humans perceive items and benefits enjoy through mastering, implicit, or express. it is also essential to add that conduct performs an essential function in gaining knowledge of, in particular when it comes to implicit getting to know.

Wondering

The Cognitive studying principle explains why the brain is the maximum super network of information processing and interpretation within the frame as we research matters. This theory can be divided into two unique theories: the Social Cognitive concept (SCT), and the Cognitive Behavioural concept (CBT). While we say the phrase "studying", we normally suggest "to suppose using the brain". This basic concept of learning is the primary point of view in the Cognitive gaining knowledge of idea (CLT). The principle has been used to explain intellectual techniques as they're prompted by using each intrinsic and extrinsic factor, which result in mastering in a man or woman. The cognitive learning concept means that the special techniques regarding learning may be defined by reading the intellectual tactics first. It posits that with effective cognitive procedures, studying is easier and new records can be saved inside the reminiscence for a long time. On the other hand, useless cognitive techniques result in getting to know problems that may be visible every time during the lifetime of an individual.

Social Cognitive concept: inside the Social Cognitive idea, we are thinking about 3 variables:

- Behavioural elements
- Environmental factors (extrinsic)
- Personal elements (intrinsic)

Those three variables in the Social Cognitive principle are said to be interrelated with every other, inflicting getting to know to occur. A man or woman's private experience can converge with the behavioral determinants and the environmental factors. internal person-environment dating, person wondering, standards, and cognitive competencies typically are altered with the aid of manner of outside elements say for instance an aid figure, tense surroundings, or maybe a warm climate. Inner person-behaviors relationship, the particular cognitive operations of the person affect his behaviors; moreover, a standard overall performance involving this sort of behavior can also adjust how he or she believes. Lastly, the specific environment-behavior dating, outdoor factors can remodel how you show the precise behaviors. Moreover, your behaviors make a distinction and regulate your environment. This specific type truly means that for useful and optimistic gaining knowledge to occur anyone should have constructive personalized functions, present perfect behavior and stay in any aid environment. Additionally, Social Cognitive speculation publicizes in which completely new encounters should be evaluated via the Spanish scholar using way of inspecting his past encounters even as using specific equal determinants. Locating out, therefore, is because of an intensive evaluation with the present-day knowledge versus manner back whilst. The Social Cognitive hypothesis includes many essential techniques with a purpose to monitor now not in reality at some stage in older humans however further at some stage in toddlers, children, and teenagers. Locating out from others by using a way of seeing these people is a powerful technique of reaching expertise and converting conduct. accomplishing things when there is truly a good to take the time to properly beautify the repeating of the behavior through the way of placing your particular within a secure environment having commonly available products for you to inspire him or her so that it will aid the absolutely new know-how and conduct learned and exercise these human beings. Self-efficacy; the specific observe route whilst the particular Spanish scholar will increase his these days found out know-how or maybe behavior by way of placing the object instantly into the workout. Over emotional; exceptional coping systems next to anxious surroundings and destructive customized functions can cause beneficial finding out, mainly all through older humans. Self-regulation is the ability to control behaviors even in destructive surroundings. Cognitive Behaviour speculation: Cognitive Behaviour speculation describes the precise motive regarding knowledge (knowing) a good way to determining and forecasting the specific behavioral recurring of a person. This unique concept was evolved through Aaron Beck. The precise Cognitive Behaviour hypothesis states ladies and men tend kind self-concepts wherein affect the unique conduct they will display. Those varieties of strategies are normally constructive or maybe unfavorable which enable it to be laid low with any man or woman's environment. The behavioral getting to know hypothesis states that people's behaviors are found out, as a result, many behaviors are normally unlearned and new behaviors are learned for the duration of their spot. Behaviorism can be worried in general about having the observable and measurable factors of a person's behavior. Consequently, any time behaviors become mistaken, they may be unlearned. Behaviorism landscapes improvement due to the fact a continuous process at some stage in which children enjoy a passive motive. It's also a popular method that's utilized in lots of specific settings which encompass both clinical and academic. Behaviorists count on how the virtual stuff normally is actual (or at the least well worth reading) could be the items we will easily discover and observe. Maximum of us cannot begin to see the thoughts, the specific identity, or maybe the specific other than conscious, nonetheless, we can easily examine how persons behave, respond and conduct themselves. Through conduct, lots of us just may help to make inferences approximately the brains and additionally the mental schools, but they aren't the primary emphasis with the evaluation. Precisely who accomplish, genuinely not what precisely they will trust or even actually experience, will be the difficulty can be analyzed? Likewise, the particular behaviorist doesn't take a look at out as their pharmaceutical counterpart or maybe the mind as a way to apprehend the reasons for abnormal behavior. This person assumes how the conduct represents certain found out exercises, and his or her efforts to view that they usually are learned. The unique stuff that's researched is obviously conducted. Certainly due to the fact behaviorists aren't eager on as their pharmaceutical counterpart, or maybe their plenty more ratified equivalents for instance psyche and heart and soul, inferences approximately the occasions wherein hold and bolster human conduct is normally made from the take a look at regarding canine behavior. Creature studies have supplied a crucial foundation in your behavioral method. The behavioral researcher is keen on understanding the particular systems underlying the behavior related to both everyday men and women and those having troubles that can be referred because of "mental contamination". Within the occasion the behavioral kind is applied to mental contamination, the item is generally for numerous introducing issues. It's most possibly greater power for the duration of the treatment of behavioral issues and troubles of impulse control, for example, excessive drinking, weight issues, or maybe erotic issues. Behavioral strategies can be quite helpful all through remedy approach concerning stress and tension and feature in reality once in a while been recently beneficial at some point of the management related to extra excessive mind problems as schizophrenia.

Records of Cognition and getting to know

Ivan G. Pavlov is Russia's maximum famous scientist. This individual first received outstanding differences for his research around the physiology of the gastrointestinal tract. Pavlov encountered any methodological issue that became ultimately for you to verify more vital and plenty greater useful in contrast along with his physical research. This character had found "conditioning". Concerning Pavlov, many behaviors had been reflexive. But take region this kind of behaviors fluctuate from the specific conduct generally named "instinctive"? Instinctive behavior would possibly likely be suggested to be endorsed. The pet has to be hungry; if you want to sexually become on, to have nest-constructing hormones preceding to those styles of instinctive behavior can take area. However, Pavlov concluded that at this time there seems to be no foundation for precise concerning reflexes and what exactly possesses normally been currently checked out as non-reflexive conduct. To be a shrink, Pavlov has been worried approximately the frightened approach, and in particular the specific cerebral cortex, honestly not having nearly any lawfulness that he would possibly uncover in the course of behavior. Bob B. Watson has been one of the most vivid personalities for the duration of history regarding mindset. Even though she or he failed to invent behaviorism, he or she has become widely recognized because of their key spokesman and protagonist. Watson has been expanded internal not unusual history: machine factors out conduct. Inside a popular eBook (Watson, 1914) she or he said how the analyzing of the mind would be the area concerning college of thought; it's the field concerning supposition and infinite idea online video games. As their pharmaceutical counterpart does not have any put in place mindset. Studies of psychology need to be determined via goal phenomena and additionally, the very last rationalization needs to become obtained inside the precise center worrying technique. It had been Watson, extra than Pavlov or maybe any other person, who satisfied psychologists how the actual evidence related to behavior put inside the traumatic device and in which as quickly as a lot of us grasped the thoughts a touch higher, the sizeable majority of the mysteries should vanish. in addition, it honestly changed due to the reality regarding Watson in which so many psychologists stumbled on assuming that what exactly they will call conditioning has been so critical. Preceding behaviorism has been involved approximately stimulus-response connections. Skinner checked the mastering process internal contrary technique, checking out the wayfinding out has been tormented by stimuli shown right after an amazing behave turned into carried out. This person determined any precise stimulus induced the particular affected character to reflect an excellent act more regularly. This character named stimuli with this species affects the precise "re-enforcers". Watson observed in which through giving reinforcement within a methodical approach an unmarried ought to shape the unique behavior at some point of famous suggestions. Url to operant instructors have benefited probably the maximum from Skinner's vital function in reinforcement as a way related to stopping and inspiring university student behavior. Its various applications so that it will lecture room exercise are usually named "behaviors modification", a way many teachers bear in mind to get absolutely considered one of their most important tools for improving each locating out and behavior of their scholars.

Operant conditioning: Operant conditioning (or a key component conditioning) is a form of locating out at some point of which a person's behavior is altered using their antecedents and outcomes. A key thing conditioning becomes initially found out and printed by Jerzy Konorski and has been added called type II reflexes. Mechanisms related to a key thing conditioning declare that the particular behavior may also adjust during type, frequency, or even power. The unique expression "operant conduct" and "respondent conduct" ended up popularized using B. F. Skinner who labored on imitation regarding Konorski's research. The unique ex- is the time period for "an item related to conduct that's at the beginning spontaneous, rather than a response to any previous stimulation, although as their consequences may bolster or even avoid recurrence of the behavior". Operant conditioning: this conditioning is thought from established conditioning (or respondent conditioning) due to the fact operant conditioning refers back to the precise reinforcement and outcome to replace behavior. Operant behaviors run across the surroundings and are likewise preserved through their antecedents and results, even though established conditioning is preserved by way of conditioning regarding reflexive (reflex) behaviors, which are probably elicited by way of antecedent circumstances. Behaviors skilled through an established conditioning method aren't preserved by way of results. These human beings each, however, type the precise crucial involving conduct evaluation and feature absolutely produced straight into professional strategies. Time-honored conditioning: even though operant conditioning takes on the largest cause during talks related to behavioral structures, hooked up conditioning (or Pavlovian conditioning or maybe respondent conditioning) is moreover a vital behavior-analytic technique that requires absolutely now not consider thoughts or maybe different inner operations. Pavlov's studies having pet puppies offer most of the people of acquainted example with the mounted conditioning manner. inside clear-cut conditioning, the dog has been supplied any stimulation say as an instance lighting or maybe a valid, and then meals have been slipped into the particular canine's lips. From a handful of reps on this series, the precise lights or even sound alone precipitated the canine for you to salivate. Although Pavlov recommended some touchy physical operations that would be worried about installed conditioning, that kind of never had been currently set up. Whilst cognitivism and behaviorism usually are each sensible finding out hypotheses, cognitivism possesses overshadowed behaviorism due to the fact the fundamental point of view.

For the ultimate decades and lots greater strictly inside the alternate with the century, behaviorism will now not keeps the precise dominance the item while offered like a locating out concept. sadness having behaviorism as a thoughtless manner for finding out, cognitivism and its subcategories regarding a couple of cleverness, brain-primarily based finding out and learner-fashion locating out have usurped behaviorism because most of the people of broadly appropriate and carried out hypotheses in recent times. Even though behaviorist hypotheses monitor finding out when it comes to firmly seen behavior even as the use of Spanish student like a passive man or woman related to knowledge through manner of stimulus-response dating at the same time as the usage of surroundings, cognitivism views the unique Spanish student simply as one energetic participator interior locating out process. Cognitivist spot better fascination with knowledge, this means, motives, feelings, ingenuity, expectations and concept tactics in addition to cognitive set united states and operations for example ram, expertise, problem-fixing, expertise, hobby, and idea- finding out. No matter the giant large distinction between the two hypotheses the truth that behaviorists will not keep in mind the mind operations in which underlie cognitive finding out concepts cognitivist and behaviorists speak about the same thinking. The two assume locating out hypotheses has to be goal and counting on the final results involving empirical research. The two take notice of the responses men and women help to make so that you can numerous stimulation situations. The two hypotheses trust in comments. The two focus on the particular effect environment possesses upon the precise Spanish student.

Sooner or later, each thinks information influences locating out. You could discover, needless to mention variations inside the specifics of the idea. On account of that accomplishes modern cognitivism, behaviorists offered the belief that finding out concept must be objectively counting on the outcome regarding empirical records. However, behaviorists cannot examine the internal cognitive operations in which create the unique responses they will document thinking about that the technological innovation has been non-existent. Â Behaviourists selected never to comprise thought conditions within their finding out hypotheses, quarreling in which this form of conditions ended up now not viable to see and evaluate consequently can't emerge as researched objectively. Cognitivism agrees wherein payback aids affect finding out and behaviors. Those human beings simply take difficulty concerning the motive of in which pay returned. Mind-primarily based studies have tested how the intellectual faculties include an innate pay lower back method named endorphins. Cognitivism appears a lot greater in the manner men and women process the particular stimuli they will come upon.

Cognition and learning styles

Cognitive styles are described as man or woman variations in modes of organizing and processing data in memory. Frequently, cognitive patterns are described as the hyperlink between character and cognition or a missing piece in know-how self. Over thirty unique fashion labels are classified into fashion households, the Wholist-analytic (WA) and the Verbalizer-Imager (VA) dimensions. Those dimensions of cognitive styles are fundamental as they develop early in lifestyles and are pervasive as they have an effect on social behavior, decision making, and mastering conduct (Sadler-Smith and riding, 2000). The overall idea even as designing getting to know materials and training is that each one people analyze comparably. Consequently studying substances and training, at the same time as designing, are standardized and fail to house cognitive patterns and getting to know styles inside the design technique. Furthermore, schooling layout methodologies even though acknowledge learning patterns, but lack the theoretical and empirical bases to deal with the critical role performed using cognitive styles in figuring out studying performance. The belief that every one individual examines similarly ignores person variations in cognitive patterns. It was advised that one of the causes for variations in the performance of individuals throughout an expansion of corporations is the effect of cognitive style. Conventional schooling design methodologies fail to acknowledge the essential role performed by way of cognitive fashion in figuring out getting to know overall performance. Hence, it's far vital to recollect the connection between getting to know performance, gaining knowledge of strategies and cognitive style. it is also essential to signify ways wherein human resource improvement practitioners may accommodate person variations in fashion such that the effectiveness of schooling and improvement interventions can be improved. Kim Buch and Susan Bartley (2002) investigate the connection between gaining knowledge of fashion and desire for education delivery mode. The look explores the subject by using the Kolb studying style tool to measure schooling delivery mode desire. The consequences confirmed a courting among the two variables depicting that convergers confirmed a more potent preference for laptop-based totally transport and assimilators confirmed a more potent choice for print-primarily based shipping. The consequences additionally found out an average desire for lecture room-based delivery for adults at the take a look at, irrespective of their studying styles. The thing additionally discusses the implications of these consequences for training design and delivery, thereby implicating the significance of getting to know patterns in the layout method of training. The type of gaining knowledge of style is not notably powerful on the students' achievement and studying overall performance in unique learning environments. The study investigates the effects of getting to know styles on students' fulfillment and studying overall performance in extraordinary getting to know environments designed in keeping with ideas of the Generative idea of Multimedia mastering. The inferences were made using reading a examine group in three distinctive studying environments at one-of-a-kind instances. The research made use of two unique learning instruments along with a pre-posttest experimental technique to pick out college students' success scores and Kolb's learning fashion inventory to measure college students' gaining knowledge of patterns. The design and application of distance studying are of primary concern to many educators. Studies have been carried out from an expansion of views on this region. Yuliang Liu and Dean Ginther (1999) discover approaches to adapt the design of distance schooling to college students' cognitive patterns. Their paper gives an overview of the assembling of cognitive patterns in conjunction with the fundamental dimensions and traits of cognitive styles. The researchers also gift some packages of cognitive styles to the layout of distance training. Steven John Simon (2000) indicates that trainees whose learning style suits the schooling method are more a hit in training effects, have higher computing delight, and have higher stages of laptop use. The take a look at examines the connection of studying style and training approach to computer pleasure and pc use. The researcher uses structural equation modeling to look at and understand the consequences of a field test to determine the optimum approach of education newbie laptop users, and to evaluate the function of mastering styles in computing machine schooling. Trainees' learning fashion was decided by the usage of Kolb's studying patterns inventory. John Hayes and Christopher W. Allinson (1997) evaluate the studies on the interplay impact of gaining knowledge of style and the studying style orientation of the gaining knowledge of environment on mastering results and talk about how the findings from educational research can improve education and development practice. Their paper attempts to indicate the effect of cognitive gaining knowledge of patterns on schooling and improvement exercise and discusses the want for extra research in work settings and the lack of legitimate and reliable measures of cognitive learning style. The presence of a legitimate and reliable degree of cognitive studying fashion can be easily administered to personnel and is considered as a thing that may also have inhibited studies in this region. Moreover, the benefits and downsides of several measures that could be utilized in work settings also are mentioned within the paper. Christopher W. Allinson and Lucinda Willis (2010) look at the range of enterprise getting to know styles in a population consistency of yank and international commercial enterprise college students. The research makes use of the productiveness Environmental preference Survey to decide mastering patterns in both working and studying environments. The study's findings suggest that learning styles are uniquely related to geographic locations. Studies show that people fluctuate in the way they technique records due to their learner characteristics. It also shows the presence of eleven dimensions of learner traits. Researchers use a clean method to instructional design and emphasize the importance of cognitive style as a learner feature. Noting that cognitive styles are solid, proof against alternate by using schooling and endure little relation to popular capability, the authors advocate helping the learner whose facts processing pattern is not like-minded with the mission to be found out by using involving specific alteration of the assignment requirement with which the learner is having difficulty. consequently, the look at proposes to design the training a good way to accommodate studying patterns using a three-step instructional design plan with which to move beyond person education to individualized training. This kind of plan would permit for variations in learners to no longer result in variations in getting to know. If you want to optimize character overall performance, managers and human resource practitioners have an important position to play and some human useful resource interventions are required to facilitate a versatility of style at both the person and the organizational ranges. The studies describe the cognitive style as a vital determinant of individual behavior and consider it vital to organizational studying and the innovation technique. The researchers argue that it is an essential determinant of individual and organizational behaviors and manifests itself in individual place of business moves and organizational structures, tactics, and workouts. This provides some of the propositions which improve some implications for studies into cognitive patterns and their effect upon innovation and organizational mastering and education. The take a look at Eugene Sadler-Smith (1996) argues that gaining knowledge of fashion alongside gaining knowledge of alternatives and cognitive styles may be included under the term personal style. The evaluation aspect of the personal fashion framework and considers its courting to mastering overall performance on the reaction, studying, conduct, and results in degree. It additionally describes the gadgets which can be used for profiling personal fashion and show that personal style profiling is of cost to human aid improvement practitioners as it can help them become aware of their very own styles, turn out to be privy to any bias or imbalance within the education and mastering techniques which they rent and layout and develop gaining knowledge of occasions which accommodate or well known the personal forms of the novices. Eugene Sadler-Smith (1996) explores methods in which person differences among newbies regarding their cognitive styles and experiential learning model can be accommodated at the same time as designing self-academic learning materials. The take a look at gives suggestions to broaden balanced instructional materials that are well known at every stage of the learning cycle and character differences between freshmen in terms of verbalizer-imager (VI) and who list-analytical (WA) dimensions of cognitive style. It also critiques the studying cycle, the related mastering patterns, and the verbalizer-imager/who list-analytical version of cognitive fashion to make hints. The studies argue that the learning cycle notions cautioned via Kolb and Honey and Mumford and the cognitive fashion version via driving may additionally provide useful hints for accommodating individual variations among newcomers whilst designing self-educational substances which might also allow; learning difficulties to be predicted and addressed, the effectiveness and efficiency of self-training to be advanced, novices to grow to be privy to the learning system enabling them to be self-reliant and self-reliant, and inexperienced persons and designers to undertake a "complete-brain" method. Implications of cognitive fashion for control exercise mainly at the same time as designing and turning in training is studied by using John Hayes and Christopher W. Allinson (1994). The paper identifies some important dimensions of cognitive fashion, addresses semantic problems related to the character of cognitive style, and examines ways in which styles can be classified. Research concerning learning patterns is rising from an expansion of disciplines and is conducted in domains outdoor psychology from which among the principal concepts and theories originate. Those domain names in the main consist of clinical and health care schooling, management, enterprise, vocational training, and training. Moreover, the programs of these principles are very large because of the significance of studying in every field and to each thing of existence. But, the topic has become fragmented and disparate because of the varied ambitions of the research and the variety of disciplines and domains in which the research is performed. Consequently, this has rendered the topic to be complicated and tough to understand and assimilate. Therefore, it is vital to present an account of the vital issues and problems surrounding studying patterns and to keep in mind the gadgets to be had for the size of favor. Using Simon Cassidy's (2004) opinions the theories, models, and measures related to learning styles are very important. The take a look at tries to clarify commonplace regions of ambiguity specifically issues surrounding dimension and appropriate contraptions. It also targets to convey collectively necessary additives of the place to be able to allow for a broader appreciation of learning styles and to tell readers regarding possible equipment for measurement of studying styles. It anticipates selling research in the area by making it greater reachable to new practitioners and researchers and by developing an extra appreciation for the region throughout disciplines. Samuel Messick (1984) examines feature capabilities of cognitive styles and the approaches in which studying styles fluctuate from each other. These distinctive traits are incorporated to form a framework that serves to outline cognitive patterns in contrast not simplest to skills however to other kinds of stylistic variables. The paper additionally discusses implications of cognitive styles in terms of improving instructional techniques, enriching teacher conduct and conceptions, enhancing scholar getting to know and thinking strategies, expanding guidance and vocational decision making, broadening academic dreams and effects, and tuning the stylistic demands of tutorial environments. The writer also addresses the reasons why cognitive patterns have an instructional impact and why such educational benefits are difficult to comprehend. Eugene

Sadler-Smith (2001) explores the assemble validity of gaining knowledge of fashion as defined within the learning styles inventory (LSI) and its courting with cognitive styles as measured by using the evaluation of the Cognitive pattern (CSA) by using R. using (1994). The look at also examines the relationship among patterns and mastering possibilities and shows that the LSI assesses dimensions as described through Kolb (comprehension and transformation) and that the getting to know the style and cognitive styles are impartial and the connection among style and desire is mediated via gender. Adrian Furnham (1991) reports three research involved with personality correlates of studying patterns. The Eyesenckian dimensions of Extraversion, Neuroticism, Psychoticism and Lie correlated with three one-of-a-kind measures of getting to know fashion; the Honey and Mumford (1982) gaining knowledge of fashion Questionnaire (LSQ), the Whetten and Cameron (1984) Cognitive fashion tool (CSI); and the Kolb gaining knowledge of style stock (LSI). Character measures, specifically extraversion and psychoticism were strongly correlated with studying/cognitive styles in each case. The examination also discusses the implications for assessing gaining knowledge of and cognitive styles in phrases of the incremental validity of the use of studying fashion instruments. The effect of text-plus-textual content versus text-plus-photo computer presentation situations and the scholars' cognitive styles at the mastering overall performance is investigated within the paper via R. riding and G. Douglas (1993). For the look at, fifteen-sixteen-year-old students in a secondary faculty were randomly assigned within sexes to one of the situations. Inside the text-plus-textual content situation, the studying cloth content material described the running of car brake structures even as the text-plus-image situation consisted of text with additional pictorial statistics. The scholars had been given a put up-take a look at standard gaining knowledge of overall performance in conjunction with the analysis of the Cognitive patterns (CSA) which measures an individual's role on cognitive fashion dimensions; Verbal-Imagery and Wholist-Analytic. They have a look at concluded that the Verbal-Imagery cognitive fashion and presentation circumstance interacted in their impact on average gaining knowledge of performance. In the textual content-plus-photo circumstance, Imagers have been advanced to Verbalizers, while within the text-plus-text condition the Verbalizers did better than Imagers. The authors additionally located that Imagers used more diagrams to demonstrate their answers than Verbalizers. The look at also discusses the effects in phrases of their implications for coaching. Elizabeth R. Peterson, Ian J. Deary, and Elizabeth J. Austin (2003) check and examine the reliability of driving's Cognitive styles evaluation take a look at (CSA) via comparing the overall performance on the original CSA take a look at and a new parallel model. Each takes a look at versions was finished twice by using 50 participants, but, the second one time the take a look at changed into completed about every week later. The reliability of the take a look at changed into measured the usage of parallel paperwork, check-re-check, and cut up half analysis. Correlations of the Verbal-Imagery (VI) and Wholist-analytic (WA) ratios from each take a look at versions were low. But, whilst the CSA and parallel form records have been mixed, the split-half evaluation of the

Wholist-Analytic (WA) style ratio turned into strong however the Verbal-Imagery (VI) style ratio remained unreliable. control education and improvement practitioners need to understand that individuals' mastering choices are likely to differ due to cognitive style and that this diversity has to be acknowledged and accommodated using practitioners via using a selection of educational techniques. Researchers also argue that management training and improvement will benefit from adopting a spread of modes of presentation as a way to enable individuals to procedure records in their routine modes (i.e. visual or verbal) and the usage of educational devices (overviews, summaries, and different forms of strengthening organizers) which compensate for the weaknesses of people' ordinary modes of organizing and structuring data in reminiscence. On the way to encourage self-recognition and for this reason, facilitate learning and method development, management schooling and development practitioners should use the notion of fashion and its assessment. Consequently, it's now imperative to fully make use of the notion of favor in the training and improvement of managers in the twenty-first century. The take a look at Eugene Sadler-Smith and Richard riding (2000) targets to recollect the results of the Wholist-Analytic (WA) and Verbalizer-Imager (VI) dimensions of cognitive fashion for management schooling and development. The study gives and examines that at a realistic level, the fashion might also exert a power overmastering behavior in some of the methods; with the aid of interacting with the model or shape of the presentation of statistics; with the aid of influencing a person's propensity to have interaction particularly styles of getting to know conduct (mastering choices) or thru the usage of attention of character's private styles as a foundation for meta-cognitive consciousness (gaining knowledge of approach development). With the aid of Eugene Sadler-Smith and Peter J. Smith (2004) gives strategies for accommodating man or woman's patterns and preferences in bendy studying applications. This argues that tremendous boom and development has taken region within the use of flexible methods of transport for administrative center gaining knowledge of and improvement. but, while designing programs for flexible gaining knowledge, the designers frequently anticipate that rookies exhibit uniformity in their capacity to method and organize statistics (cognitive fashion), in their tendency in the direction of unique mastering formats and media (academic options), and the aware movements that freshmen appoint to deal with the needs of particular getting to know situations (gaining knowledge of techniques). Because of such assumptions, the designers of mastering materials and training can also danger ignoring vital elements of character differences in patterns, preferences, and strategies. The ambitions to do not forget some factors of individual difference that are tremendous to the delivery of flexible mastering within the place of business, identify some of the challenges that may improve for instructional designers and gaining knowledge of facilitators primarily based on variations in styles and choices between people and endorse methods to house and renowned individual variations in patterns and options in the fashions of bendy learning design and transport via using more than a few instructional layouts, learning and help techniques. Pat Burke Guild (2001) examines the results of diversity, getting to know patterns and way of life on the studying overall performance of freshmen. The author argues that educators do now not accept as true with that each one beginner's research in an equal manner, yet, educators during the sector maintain to deal with all newbies alike at the same time as acknowledging range. Educators, today, are aware that scholars learn in one-of-a-kind ways. Theories and big studies illustrate mastering variations amongst people. Newcomers convey their personal individual technique, talents, and interests to the mastering state of affairs in terms of studying patterns, cognitive patterns, or multiple intelligences. Furthermore, person newcomers' subculture, circle of relative's history and socioeconomic stage additionally affect the gaining knowledge of technique. As a result, those theories and ideas have a critical impact on the opportunities for success for each scholar in schools. Teng Pei-Shan, DengchuanCai, and Yao-Jen Fan (2009) check out the connection between layout questioning and design performance in exclusive kinds of cognition. Designers have the duty to recognize and care approximately users' cognitive habits to distinguish the distinction between thinking and performance in distinct cognitive styles. The examination makes use of the Cognitive fashion Index (CSI) and classifies it into corporations; analysis and instinct. The research uses revel in and questionnaire strategies to test two businesses with unique cognitive styles, to expose the difference of design technique performance in wondering and caricature ability while executing the identical project. The primary results of the study concluded for the design system that; humans in instinct organization decide upon picture wondering and those in evaluation institution select phrase questioning; people in intuition institution have better overall performance than those in an analysis organization. Eventually, cognitive style may be carried out to design training and work such that educators admire the studying modes of different customers and make use of the right approaches to advantage better gaining knowledge of overall performance. James B. Wells, Benjamin H. Layne, and Derek Allen (1991) have a look at the appropriateness and applicability of multimedia educational strategy inside the management improvement schooling. It also reveals widespread variations inside the mastering types of supervisors, center managers, and top managers. It additionally provides a few motives for the existence of getting to know fashion differences and indicates schooling media and academic strategies maximum ideal for the dominant mastering style of each level of control. They have a look at provides diverse methodologies and media approaches that may be planned to meet the wishes of the schooling participants.

Metacognition

Metacognition is the potential to examine how you technique mind and feelings. This capability encourages students to understand how they examine pleasantly. It also facilitates them to increase self-recognition abilities that grow to be crucial as they become old. Humans who have advanced metacognition are capable of checking their idea approaches and reframe the way they assume to conform to new conditions. With the use of metacognition, college students advantage expertise in the situations, processes, and techniques that work satisfactorily for them. They will discover that a method that works for one class doesn't work for they all or that analyzing for one challenge might require more time than any other. Through the technique of trial and mistakes, college students reach some methods and fail in others earlier than trying again. Teachers can assist students to expand metacognition with some techniques. To start, instructors can offer students information about how the brain techniques statistics, how it forms understanding and recollections, in addition to the impact strain has on these talents. Instructors can also encourage students to understand what they don't apprehend and speak how confronting the unknown is a fundamental part of gaining knowledge of experience. To assist students to apprehend how they research best:

• Schedule time for college kids to reflect on the mastering technique and notice how their understanding has changed.

• Offer opportunities for students to reflect on what became difficult for them to analyze versus what was easy and why and which look at conduct or strategies worked and which of them didn't and why.

• Encourage students to recognize how humans get solutions, each incorrect and proper, and the techniques used to get to those factors.

Some assignments can assist students to exercise reflexive questioning, which is an interest that encourages metacognition. For example, essay tests inspire better-stage wondering, supporting college students' spark off additional information in the gaining knowledge of technique. Teachers also can assign college students to assess their very own beliefs concerning problems like race, bias, or different held ideals. This evaluation pushes each personal increase and understanding of how beliefs are formed and the way they could evolve. In brief, any challenge that encourages students to parent out the solutions on their own enables them to work through the mastering manner and refine they're getting to know capabilities. Institution work and collaboration further enable students to expand metacognition as those abilities assist students to work thru troubles in new methods. Operating with others enables college students to take a look at troubles from new views and helps them to understand how they may better technique issues in the future but can be successful in their educational and expert careers. The better able a student is to understand how she or he learns, recollects, and strategies records, the extra statistics he or she will ultimately hold. This capability is in addition connected to growing better reminiscence capabilities, which is a predictor of destiny academic success. Students who apprehend how they learn are better capable of creating conditions that sell learning. For instance, novices might recognize that they need to take a look in a quiet room, at a positive time of day, or with notecards in a class that requires several memorizations. Alternatively, he or she might recognize that writing requires a distinct kind of putting or time allotment altogether. Whilst there is lots to train in a day, encouraging time for mirrored image on the gaining knowledge of technique permits students to better apprehend their own gaining knowledge of processes. This, in flip, affords college students with the competencies to take a look at and complete coursework more successfully and successfully. Techniques that concentrate on college students' metacognition and their capacity to reflect on consideration on wondering can close a gap that a few college students enjoy among how organized they experience for a take a look at and the way prepared they absolutely are. In a new look at, students in an introductory college information class who took a quick online survey earlier than each exam asking them to consider how they might prepare for it earned better grades inside the route than their friends; a third of a letter grade better, on common. This low-cost intervention helped college students gain insight into their examination strategies, boosting their metacognitive skills and giving them equipment to be greater independent beginners. Patricia Chen, a postdoctoral researcher at Stanford and the lead creator of the study, says she frequently had college students coming to her lamenting their bad check ratings. "Many college students have come to me after their tests seeking to recognize why they did not do as well as they'd predicted, despite their hard work," she remembers. She suspected that the difficulty turned into that they lacked recognition of the way unwell-organized they were metacognitive awareness and that brought about the abruptly low scores. The idea they understood the cloth higher than they really did. Almost two a long time in the past, Cornell psychologists David Dunning and Justin Kruger carried out a landmark study searching at this belief hole. In a chain of experiments, they observed that many college students who carried out poorly on exams of good judgment and grammar had puffed up their overall performance, believing themselves to be above average. This phenomenon, the Dunning-Kruger impact, explains why many college students experience the confidence that they'll bypass a take a look at despite being underprepared. Overconfidence leaves college students "with the fallacious influence that they're doing just best," according to Dunning and Kruger. Extra recently, a crew of psychologists and neuroscientists posted a comprehensive evaluation of ten learning strategies normally utilized by students. They discovered that one of the maximum famous strategies rereading cloth and highlighting key points is likewise one of the least effective because it leads college students to develop a false sense of mastery. They evaluation a passage and flow on without figuring out that they haven't thoroughly understood and absorbed the cloth. This has serious implications for getting to know: It's some distance too easy for college students to overestimate their information of a topic sincerely due to the fact they're familiar with it. Metacognition facilitates college students to apprehend the distance between being familiar with a subject and expertise it deeply. However weaker college students frequently don't have this metacognitive reputation which ends up in disappointment and might discourage them from attempting tougher the next time. Research suggests that even children as young as three advantage from metacognitive activities, which help them replicate on their very own mastering and increase better-order thinking. To promote college students' metacognition, middle and excessive faculty instructors can put in force the following techniques. Simple instructors can model or adjust those strategies with their college students to provide more scaffolding. The key to metacognition is to encourage students to manage their very own mastering as opposed to passively soaking up cloth. Donna Wilson and Marcus Conyers use the phrase "drive your brain" as a metaphor to explain to students how they could grow to be extra aware of their mastering. In addition, selling an increased mindset facilitates college students to take into account that getting to know isn't constant: thru dedication and hard work, they can discover ways to be greater resilient and triumph over many challenges that may otherwise sense impossible. Surely being conscious that there's a distinction between a hard and fast and an increased mindset is one of the best metacognitive techniques that students can benefit from. All through elegance, encourage students to ask questions. Remember the fact that suffering college students won't realize what questions to ask, or may feel too embarrassed to ask any. Don't count on that every student understands the material simply due to the fact nobody asks a query. Use low-stakes formative assessment techniques like exit tickets, pop quizzes, or the traditional "One-Minute Paper" to discover gaps in expertise and manual future training.

During class, students must ask themselves:
- What are the principle ideas of today's lesson?
- Become something perplexing or tough?
- If something isn't making sense, what query ought to I ask the teacher?
- Am I taking proper notes?
- What am I able to do if I am getting stuck in a trouble?

To close the distance between what your students recognize and what will be on a check, encourage them to quiz themselves in place of simply rereading and highlighting a text. This no longer best boosts long-term retention however additionally bridges the gap among familiarity with a topic and deep know-how of it.

Earlier than a take a look at, college students should ask themselves:

- What is going to be at the test?
- What regions do I battle with or feel careworn about?
- How much time ought to I set aside to prepare for an upcoming take a look at?
- Do I have the necessary substances (books, faculty resources, a computer and online get admission to, and so on.) and a quiet place to examine, without distractions?
- What strategies will I take advantage of to take a look at? Is it enough to actually study and review the fabric, or will I take exercise assessments, study with a friend, or write observe cards?
- What grade could I get if I have been to take the check right now?

The technology at the back of metacognition (particularly in training) has been drastically researched as it covers a totally large place. The latest proof shows that it could upload up to 7 months of extra mastering for college kids. Metacognition can be better through improving your potential to expect how well you'll perform on a task. Other recent research has determined that reflecting on which take a look at resources to apply, why those sources are beneficial, and how you'll use them improves metacognition, self-mirrored image, emotional control, and grades.

Chapter Three

Cognitive Psychology

Cognitive Psychology is described as the take a look at thoughts, emotions, and behaviors. One main angle inside psychology is known as cognitive psychology, which is normally worried about the reason of thought procedures through the improvement of theoretical mental structures. Cognitivism is relatively broad in its psychology methods and most effectively connected in its purpose to create hypothetical intellectual systems to explain behaviors. The exact origins of cognitivism are tough to pinpoint. Ideas that make up the perspective had been traced returned to historical Greece. Its objectives to apprehend the intellectual accompaniment of everyday perceptions and movements. using devising intellectual systems of mental features and how facts are processed, it may then be possible to explain observable behaviors. The maximum large idea of cognitivism is the computer or statistics processor metaphor. It underlies most people of theoretical and empirical studies in the subject. This analogy related the thoughts to a pc with sequences of computational processes. A Mathematical concept of communication turned into an influential paper written using Claude Shannon which first supplied the concept that to be communicated; records needed to journey via alerts through a sequence of ranges and variations. Such theories gave a notably greater complicated view of human behaviors, particularly in assessment to less complicated stimulus-reaction theories formed in behaviorism, by way of adding the important measurement of the mind. This concept gave a mechanical view of human thoughts and behaviors, implying that the brain works, in addition, to a piece of computer software program programmed to perform pre-described capabilities. Additionally, cognitivism added the concept of an intervening method between stimuli and responses. Cognitive psychology is likewise the have a look at of intellectual strategies. The yank mental association defines cognitive psychology as "The look at of better mental approaches inclusive of interest, language use, reminiscence, perception, hassle solving, and thinking. Lots of the work derived from cognitive psychology has been incorporated into various modern disciplines of mental have look at which include social psychology, personality psychology, strange psychology, developmental psychology, and academic psychology. Cognitive psychology is the clinical investigation of human cognition, this is, all our intellectual abilities; perceiving, mastering, remembering, questioning, reasoning, and expertise. within the mid-20th century, three predominant effects arose that would encourage and form cognitive psychology as a formal school of thought: With the improvement of the latest battle generation all through WWII, the need for more knowledge of human performance got here to prominence. Troubles together with how to excellent educate soldiers to use new technology and the way to deal with topics of interest whilst below duress became regions of need for navy employees. Behaviorism furnished little if any perception into those subjects and it became the work of Donald

Broadbent, integrating standards from human overall performance research and the lately developed facts idea that forged the manner on this place. Traits in computer science could result in parallels being drawn between human concepts and the computational capability of computer systems, starting entirely new areas of mental notion. Allen Newell and Herbert Simon spent years developing the concept of artificial intelligence (AI) and later labored with cognitive psychologists regarding the results of AI. The effective result turned into more of a framework conceptualization of mental functions. Cognitive psychology is an essential subject because it studies everything that makes up who someone is, primarily based on what they recognize, assume, and experience. Understanding cognitive psychology can help people make higher decisions and help understand how humans accomplish excellent matters. as an example, if a person is having a tough time focusing on elegance and that they discover when the chatty humans in the back of them do now not display up they take better notes than it's miles useful for them to cognitively decide to sit someplace else. This case indicates how understanding cognitive psychology can permit someone to get to recognize him/herself better, consequently making better private choices. Getting fundamental know-how of cognitive psychology involves four fundamental standards: the intrinsic limitations of introspection and behaviorism, operating reminiscence, the role of the amygdala, and the structure of a neuron and synapse. The idea of cognitive psychology came about inside the Fifties, found by using psychologists named Wilhelm Wundt and Edward Titchener. It was formerly thought that psychology couldn't have a look at the world at once, however, these researchers founded the idea of introspection, meaning to examine and document our own intellectual lives. Even though introspection appeared like an inventive manner to immediately have a look at people, it became out to have a couple of intrinsic obstacles. First, it did no longer account for subconscious thoughts. Cognitive psychology commenced around 1nineteenth century. One-of-a-kind strategies were used to trace the roots of psychology. It is psychology changed into outnumbered by behaviorism however later revived, bringing into being cognitive revolution. The paper discusses cognitive revolution in the records of cognitive psychology as the maximum influential part inside the practice of present-day psychology. The advent of a scientific department of psychology that is involved with the study of cognition is referred to as cognitive psychology. Cognition has components concerned with mental methods that encompass perception, attention, reminiscence, trouble fixing, reasoning, and decision making. As noted via Benjamin (2007), cognitive psychology is an illustration of a slow shift in idea and methodology borrowing expertise from different fields which includes computer systems, theory of information, the idea of linguistics, and communication networks amongst others. It keeps today inside the research of cognition. As an instance, neurophysiology is reached via neuroscience and biochemistry for better information of cognition. Cognitive revolution supplied information-processing approach as a new manner of mind have a look at. The introduction of virtual computers, devices for processing information, stimulated many psychologists who began to view thoughts as the foundation of records processing. The capability of computer systems to manner records in stages captured the attention of many cognitive psychologists. By using expertise that data in a pc as it is first acquired by input processor, then stored in memory unit follows, and ultimately processing in the arithmetic unit, many cognitive psychologists experimented and carried out this layout. For example, Goldstein (2007) suggests that Cherry, a psychologist, experimented on attention where he offered one-of-a-kind messages at a visit to human beings and later instructed them to copy the messages. He found out that human beings be aware of one message amongst many.

Mind characteristic

Records processing systems within the mind are studied beneath Cognitive psychology. Cognitive psychology is an extensive range of observing, which includes the look at internal intellectual situations, wondering, and language, solving issues, processing facts, artificial intelligence, development of toddlers, feelings, and how the mind plays those capabilities. improvement of Cognitive psychology has supplied many significant factors in studies and has become out to be a most important field in psychology that appears in the mental methods, as an example, fixing issues, language, and memory, the have a look at how a person thinks, perceives, remembers, learns, after which behaves. Inside the later part of the nineteenth century, several psychologists have become more and more inquisitive about the sphere of cognition. Thinking about theories of advanced behaviorists, as an instance Jean Piaget inside the early part of the 1nincteenth century along with his interest in the mind of kids, B.F. Skinner within the mid-nineteenth century together with his operant conditioning, or Noam Chomsky who challenged B.F. Skinner's concept a few years later. After many doubts and uncertainties of the capacity of the research attained from the behaviorists, presently what's known as cognitive psychology changed these theories. consequently, the interest with the have a look at of cognition starts to increase and cognition seems to be a huge idea in psychology, which has been referred to as the cognitive revolution, and then became to be known as cognitive psychology. A considerable factor within the advancement of cognitive psychology begins with a psychologist named Wilhelm Wundt, who become the primary individual to pick out the problem of psychology, inside the ultimate part of the 18th century. Wundt's idea that psychology dealt with the exam of enjoy (structuralism), which he defined in a table of the brain that was just like the periodic table. Every other psychologist, using the call of William James, challenged Wundt's findings, and the studies that James performed, allowed James to understand that "mental approaches ought to have a motive; they should be for something". In other phrases, the enjoyment of a man or woman turned into no longer what became critical but that means of the enjoy to the individual (functionalism). Additionally, William James took part in the James-Lange theory. This theory suggests that an individual's emotion that is experienced is based totally upon the determined action wherein the individual engaged in. After structuralism (Wundt) and functionalism (James), a theorist emerged to project the theories of James and Wundt, this theorist was named John Watson.

Watson's theory is called behaviorism and turned into based totally upon his own beliefs. After Wundt's structuralism and James' functionalism, a theorist named John Watson emerged and challenged each of Wundt's and James' theories by using his own beliefs, which are referred to as behaviorism. Behaviorism may be described as what a character is doing or is located to be doing with the aid of any other person. Watson's concept indicated, first look at the person's behavior and make an assumption, then decide the basic members of the family between the stimuli and the reaction. Watson believed that stimuli and a reaction can be interchangeable. After Watson's theories of behaviorism, the decline of behaviorism started and every other concept turned into commenced to have a look at the thoughts, this different theory compared the thoughts to a laptop. This idea turned into the bond connecting behaviorism and cognitive psychology. As generation superior, this assessment of the thoughts to a PC allowed psychologists to apprehend more of the internal human, which became a chief element in how theorists studied human idea procedures and behaviors. Behavioral observation of psychologists' converted interest in the intellectual process became introduced by way of the improvement of the computer. This development supplied a charming image of the human mind, which related the laptop to the mind. The computer codes used, offered a step-with the aid of-step version of ways statistics obtained from the environment every day are recorded, saved, and recovered to offer a response. The formation of computer contrast gave psychologists the idea to begin a plan for information processing fashions of the human concept process and behavior. The term behaviorism becomes founded by using John B Watson. It refers back to the school of psychology that believes that all behaviors may be measured, modified, and skilled. Behaviorism additionally referred to as behavioral psychology is primarily based on the theory that everyone's behaviors are acquired via conditioning. Conditioning happens via interplay with the surroundings. Behaviorists trust that the responses to environment stimulus form the conduct. Behaviorists ignore mental strategies as something to be studied. In well-known, behaviorists are concerned only with observable behaviors, in preference to investigating the inner procedures of the thoughts. Behaviorists studied behavior in a scientific and observable way and definitely ignoring the inner intellectual states, including cognition, emotions, and moods due to the fact they may be too subjective. Two primary types of conditioning are Ivan Pavlov's concept of classical conditioning and B.F. Skinner's concept of operant conditioning. Behaviorism changed into a primary fashion in psychology that at once accompanied functionalism, which turned into a branch of psychology that examines intellectual tactics and how they relate to human behaviors. Behaviorist principle turned into that it rejects the unique nature of mental events. It does this by asserting that Psychology is the observing of simplest observable behaviors. Therefore mental activities and occasions that show up outside the explanation of conduct became no longer a challenge for Psychology. In definition, behaviorism is the take a look at the connection between a person-environment and their behaviors, without taking into concern what occurs within their minds. For the reason that behaviorism dismisses the look at steel states, there have been but many efforts made to repair the thoughts additionally known as cognitive strategies. That is what led to the "cognitive revolution". This revolution causes the rise of cognitive psychology and also cognitive technology. It is said that the cognitive revolution caused the substitute, decline, or even dying of behaviorism along with behavior analysis.

This behaviorist motion receives vast help from scientists who claimed that other theories of psychology have been invalid and now not empirical and as a result now not quantifiable. Behaviorism takes an objective stance to ensure that study's findings can be legitimate and capable to rely upon. Behaviorist achieves it by ignoring what they referred to as the" black box" of the mind because human beings cannot measure what is going on within the individual minds. But, people can degree and look at behaviors through interaction with their surroundings. Behaviorism changed into ruling psychology fields for many years, but there was a primary flaw. Behaviorism dominance over psychology limited the technology of observable behaviors. Behaviorists regarded psychology as herbal technological know-how with crucial deductions, first of all, psychology must be the goal, and secondly, psychology regarded as a technology area should be empirical as nicely. Concepts along with attention were taken into consideration to be outside the domain of psychology, whereas, cognitive psychology concentrates on the intellectual states. The criticism of behaviorism is that it's far a one-dimensional way of analyzing behavior and behavioral theories do not account totally free will and inner impacts together with thoughts, moods, and feelings. Behaviorism gaining knowledge revolves around reinforcements and punishments and does not account for other types of learning. The strengths of behaviorism are since it examines observable behaviors, information and statistics' might be easier to acquire while conducting research. Effective therapeutic strategies along with in-depth behavioral intervention, behavior analysis, and cognitive psychology are all rooted in behaviorism, even as behaviorism isn't dominant within the modern-day world in comparison to the middle of the twentieth century; it still stays as an influential pressure in psychology. Those approaches are very useful in changing undesirable or harmful behaviors in adults and children. Animals' trainers, teachers, and dad and mom employ behavioral techniques to inspire new behaviors and discard unwanted behaviors. Many psychologists have disagreed with behaviorism and reject this attitude and became to the take a look at of wondering and attention, referred to as cognitive psychology. Cognitive psychologists are fascinated to recognize greater how a person is familiar with and resolve issues. Cognitive psychology is a more modern college of thought in psychology because it commenced growing within the 1950s and the early 1960s. It had will become the dominant perspective in psychology in the 1970s. People have been more attracted to the cognitive method and upset with the behavioral perspective. The development of better experimental techniques and the improvement of the pc contributed to the cognitive attitude dominance. Cognitive psychology is set reading cognition, in particular, it affects getting to know and behavior. It explores internal mental strategies along with language, hassle solving, and reminiscence. One of the most influential psychologists in this field is Piaget's concept of cognitive improvement. There are some assumptions based totally on cognitive psychology. Firstly it's miles a natural technology-based totally on broadly speaking laboratory experiments that is a form of deductive reasoning. Every other assumption is that the brain works very much like a laptop, like how the thoughts operate and manner statistics. The mind enters, shops, and retrieves records very similar to how a computer operates. Cognitive psychology is very beneficial and popular because it could be applied to many fields in psychology, which include reminiscence, attention, notion, baby development, hassle solving, and eyewitness testimony, and gender role development. Cognitive psychology has many sensible programs, like cognitive ideas, are often utilized in the creation of educational curriculum and software program layout. Some prominent cognitive psychologists are Jean Piaget, Wilhelm Wundt, Aaron Beck, and Albert Ellis. Cognitive psychologists research human mind procedures. Cognitive psychologists work in lots of regions like universities, government agencies, company groups. They look at questioning, notion, decision making, reminiscence, and judgment. It examines how someone gathers, process, shops and recollect data. This branch of psychology prefers to carry out studies for the theories to be proved. Cognitive psychologists normally finished their research on humans. They may complete experiments on how to improve reminiscence, and to better understand why a few humans can don't forget statistics quicker than others, studies may be performed on what affects decision-making. Groups are one of the fields that benefited from cognitive psychology, as groups additionally hire cognitive psychologists. Organizations will need their employees to carry out to the exceptional. Cognitive psychologists will work with the pinnacle management on how to improve the working surroundings and to advanced techniques to assist personnel to improve the work performance. Having a terrible operating environment, the workers will therefore be sad, less effective, and most likely resign for a higher task. Because the turnover costs may have a huge monetary burden for businesses because companies will need to find an alternative, find answers to get the work achieved as the location is vacant, as training the brand new personnel takes time and money. The new employee may also need to attend courses take required them to carry out the activity and greater time is wanted to manual the brand new personnel at the task scope. As it's a completely tedious process to retrain a brand new employee and looking them go out of the organization after a brief stay at the enterprise. it will be extra effect whilst numerous employees exit the organization at around the identical time, and the brand new personnel aren't as revel in to address the activity consequently compromising on the productiveness and the personnel running inside the businesses for years will coach and manual the brand new personnel along making the personnel now not running to the first-rate in their abilities and making them unproductive. Businesses might need to rent individuals who can work for a long time period for the agency and need their employees to be satisfied operating their positions. Therefore a psychologist can help the groups in a lot of these situations. Whilst advertising department loves to examine extra approximately what influences the client to shop for their merchandise. Cognitive psychologists can be beneficial to explain what impacts the consumer selection-making procedure. The cognitive dissonance idea shows that our attitudes and ideals ought to cross in concord with each different and keep away from disharmony referred to as dissonance. Cognitive dissonance refers to a situation concerning conflicting attitudes, beliefs, or behaviors. This in turn will produce a sense of soreness to cause exchange in one of the attitudes, beliefs, or behavior to lessen the pain and repair harmony. Human beings are difficult-stressed out to be very uncomfortable with statistics that struggle with what they consider in. Cognitive dissonance can be beneficial to enhance the sales of the business. sales strategies like foot-in-the-door are beneficial to boom sales like firstly to study the clients and what they are hoping for and lead the customers the goods with a purpose to get them what they desire for and the client's hopes are always approximately how they experience in the direction of the products and not to get customers to shop for what they do now not want. As the job market is becoming growing competitive, much research has shown and supported that fashionable reasoning capability is definitely correlated with activity performance within a career. Therefore employers will look for people that the overall reasoning abilities are above the minimum necessities for the profession. The next field to gain from cognitive psychology might be clinical and patients tormented by memory issues including Alzheimer's disease. Alzheimer's ailment is an innovative loss of recollections beyond regular time. Some researchers propose that the semantic deficit reflects the worsening of the semantic network itself, while others attribute the deficit to impaired retrieval from the network. As humans are elderly, their cognitive features become worse time beyond regulation and now not characteristic as sharp as earlier than. Psychologists help them to develop techniques and strategies to maintain their minds and our bodies sharp like using the memory retrieval theory to help the sufferers. As emotions have an effective and vital effect on our cognitive techniques, as it's nicely mounted that memory influences liking. Alzheimer's patients can consider if you set off them to remember. Its first-rate to attempt to elicit recollections thru activities in their earlier years as it robs people of their brief time period reminiscences, however, their long-term recollections can stay largely intact. Activities like sitting down and searching at the vintage circle of relatives pix, making a song their famous music of their teenagers because music can influences moods, interest, keep in mind and attitudes. Watching movies or TV shows that they like, getting them to be involved in holidays, as holidays typically may have an emotional impact on people, like in the course of festive seasons they've circle of relatives gatherings and experience themselves collectively. All of the activities have an emotional impact on Alzheimer's patients and sturdy emotions can trigger lower back reminiscences. Using reminiscence techniques can help the brain to develop new pathways for getting to know and enhance reminiscence even for people displaying early signs and symptoms of Alzheimer's. Humans with slight cognitive impairment (MCI) have stepped forward memory after the use of memory strategies along with mnemonics and phrase lists. Magnetic Resonance Imaging (MRI) indicates that reminiscence techniques improved activities in the brain related to language, learning capabilities, and remembering areas and gadgets. As the brains of MCI also have plasticity, there has been decreased activation of the hippocampus in comparison to adults without MCI. Adults with MCI go through a reminiscence training application and observed that the MRI proved a growth activation of sure elements of the brain answerable for language processing, getting to know abilities, and remembering areas and objects. The findings display that there may be no personal area of the mind that shops all memories; however the mind can atone for the lower activation of the hippocampus by growing activation in different elements of the brain.

Cognitive psychologists work with the sufferers and households to improve the cognitive functioning of the patients. Alzheimer's disorder is excellent regarded for inflicting loss of memory and cognitive performance capability. Some specialists agree that psychotherapy could be at the same par as medicine remedy. A few argued that it is even extra effective in the early ranges. Psychotherapy can assist the affected person to address melancholy, anxiety, and all other terrible feelings nicely. But as Alzheimer's disorder progress to an extra superior level, the effectiveness of psychotherapy is much less effective because the patient cognitive functioning decreases. Another area that benefits are schooling. Cognitive psychologists can also work with children who're struggling in faculty and have mastering difficulties to improve their memory and additionally to introduce specific look at techniques and techniques. An FMRI observation on musicians confirmed that tune sports activate the "spatial regions" of the mind. Schmithorst and Holland (2003) determined activation of the inferior parietal lobules at some point of melodic and harmonic processing, and those regions are also activated in range comparison duties advocate that shared areas are involved in quantity and song processing. Consequently, it could be proposed that track education will increase spatial competencies and performs a tremendous position in mathematics fulfillment. Perhaps music can be brought to assist the scholars with getting to know issues. As gaining knowledge of and memory are inseparable and having a deficit on reminiscence will have an effect on how a person learns which will therefore influence behavioral and brain development. Cognitive evaluations are regularly given out to get admission to the scholars to look if they're eligible for the gifted program as it is a completely common method of having access to intelligence. It can be helpful to the police to enhance eyewitness testimony by using lowering factors together with fending off main questions and improving the memory of the witness. Cognitive psychology has made contributions to our understanding of eye witness memory specifically within the obstacles and failures of the eye witness memory which leads to wrongful prison phrases. Cognitive psychology has discovered that the memory for eyewitnesses can be altered via the phrasing of questions used to elicit data after the event has taken place. This proposes that interviews with the eyewitnesses with the police after the incident had taken place, can lead to a reconstruction of the character's memory of the event. In end, many fields have benefited from cognitive psychology. it could assist in commercial enterprise to increase its income, assist employees to work at its height, assisting teachers to advantage by getting to know approximately how people system, take in, study and consider data and helping patients laid low with Alzheimer's to consider reminiscences that had been valuable to them. it can also help in getting to know to help college students with gaining knowledge of issues to carry out better in school and ultimately to help the authorities which include the police to help in investigations. As cognitive psychology touches on many others disciplines, this department of psychology is therefore studied by numerous humans in distinctive fields. Many common features inclusive of wondering, hassle-fixing, mastering, reminiscence, language, and greater come are defined by way of Cognitive psychology. With those essential capabilities, you may marvel, simply what's Cognitive Psychology? Cognitive psychology is a branch of psychology that covers the mental strategies of the way people acquire, preserve and hold close records and situations. The time period "cognition" stems from the Latin phrase "cognoscere" or "to recognize". Essentially, cognitive psychology studies how humans collect and observe knowledge or information. It's far intently associated with cognitive technological know-how and stimulated using pc science, philosophy, neuroscience, linguistics, biology, physics, and anthropology. Cognitive psychologists are inquisitive about how people apprehend, diagnose, and solve problems, regarding themselves with the intellectual approaches which mediate between stimulus and response. Currently, cultural and social elements have additionally ended up part of cognitive psychology in conjunction with emotion and recognition. There are numerous regions of cognitive psychology that I accept as true with strengthening the expertise of our bodies and brains. The three important approaches to cognitive psychology consist of computational cognitive psychology, neural cognitive psychology, and experimental cognitive psychology. Computational cognitive psychology develops mathematical and computational models of human cognition based totally on dynamical structures and symbolic representations.

Unarguably, scientists have a look at the human mental and cognitive features that have caused many discoveries and observations. Fundamental, diverse psychologists and anatomists have tried to trick the human cognitive human processes. As an example, history elicits that Plato turned into a few of the first people, who tried to explain how the human mental strategies feature. Cognitive psychology entails the scholarly and sensible observation that attempts to recognize the manifestation of the various intellectual procedures. Certainly, the brain is a complicated organ that operates in a complex way to process and coordinates the diverse processes in our bodies. For that reason, cognitive psychology tries to define how the brain compartmentalizes capabilities together with memory, belief, language, purpose-made, and notion. It is applicable to say that this look emphasizes how intellectual processes affect the manner people act, operate, or feel. Moreover, it is essential to add that cognitive psychology requires knowledge of cognitive technological know-how and the essential foundations of cognition. As noted earlier, cognitive psychology utilizes numerous research and studies that intricate the various intellectual strategies. As a consequence, this takes a look at has hyperlinks to the numerous branches of psychology. For instance, these ideas exist in the fields of character, social, academic, and developmental psychology. Diverse standards entail the functioning of the mind regarding intellectual procedures. Plato came up with the notion that the brain is the inspiration of various cognitive tactics. Various philosophers and psychologists have argued for or against this perception. History elicits that there were pupils, who argued that human notion became innate. This concept attempted to reveal that human notion turned into not experiential. Alternatively, different philosophical debates attempted to complex that human notion trusted the sensory situations. In truth, philosophers along with John Locke significantly supported this concept. Crucially, comprehension of the numerous cognitive capabilities calls for a knowledge of the anatomy and functioning of the brain. Appreciably, the eighteenth century paved the manner for this know-how. Broca's place is an anatomical part of the temporal location of the mind associated with language development and manufacturing.

Paul Broca discovered that this anatomical place decided the nature of language production in human beings. This discovery turned into very important, on account that, it bolstered the rules of cognitive psychology. Consequently, Broca's aphasia pertains to the dysfunctional manufacturing of language. Carl Wernicke identified the region related to the processing and know-how of language. Damage to the Wernicke's location due to trauma, infections, or congenital malformations reasons Wernicke aphasia. Fundamentally, numerous situations and occurrences in history improved the attention of cognitive psychology. In reality, psychologists drew diverse standards from the numerous events in records. For instance, the advent of the laptop generation brought on various standards regarding cognitive psychology. The information of the way synthetic intelligence influences the laptop's overall performance become very vital. It enabled psychologists to attract contrasts and comparisons between this process and how the mental functions function. It's fundamental to be aware that laptop professionals along with Herbert Simon and Allen Newell cooperated with cognitive psychologists. These synergic efforts helped the evolution of cognitive psychology. Considerably, world warfare II caused various insights regarding the expertise of behaviorism. There was a preferred motivation for scientists, who desired to increase the performance of soldiers. Various people, inclusive of Donald Broadbent evolved principles of behaviorism that supplied extra perception about the field of cognitive psychology. Indeed, human cognitive functions play various roles within the survival of human beings. Sensory input plays the role of records within the human mind. Consequently, it has to go through various transformational and conversion stages so that it will produce relevant interpretations. It's far critical to mention that cognitive psychology can also have numerous distinctions or branches relying on that improve the general comprehension of cognitive psychology. The principle distinction involves a class of the numerous assets of statistics related to cognition. As noted in advance, intellectual procedures and computer capability have multiple similarities. Consequently, the principal branches include cognitive neuroscience, experimental psychology, and pc analogies method. With the use of this classification, individuals may additionally realize how intellectual cognitive features operate. Cognitive neuroscience includes how the brain features when underneath various forms of pressure or duress. As an example, cognitive dysfunction might also occur because of trauma, congenital malformations, infections, or mind tumors. Consequently, a knowledge of how these factors affect the overall cognitive capabilities explains the scope of cognitive neuroscience. Human experimental psychology includes the observation of the numerous intellectual activities and how they interrelate with the sensory enter. The impact of numerous situations on language or memory might also enhance the comprehension of human experimental psychology. Drastically, computers receive statistics enter and methods it thru various sequential tactics. As a result, there's a branch of cognitive psychology that dwells on the comparisons and contrasts among laptop functionality and mental techniques. In summary, this paragraph presents extra insight into how the numerous cognitive psychology ideas evolved. Human beings continuously get hold of facts within the form of sensory input. The various sensory perceptions include the feel of sight, scent, flavor, sound, and touch. Body structure explains how those senses coordinate the behavior and nation of humans. Sensory enter travels via nerves to the fearful device. The relevant fearful machine includes the brain and the spinal wire. For this reason, these organs have the capability of deciphering statistics and changing them into useful statistics. Notably, the cerebral cortex performs a vital function in changing the sensory enter. For instance, the occipital cortex techniques visible stimuli. The body, consequently, utilizes the records to perform bodily capabilities that happen as responses. The body may additionally react to painful stimuli using shifting that a part of the body. Certainly, the fundamental regions of observation in cognitive psychology contain intellectual functions that have an impact on conduct. This essay shall intricate the contents of the main mental processes. These include attention, perception, reminiscence, language, and metacognition. Predominant, interest influences the manner humans to behave and act. There is no proper definition for this time period. But, it defines the presence of alertness toward a sure sense of perception. Attention has two essential branches. Psychologists categorize attention as relying on the kind of manipulate kind. As a result, attention can also have exogenous or endogenous manipulate. This distinction aids in elaborating the numerous approaches wherein interest operates. In reality, psychologists use numerous models to explain how they affect attention on our behaviors and moves. The endogenous kind of interest originates from the brain, particularly, from the cerebral cortex. In this model, the mind actively sends impulses that manipulate the awareness of the sensory input from the external environment. As an instance, a person reading a segment of an e-book elicits this sort of attention. Rather, the exogenous type of attention refers to the focus of sensory impulses from the peripheral regions of the frame. Exogenous interest, often, manifests in our day-by-day sports. The significance of interest is obvious when the mind is receiving distinct styles of stimuli from the environment.

The brain discriminates among the crucial and beside-the-point types of sensory enter. Therefore, attention enables the mind to carry out its cognitive capabilities correctly. It filters and choices out the crucial factors of records. This impact allows the mind to concentrate on the diverse components of data within the environment.

Unarguably, many cognitive psychologists have studied the diverse factors of divided attention. Humans can critically analyze and procedure various forms of sensory enter. This phenomenon happens because of divided attention. Accordingly, friends at a noisy celebration can talk to every different and, simultaneously, recognize the respectable song at the historical past. Researchers are nonetheless seeking to determine how the mind picks interest and how it techniques sensory input as a way to produce data. In summary, attention is important, seeing that, it avoids the overload of information in the brain. An excessive amount of unfiltered statistics may also lead to confusion and terrible concentration. Language is an essential thing of cognitive characteristic. Cognitive psychologists notably research and behavior various experiments in this area of look. Language involves using phonetic and articulation sounds to communicate. This cognitive feature affects the manner people relate to each other. There are numerous disorders related to the bad development of language. Dysarthria refers back to the bad articulation of sounds about talking or speech formation. Rather, dysphonia describes the incapacity to produce speech sounds. Frequently, it manifests due to the impairment of the vocal organs which consist of the tongue, throat, mouth, and lips. This elaboration emphasizes the relevance of language in the lives of human beings. In reality, the primary form of verbal exchange in people is thru the use of language. It acts as an auditory form of sensory input. Hence, language isn't always a conversation tool inside the auditory impaired individuals. As noted earlier, cognitive psychology includes the observation of the way cognitive features influence the way human beings behave. Language is a precept factor that impacts the manner human beings act or behaves. The temporal place of the cerebral cortex takes part in the improvement, manufacturing, and processing of language. The Broca region of the cerebral cortex plays a critical position in language manufacturing. Paul Broca provided the perception approximately how the brain perceives enters and produces language. He discovered that the cerebral cortex coordinated the audio output through this region of the mind. Physiologists and psychologists seek advice from the dysfunction of language production as Broca aphasia. Broca's aphasia has diverse reasons. However, the principal purpose of this sort of aphasia occurs due to brain injury in Broca's place. On the other hand, the Wernicke location participates in the processing of language. It is relevant to mention that the human frame perceives the various forms of sensory input and undergoes a sequential process to provide applicable facts. These records may be inside the shape of audio input. Physiologists and psychologists have substantially studied this location in a bid to recognize how this place incorporates signals to supply output. Indeed, language is a vital aspect of human development. In reality, pediatricians focus on language development in babies due to the fact it could predict the cognitive feature. Various factors influence the manner human beings expand language. For example, memory and socioeconomic fame are important determinants of language improvement. Substantially, memory is an essential element of cognitive capabilities. There are primary distinctions of reminiscence. Short-term memory defines reminiscence over a quick time frame. Cognitive psychologists devote most of their research to analyzing the aspects of reminiscence. Amnesia is a commonplace symptom of patients, who have suffered from concussions. It refers to the dearth of reminiscence. Different factors may additionally affect reminiscence. Of course, individuals range in the manner they bear in mind events, humans, or names. For that reason, genetics affect memory. In fact, studies suggest that gene variations may additionally influence the functioning of the cerebral cortex in terms of the formation of the neural circuits. Consequently, this effect may also intricate the variations in getting to know charges. Amnesia happens after concussions due to the annoying damage of the head. Practitioners and psychologists use various approaches to gauge the reminiscence ranges of various people. For instance, a practitioner might also ask a patient to tell him or her the call of the president as a style of gauging the long-term reminiscence. There are various principles that cognitive psychologists make use of, too difficult the one-of-a-kind instances of reminiscence. As an example, the Ebbinghaus test includes the naming of a list of items. This test elicits that it is less complicated for human beings to bear in mind objects noted at the start or the cease of a list. However, some words in the list can also attract extra interest greater than others. Long-term memory has numerous kinds. A not unusual sort of long-time period memory is the semantic memory, which people use to pick out famous matters or names. Cognitive psychologists appreciably examine how the intellectual procedures technique and dedicate records. For that reason, they make use of diverse tactics to analyzing the effect of those mental capabilities on behavior. A great instance of a mental technique is the reductionist technique. This approach refers back to the ideology that irrespective of the complexity of human behavior, filtering of cognitive capabilities is possible. For that reason, it's far essential to emphasize the function of sensible studies and programs at the observe of cognitive psychology Of path, clinical research requires realistic packages and studies that prove the accuracy and legitimacy of the concepts. Therefore, cognitive psychology also requires a laboratory utilized for checking out the credibility of the various theories. Nonetheless, it's far important to mention that some laboratory studies might lack the proper laboratory validity. Considerably, this department of psychology includes the significant use of experimental methods. Cognitive psychology has theories that oppose some of the concepts of behaviorism and conditioning. It also antagonizes the standards of the various psychoanalytical theories developed through famous psychologists along with Sigmund Freud. Crucial evaluation of the various cognitive procedures indicates that the discovery of the computer systems caused an elevating hobby inside the comprehension of the whole idea of wondering. Psychology pupils agree that the sphere of cognitive psychology step by step advanced during the nineteen sixties. Well-known psychologists such as Jean Piaget laid the foundation for the improvement of ideas concerning cognitive wondering and reasoning. The synthetic intelligence device of the computer systems resembles how the various mental functions. Computer analogy gives a rough description concerning how the laptop strategies information. Consequently, cognitive psychologists hyperlink this system to the sequence of cognition. The paradigm of cognitive facts starts with the notion of numerous stimuli from the environment. It's applicable to point out that there are differences between behaviorism and cognitive psychology. Behaviorists continually take a look at the outside manifestations of human behavior. For that reason, they could most effectively take a look at the frame stimulus and response. Consequently, they handiest have a look at the center and output. As an alternative, cognitive psychologists agree that human behavior has an outside and internal thing. They, consequently, observe the input and response. Additionally, they look at how the inner procedures coordinate to mediate the production of a reaction after stimuli notion. As mentioned in advance, these coordination methods may also involve language, interest, and memory. Significantly, perception is a critical determinant of people's conduct. It entails the ability to feel the outside stimuli. Belief regularly occurs in the peripheral organs. They include the skin, eyes, ears, tongue, and nose. Those organs have nerve endings that could acquire stimuli from the outside surroundings. Consequently, conversion of stimuli to nerve impulses takes vicinity at these sites. Visual and auditory stimuli are several not unusual stimuli. Cognitive psychology deals with how the central worried gadget interprets those stimuli.

The notion is an example of a cognitive process that takes place constantly in regular human beings. Comatose patients may have an inadequate or impaired notion. Unarguably, the take a look at cognitive psychology involves a group of various concepts from the diverse fields of observation. Cognitive technological know-how and cognitive psychology percentage certain similarities. It is hard to distinguish among these areas of taking a look at. Even though crucial examination elicits various contrasts. Essential, cognitive psychology entails the knowledge of the motivating factors of human behavior. Hence, it seeks to explain why people act in specific methods after publicity to the identical sort of stimuli. Rather, cognitive science includes an accumulation of numerous standards from diverse topics of having a look at, especially, neuroscience. It extensively relies upon practical research and the usage of case studies.

History of Cognitive Psychology

History of Cognitive Psychology consistent with G. Miller of Princeton College, cognitive psychology is a method to psychology that emphasizes inner mental techniques. So, "for the reason that they start of experimental psychology inside the 19th century, there had been hobby inside the have a look at of higher mental procedures. however something discontinuous passed off within the late fifties, something so dramatic that it's far now referred to as the 'cognitive revolution,' and the view of intellectual processes that it spawned is known as 'cognitive psychology.' over time psychology, there were many scientists and psychologists who've taken it upon themselves to have a look at cognitive psychology. Such research has made predominant contributions to the arena of cognitive psychology. One contributor in the direction of cognitive psychology changed into George Armitage Miller. "Miller is an amazing subject to observe, for he literally embodies plenty of the records of cognitive psychology and cognitive technology. His career spans the cognitive revolution. He started as a great behaviorist but later came to reject behaviorism, turning into, in a single historian's words, 'the single best chief of the cognitive psychology.' similarly to being a modern thinker in his own proper, he additionally played the vital role of translator, introducing thoughts from different disciplines into psychology. Additionally, as co-founder of the Harvard Center for Cognitive research, he helped to institutionalize the cognitivist approach to psychology. In short, he did a great deal to offer current psychology its gift form" "at some point in the 1970s, Miller became one of the main advocates for the sector of cognitive science. His eBook, Language, and notion (1976) with Philip Johnson-Laird, helped to set the schedule for the field". Every other contributor to the cognitive psychology global might be Albert Bandura. "Bandura's initial application of studies at Stanford focused on the centrality of social modeling in humans. Whilst explorations of human cognition can be traced returned to

The works of Wundt, Cattell, and James can be credited with the beginnings of the cognitive approach to mental inquiries. In the Fifties, when researchers started to broaden theories of thoughts based on computational strategies and complex representations, the Cognitive Revolution commenced. Cognitive psychology, as a systematic field, is encouraged by way of philosophy, computer technology, and neuroscience, amongst many different disciplines together with biology and linguistics. However, not like many other psychological perspectives, cognitive psychology has constructed a reputation based on experimentation and the scientific approach. To apprehend cognitive psychology and assumptions, one must be aware of the important thing milestones that brought about its improvement and the function behaviorism performs in trying out the theories in cognitive psychology. Before the Cognitive Revolution, behaviorism dominated American psychology. Behaviourism is the "observe of laws touching on observable conduct to goal, observable stimulus conditions with none recourse to inner mental techniques". The success of behaviorism changed due to its emphasis on the behavior being observable and its purpose to simplify complex problem count numbers by breaking them down to their maximum primary units. The upward thrust of cognitive psychology is basically because behaviorism fails to talk about and account for internal intellectual techniques, along with grammar and language, techniques, complicated learning, and memory. It changed into these insufficiencies, fundamental to cognitive psychology, which brought about behaviorism's undoing and the Cognitive Revolution. A powerful effect at the beginning of cognitive psychology became the metaphor comparing human thoughts to a PC. However, the method of the use of metaphors to explain human thoughts isn't always a current occurrence. Descartes proposed a hydraulic machine of nerve characteristics and in the nineteenth century, researches in comparison the thoughts to a telephone switchboard. The similarities between the human mind and the computer prompted new questioning for the observation of thoughts. This metaphor was so influential that it has become known as the information processing model. The records processing version operates underneath the assumptions that human beings are processors of facts, which aid human concept and conduct; that representations of objects or activities and processes that perform on these representations underlie facts processing; and that information processing usually occurs within in large part isolated modules, which might be prepared in ranges and processing. Even though the metaphor did now not provide a complete reason for all human internal approaches, it did promote in addition questioning. Scientists have been cognizant that they wished aid for the idea that summary constructs could be fine to technology. The help they needed got here from fields, computer science, and neuroscience. With artificial intelligence, that is the pursuit of intelligent conduct through a pc, scientists have been capable of use sophisticated machines that were capable of logic and strategy to support theories of summary constructs. As you may bear in mind, behaviorists disregarded unobservable phenomena, and using a computer to measure unobservable conduct becomes taken into consideration to be unscientific. Allen Newell and Herb Simon (1956) developed software in the mid-1950s that proved theorems informal good judgment. There have been three important matters approximately this software and what it represented.

Limitations of Cognitive Psychology
Cognitive psychology is a critical field as it researches everything that makes up who someone is, based on what they recognize, think, and sense. Knowledge cognitive psychology can assist human beings to make better choices and help apprehend how people accomplish splendid matters. as an instance, if somcone is having a hard time

focusing in elegance and they discover whilst the chatty people in the back of them do now not display up they take better notes than it's far beneficial for them to cognitively determine to take a seat somewhere else. This case suggests how know-how cognitive psychology can allow a person to get to realize himself or herself higher, consequently making higher private decisions. Getting basic expertise of cognitive psychology includes 4 fundamental concepts: the intrinsic limitations of introspection and behaviorism, running reminiscence, the position of the amygdala, and the structure of a neuron and synapse. The idea of cognitive psychology took place within the Fifties, found through psychologists named Wilhelm Wundt and Edward Titchener. It changed into previously thought that psychology couldn't look at the world without delay, however, these researchers based the concept of introspection, meaning to take a look at and report our very own intellectual lives. Although introspection is regarded as an ingenious way to without delay have a look at humans, it turned out to have a couple of intrinsic limitations. First, it did now not account for the unconscious mind. The cognitive approach to psychology research inner facts strategies consisting of notion, attention, language, and memory. Cognitive psychologists look at those inner strategies and the way they affect our feelings and behaviors. while cognitive psychology has been very beneficial in growing new theories and finding out more about how thoughts work, there are some limitations to this approach.

1) Lacks ecological validity. This means researchers inside cognitive psychology regularly conduct their research within a 'fake' putting or one that does now not constitute

the real international. for example, a have a look at researching memory might involve testing contributors in a lecture room surroundings wherein they will feel under greater pressure to carry out properly, and their reminiscence overall performance may also consequently be worse than if it changed into measured of their own home. This loss of ecological validity makes outcomes of the study less consultant to everyday life and will suggest they are no longer applicable outdoor to the study surroundings.

2) Reductionist. Reductionism is a time period without a doubt used to describe theories that oversimplify human behaviors. some of the processes in psychology fail to take into account all the distinctive impacts that have an effect on the human mind and our behaviors and as an alternative selected to awareness on best one a part of the reason into how the thoughts works. In cognitive psychology man or woman, differences are often ignored, and it's far assumed all internal processing is the same in one-of-a-kind people. This is reductionist because it fails to account for environmental, organic, or genetic effects on cognitive function.

3) Incapability to at once degree cognitive feature. Every other big trouble for cognitive psychologists is that it is hard to degree internal methods inclusive of attention and perception. In preference to measuring this method' at once, cognitive psychologists use tests that measure behaviors, or external capabilities that they consider are related to the inner techniques. In doing this, researchers ought to infer that the internal process which they want to investigate is honestly associated with the recorded behaviors without having any evidence of this connection.

That is some other difficulty of the cognitive technique which can lower the validity of research inside the place.

Theory of Cognitive Psychology

The principle of Cognitive psychology looks at any individual as the source of processing the statistics simply any pc which perceives the input inside the form of facts after which processing it with the help of already installed information related to it and then it's far given out as an output via following the program. It is still feasible to observe the intellectual role of the mind through meditational approaches related to interest, perception, and reminiscence. Those are the degrees in processing the records in a human mind. Objects, information, eventualities are always present right here in our environment and we respond to them thru numerous moves and reactions of our thought's functionality. On every occasion a person looks at an item through his eyes, he will look at it only whilst he'll pay attention to that object. Every time we are aware of any specific item or someone, we start perceiving all the related information approximately it that's used for perceiving his capability to figure others' country as example emotions and his traits. There has been a widespread tradition that the belief and attention each affect the memory of someone depending upon the contemporary mind and beyond experience associated with comparable scenarios seen through the character. The 'attention' that is common to all doesn't need to cause the notion of the extracted data in an identical manner. Whether or not you realize it or now not, you are constantly employing cognitive tactics so that it will characteristic at some stage in the day. The term for the study of these cognitive approaches is cognitive psychology. Rutgers University defines cognitive psychology as "the clinical take a look at of mind and mental characteristic, which include mastering, reminiscence, attention, perception, reasoning, language, conceptual development, and selection making". One place of these cognitive tactics is called wayfinding. It includes several cognitive approaches consisting of knowing the relative area of a destination to the place to begin, knowing wherein matters are within the environment, making choices approximately which destination to visit first, and which path to take to get to the vacation spot. This literature evaluation will try to reduce the number of the disorder of the wayfinding field with the purpose to focus on one precise cognitive procedure in wayfinding: direction choice. In 2009, Wiener, Büchner, and Hölscher sought to categorize and provide an explanation for the huge array of wayfinding duties and the different cognitive sources required for the tasks. The shortage of categorization inside the field has resulted in research with ambiguous language that labels very exclusive duties as absolutely "wayfinding". Navigation is made from locomotion, that is response to 1's immediate surroundings i.e. steering, heading off boundaries, and the technique of a visible object, and wayfinding, which is described as "navigation in environmental. Because of the circuit board of a laptop, information streams via the channels of thoughts at a lightning-rapid pace. But, what takes place whilst you lose this essential characteristic? As soon as lost, a person may want to right now understand the absolute need for it. The need to apprehend how records are stored and recalled become thought not so widely accompanied thru till the concept of cognitive psychology got here along. Cognitive Psychology is broadly known as the study to recognize the deep complexity of processing and recalling records that can determine our behaviors and emotions. Three principal focuses make contributions to the have a look at cognitive psychology. The first is a memory that can be checked out because of the storage of information, both without delay and stored during a given duration of time. Of direction, a properly working memory can help or prevent someone which causes it to be studied in cognitive psychology often. The second region targeted in this unique gadget is belief. Perception plays a crucial role in how we as individuals view and interpret the surroundings around us, and combines with the values and ideals on why we're deciphering this data in a particular way. Learning is the remaining of the three areas and most interesting while a person develops the idea or course to adapt to what's being presented exchange route. The take a look at of studying in the confines of cognitive psychology brings us to a psychologist who delivered. In the twentieth century, several psychologists have become fascinated with intellectual sports studies in people, which include facts techniques, reminiscence, and communique. This new direction received the name of cognitive psychology. One of the pioneers, who installed this direction in psychology technological know-how, was Swiss biologist, Jean Piaget. Piaget's discoveries and concepts have made a considerable contribution to the growth of cognitive psychology thoughts. His studies and concepts that were based on children mastering and progressing helped him to form his well-known principle of 4 developmental levels, which later discovered supporters and critics among many psychologists. Even though a great deal of his work covered analyses of baby's improvement, he defined himself as a "genetic epistemologist", no longer a baby psychologist. He emphasized that his research has been devoted to the epistemological query: How can we get the information? This essay covers data approximately his education and profession, most important accomplishments, and his theoretical techniques, consisting of the four mental growth stages of the kid's development. We're going to briefly describe each of the levels one by one and examine the significance of his research in trendy. Schooling and profession. Jean Piaget becomes born in August 1986, in Neuchâtel, Switzerland in their own family of historians. On account of their early formative years, he turned into interest by studies of the natural sciences.

Significance of Cognitive Psychology

Extensively, cognitive psychology plays an essential role in the various branches of medication. The treatment of depression makes use of the standards of cognitive remedy. Melancholy is step by step growing in various areas. Essentially, many practitioners and medical experts use pharmacological remedies to manipulate despair. But, statistics display that most effective 60% of sufferers enjoy the use of antidepressants. Antidepressants have detrimental facet effects. Many patients taking antidepressants revel in weight gain. Moreover, there are numerous reviews of patients experiencing allergic reaction reactions because of the usage of antidepressants. For that reason, the management of depression has to consist of a combination of pharmacological and non-pharmacological remedies. Non-pharmacological therapy, regularly, entails the usage of cognitive therapy. In this remedy model, the patient teaches himself to manipulate the depressive signs and symptoms. Studies show that there's a gradual development of symptoms the usage of this version. In fact, the use of antidepressants best isn't a higher opportunity because patients lose the internal ability to manipulate their moods. Crucially, character psychology has greater due to the overall comprehension of the concepts of cognitive psychology. Obviously, individuals have various personality developments. Consequently, the various methods of perception and record processing have an impact on the way people behave. In reality, research display that some persona problems may also evolve because of cognitive dysfunction. Cognitive therapy is crucial in the control of personality and intellectual disorders. It involves schooling individuals to govern their actions and behavior. Additionally, cognitive psychology has empowered educational psychology. Psychologists can now illustrate how human beings handle and process data. The numerous theories in the schooling region utilize ideas from this department of psychology. For example, the numerous differences of long-time period and quick-time period reminiscence have furnished extra insight on how students analyze. Furthermore, instructors can decide the reasons for amnesia in a scholar by the use of the memory version. Cognitive psychology has also multiplied the knowledge of know-how employers. Jean Piaget developed various ideologies and theories concerning the cognitive improvement of humans from adulthood to early life. His theories elaborated how people have various sorts of conduct. In truth, he came up with a model that defined how skipping sure childhood stages may additionally result in the manifestation of certain peculiar conduct. Cognitive psychology played a critical function in the improvement of his theories. In fact, it's miles essential to feature that the essential principles of developmental psychology relate with the ones of cognitive psychology. The cognitive development of a child significantly makes use of metacognition. Therefore, the kid focuses on their mind then it assumes that each different individual additionally has thoughts and feelings. Metacognition is a cognition process that includes an important analysis of one's thoughts. It allows human beings to gauge their intellectual performance. Vitally, cognitive psychology aids in defining the diverse reasons for social dysfunction. In accordance to investigate, anti-social people have a depressed statistics processing function. They have a confined functionality of processing social stimuli. Additionally, they cannot evolve the perfect social response or cue. Various social fashions hint at the various levels of human beings as they develop to maturity. Cognitive psychology performs a massive position in the development of humans. It includes the take a look at of ways mental procedures affect the behavior and deeds of people. It's really worth noting that cognitive psychology examines how people understand and manner statistics. It offers the inner processes that arise before the evolution of a response. As noted in advance, various cognitive techniques play a predominant position in figuring out the behavior of humans. Interest, language, memory, and notion are the principal examples of cognitive procedures. They happen in numerous ways.

As an example, interest filters the uncooked information that enters the principal apprehensive device. This information is continually in the shape of sensory enter. Nonetheless, it avoids the overload of information inside the brain. There are various criticisms of the ideas of cognitive psychology. Behaviorists together with B.F. Skinner opposes the theories of cognitive psychology. According to them, the simplest determinant of behavior was outside stimuli. They declare that there are no data processing methods that take place within the valuable nervous gadget. Moreover, several behaviorists together with Carl Rogers consider that the usage of the laboratory for sensible research is not suitable and credible. Conclusively, the theorists intricate the numerous merits of cognitive psychology. Many fields of look at utilize standards that originate from cognitive psychology. It has caused an enhanced comprehension of educational psychology. Teachers and educational professionals can now apprehend how the various forms of memory decide the gaining knowledge of costs of college students. Except, sociologists can now explain the origins of the numerous forms of social troubles. An assessment shows that aggressive individuals lack the precise schematic manner of sensory perception and data processing. The sector of developmental psychology has majorly benefited from understanding how the numerous cognitive features relate. As an instance, Jean Piaget notably applied the ideas of cognitive improvement to explain the diverse stages of development from youth to maturity. In summary, cognitive psychology is an essential section of psychology that explains the conduct of people.

Chapter Four

Academic intelligence

What's Intelligence? This has been a question for so long as we were capable of understanding human beings have minds to think. These days there are as many factors of intelligence as human beings are looking to study and apprehend it. For arguments, sake allows using the definition of intelligence, has the potential to learn about, learn from, apprehend, and engage with one's environment. Even though there won't be an agreed-upon definition of intelligence, tries to test intelligence arose in France inside the early 1900s. This is called trying out the Intelligence Quotient (IQ) of a character. The IQ, extensively described, is the degree of intelligence which can be determined through a standardized take look. The first intelligence test become created in 1905 by using Alfred Binet and Theodore Simon, in reaction to the request made using the French authorities to become aware of college students who wished extra assist mastering. As Intelligence trying out has become an excepted degree of intelligence it began to be used in several special areas. Since the inception of IQ testing, there has been steady controversy over the discriminatory and biased nature of these assessments. Human beings began to argue that those IQ tests have been biased in opposition to minorities. This notion turned into, in component, primarily based on outcomes of IQ tests always displaying African individuals scoring decrease than Caucasian kids on these standardized tests. May want to this be approximately ethnic differences in intelligence, character environments, or is it proof that IQ tests are biased? With great research, I was able to discover the origins of intelligence, theories of intelligence trying out and, troubles of validity while making use of those theories to minority companies. Intelligence is also understood because of the potential to collect expertise, to think and supply cause successfully, and to deal adaptively with the environment. This mental potential enables him within the undertaking of theoretical in addition to practical manipulation of things, gadgets, or events found in his surroundings on the way to adapt or face new demanding situations and problems in life as correctly as feasible. Intelligence derives from the potential to research and utilize what has been found out in adjusting to new situations and fixing new troubles. The idea of intelligence owes a lot to early studies of animals gaining knowledge. Approximately a century in the past, following courses of Darwin's "Origin of Species", there was a flurry of interest in the evolution of intelligence, and lots of checks were devised to measure intelligence in animals starting from ants to chimpanzees. Those were exams of studying potential. The overall technique was to dam a customary get admission to meals or to introduce a stressful element from which escape become possible. Intelligence is the potential to recognize the world, assume rationally, and use resources efficaciously while confronted with demanding situations. Intelligence represents a focus for psychologists; they intend to understand how human beings are capable of undertaking their behaviors to the surroundings wherein they live. It also represents a key component of the way individuals fluctuate from each other inside how they find out about and apprehend the sector. Mental assessments are used to measure character variations that exist amongst human beings in competencies, aptitudes, hobbies, and issues of persona. Intelligence, an easy yet complex time period, present in ordinary, layman vocabulary and argued by way of most minds of psychology. Intelligence is presently described as the capacity for goal-directed, adapted behaviors. The definition has gone a couple of revisions due to the fact we've modified our very understanding of intelligence, first of all, used to explain educational brilliance and rote memorization, the modern-day definition encompasses more fields consisting of road smarts, phrase play, interpersonal interactions, and abstract reasoning. Possibly the most interesting element of all is how intelligence modifications from tradition to lifestyle; an amazing farmer is a genius in an agricultural society and a dullard. Flynn made a stunning discovery; his studies indicated that IQ ratings have been on a non-stop upward push due to the fact the beginning of the 20th century, or greater precisely increasing at a fee of three factors a twelve months or three points a decade. This consistent growth in IQ ratings has been termed because of the Flynn effect and some thrilling theories are explaining it. higher IQ rankings had been recorded primarily based on facts from the standardized test WISC (Wechsler Intelligence Scale for kids), especially the increase in IQ isn't a standard upward thrust however instead a higher rating in two subtests that target abstract reasoning, and as a consequence, growth in summary common sense is referred to as a motive for the Flynn impact. Another possible rationalization is the current global we live, in our technological age we've got machines that want high degrees of good judgment to operate and have interaction with, moreover, those machines have an excessive price of data processing and as a result of which created a need for humans which can compute faster, and they'll, in turn, construct faster machines, putting in place a comments loop that step by step increases intelligence. First of all, Rodger says improved adolescence nutrients, secondly, time-honored schooling, thirdly, smaller families, and lastly the impact of educated moms on their children. Every other reason that supports the rise in intelligence would be the manner our subculture appears at formal schooling. until the start of the twentieth century, maximum people had only approximately seven years of training; these days findings indicate that over 1/2 of adults have at the least a few tertiary schooling. Those findings are similar reasons for growth in intelligence. Moreover, the exchange of occupations from agricultural-based ones to technical and managerial jobs has created a greater intellectual society, which has led to a boom in common sense talents and as a result of which extended intelligence check rankings.

Knowledge Intelligence

For lots, intelligence is a time period this is difficult to define, and it could mean various things to special human beings. The problem is defining what intelligence is has created a war of words amongst those studying it. Nowadays the definition of intelligence seems to be characterized via who is studying it at that second. The origins of intelligence can be traced as far back because the 1800s. at some point in the 1800's Charles Darwin and

George Romanes, in the midst of comparative research with animals, started to notice conduct that was regarded to illustrate a few degrees of intelligence. Romanes software of look concentrated, for the most element, on animal intelligence. Romanes labored diligently to show that there was continuity among animal and human intelligence. Romanes proposed that intelligence become the capability to recognize the difference between "unperceived characteristics" from "perceived characteristics". Lloyd Morgan, in 1892, criticized Romane's work and proposed that human beings and animals did no longer have commonalities about intelligence however that they, in fact, we're pretty exceptional. Morgan described human intelligence as a behavioral and neurological characteristic that allowed human beings to motive thru "rational inference". Despite how we pick to define it, attempts to broaden assessments to measure intelligence began in 1904. John McKeen Cattell turned into the first, within the observation of information intelligence, to introduce the idea of the "mental check". At some stage in the early 1900s, the French schooling machine required all kids to wait for college. This condition gave upward push to the significance of finding a way to distinguish those students who required brought help from individuals who did now not. To solve this problem, the French authorities employed Alfred Binet to broaden a test to assist discover who these pupils, were. Binet, with the assist of his assistant Theodore Simon, evolved the primary IQ exams in 1905. The primary intelligence exams had been known as "the Binet-Simon Scale". Binet did not accept as true that his method might be used to calculate an inherited stage of intelligence. He struggled with reducing intelligence to a single unit, suggesting that intelligence is some distance too vast an idea to quantify with more than a few. He believed that intelligence is influenced through several matters and its modifications over the years. Further, Binet believed that validity became received only whilst take a look at scores are in comparison among youngsters with comparable backgrounds. The Binet – Simon scale become added to the united states by using Henry Goddard in 1908. Goddard attempted to apply the take a look at as a way to show intelligence changed into an inherited trait and proceeded to show this factor along with his case observation of the Kallikak family. Goddard used those tests to aid his perception that those he diagnosed as "feebleminded" should not procreate and that this so-known as "gene" had to be eliminated. At the same time as studying at Clark University, Lewis Terman has become interested in the examination of intelligence testing and conducted an observation with 14 adolescent boys. Terman, like Goddard, used the outcomes of this observation to guide his perception that heredity changed into the prime indicator of intelligence. Terman, even as hired a Stanford University, revised and standardized the Binet take a look at, renamed it the Stanford- Binet Scale, and had it posted in 1916. While global warfare I came, U.S. army officers had to screen a massive number of navy recruits. In 1917, psychologist Robert Yerkes developed two checks called the navy Alpha and Beta tests. The exams were administered to cover a million squaddies so that you can help the military pick out which men were suitable for precise positions and others who are probably suitable for leadership roles. After the war ended, IQ checks remained in use on a variety of occasions. One specific state of affairs worried about using IQ assessments to screen new immigrants as they entered the US. The outcomes showed big numbers of immigrants scoring specifically low on those tests. This consequently resulted in discriminatory generalizations approximately entire populations and led Congress to skip immigration regulations. Goddard, Terman, and Yerkes all believed that intelligence becomes frequently genetic and surroundings had little to do with a person's overall capabilities. Others like Edward Lee Thorndike however did not. Thorndike believed that intelligence was a characteristic of experience. Thorndike believed that for you to measure character intelligence it turned into crucial to apprehend cultural background as properly. David Wechsler examined the Stanford-Binet and believed it had too many obstacles for use as the fundamental degree of intelligence, so he decided to increase a test of his very own. In 1955 the first Wechsler Adult Intelligence Scale (WAIS) was posted (Kaufman, 1990). Wechsler also evolved two assessments to use with children, the Wechsler Intelligence Scale for children (WISC) and the Wechsler Preschool and Primary Scale of Intelligence (WPPSI). The personal version of the test has been revised numerous instances since its original publication. Wechsler tests are nevertheless in use nowadays, as is the Stanford – Binet but, each having been through a chain of revisions because of what is called the "Flynn effect"(the fact that IQs have become higher every year). Other in all likelihood motives for revisions may well have been due to possible bias.

So what about racial bias with Intelligence checking out? it's far obvious that the authentic Binet-Simon scale, the navy alpha and Beta assessments, and the Stanford-Binet check had quite a chunk of bias, and has resulted in wrong assumptions about people (i.e. immigrants looking to get into the country). The query approximately the validity of IQ tests has been in debate since the first test was developed. A few humans assume that cultural biases in IQ testing act in opposition to ethnic minorities. Extensive court docket cases including parents in motion on unique education (PASE) vs. Hannonost and, Larry P. vs. Riles alleged that IQ exam questions are written in want of the white, center-class. The courts gave contradictory opinions of standardized testing in those cases. The court ruled in the PASE case that IQ assessments had been legitimate so long as different elements together with SES and environment had been used to area students in advanced classes. Inside the Riles case, however, the court ruled IQ checking out changed into biased. It's far unclear if checking out is biased or simply now not been researched sufficient to bear in mind whether there's the cultural bias or now not. Simply as Reynolds (2000) factors out, our venture is to understand why these variations exist without our feelings and beliefs entering into our manner. Could those assessments possibly be biased? Maybe. What's greater essential, I trust, is that we can all agree that intelligence is multifaceted. Intelligence is also relative and, ever converting as we keep analyzing new things. Intelligence professionals can also by no means agree on a proper definition of intelligence or how to degree it. It's far one of these "is it nature or is it nurture" questions. My personal belief is that it's a mixture of both. Various individuals have given their thought of intelligence. Intelligence is broadly related to the achievement of success or mastery in a given idea. Consequently, it seems affordable to a country that intelligence is essentially a capability. The controversy starts when people attempt to define what exactly this ability is and to what entity this capacity may be attributed. A few claim this ability is solely innate and in other nations, it is stimulated via one's environment. Consequently, time plays a crucial position in this idea. The amount of time someone takes to comprehend an idea is associated with the diploma of capacity that one has. As a result, this is why the time period gradual or retarded exists, relating to the time people take to understand an idea. However, people known to be geniuses are capable of grasp a concept in a short time without the "proper formal" education. For this reason, the duration of the concept of time is significant to the widely generic concept of intelligence. Intelligence is basically attributed to the brain. Spearman had indicated that intelligence stems from intellectual strength placed somewhere in the brain. Moreover, the manifestations of smart behaviors are because of this intellectual energy. This concept does seem to have some legitimate factors. Scientists were capable of discovering that the shape and chemicals within the brain related to our behaviors. A mind lesion at the arcuate fasciculus areas influences one's capability to copy words and non-phrases.

Intelligence is a concept Psychology
There are implicit and explicit theories of intelligence. Implicit theories are people's ordinary thoughts that surround a selected subject matter. Consequently, implicit theories of intelligence are regular thoughts that surround

intelligence. A layperson is a non-expert in a selected area and intelligence researchers have checked out laypersons' theories of intelligence. Sternberg, Conway, Ketron, and Bernstein (1981) performed a study to research individuals' conceptions of intelligence. A pattern of members had been required to list behaviors that had been characteristic of 'intelligence', 'academic intelligence', 'everyday intelligence' or 'unintelligence'. After this, another sample of contributors was requested to charge how effectively every of the listed behaviors meditated aspects of intelligence. After reading the consequences of the examination, Sternberg et al. (1981) identified three dimensions of intelligence: practical hassle solving, verbal capability, and social competence. A further look at turned into carried out with the aid of Sternberg (1985) into laypersons' theories of intelligence. In this have a look at, forty-seven individuals were asked to think about behaviors that had been characteristic of a clever character. Those hints enabled Sternberg (1985) to supply descriptors of smart behaviors. Then, college students were requested to type those descriptors into those that were possible to be discovered together in a person. Sternberg (1985) pronounced comparable findings in his 1981 examination from the results of this undertaking, however, he additionally discovered six components to intelligence: practical hassle-solving potential, verbal potential, intellectual balance and integration, purpose orientation and attainment, contextual intelligence, and fluid idea. So that you can assess the variations in the manner laypersons and professionals inside the field of intelligence considered intelligence, Sternberg (1985) asked specialists inside the discipline of intelligence to complete questionnaires. They determined a high correlation among the professionals and the laypersons in their implicit views of intelligence. Laypersons positioned greater emphasis on the social and cultural aspects of intelligence, whereas experts emphasized the function of motivation. It's also noteworthy that lay conceptions of intelligence are a great deal broader than psychologists' professional conceptions. In conclusion, implicit theories of intelligence do have limitations. Rather than presenting an account of intelligence, they offer a powerful framework that people use to organize and interpret their views of intelligence. They also lack specificity in that the kinds of behaviors that emerge from analysis of the theories could be very widespread. Those theories do additionally have strengths. Implicit theories have contextual relevance as they tend to place importance on the context wherein intelligence is displayed. They're additionally effortlessly falsified, despite being vague in their formulations. Finally, they have an excessive ecological validity and awareness greater on ordinary performance as opposed to maximal performance, in contrast to specific theories. In analyzing the outcomes of implicit theories research, it's far essential to note that they offer a basis for specific theories as a way to now be mentioned. The classical, explicit theories that nowadays have the most influence on information intelligence at the moment are considered. Specific theories of intelligence are primarily based on data collected from studies presumed to degree human beings' intelligent functioning. These express theories can be divided into differential and cognitive theories. A traditional example of a differential idea was developed by way of Spearman (1927) who argued that intelligence is constituted of two factors: widespread elements and specific elements. All through a study, Spearman (1904) observed that kids' rankings on several mental assessments were definitely correlated, and so he concluded that there may be one well-known aspect that underlies all cognitive movements, 'I'm. Alongside 'I'm, Spearman (1904) found a thing of intelligence referred to as unique abilities, or. This refers to every sort of intelligence needed for acting nicely on an intelligence project. Assist for the life of 'go has been supplied and found that mice seem to exhibit a shape of 'go. Express theories of intelligence have several excellent strengths. They provide a detailed specification of the intellectual structures and tactics which may be concerned with intelligent overall performance. Additionally, they have made it possible for researchers to move past the trivial operational definition of intelligence as what intelligence tests degree. In contrast, explicit theories also have notable weaknesses. A number of the theories have confirmed hard to falsify result of intrinsic traits that make falsification nearly impossible. express theories additionally fail to notice the contexts wherein intelligence behaviors happen, however, many psychologists have argued whether it is even possible to fully apprehend the idea of intelligence without paying attention to the context in which it's far exercised. They've also failed to provide an express basis for the selection of responsibilities on the idea of which to look at intelligence. There are many problems associated with intelligence trying out, but there are 3 which arise most often in intelligence literature: the reliability of intelligence measures, the validity of intelligence measures, and whether or not the usefulness of intelligence measures is exaggerated. The reliability of a test can seek advice from the internal reliability and the test-retest reliability. Internal reliability refers to the intelligence measure together with some of the items that correlate positively with each other, suggesting that they're measuring the identical construct. Check-retest reliability refers to how reliable a check stays over the years. An awesome intelligence check will display an excessive level of reliability through the years as one's intelligence is considered by many psychologists to be stable. Therefore, it may be assumed that if a character became to take an intelligence check on one event then take the equal check a while later they could get similar IQ scores. The main argument against intelligence checks being dependable or not entails thinking whether trendy intelligence rankings (IQ) can range and fluctuate. Intelligence researchers including Benson (2003) have estimated that this fluctuation may be as a lot as 15 IQ factors. It is recognized that different elements such as educational heritage and temper can also affect this fluctuation. The fluctuation is made even more due to the fact intelligence tests are the handiest alleged to be taken as soon as; they need to by no means be repeated. This helps to lessen the likelihood of a man or woman memorizing the questions worried within the check and eventually appearing higher ensuing in a better IQ rating. This situation of fluctuating intelligence ratings is taken into consideration so vital that a high-quality deal of studies has been carried out with the aid of intelligence psychologists over time. The primary findings of this research display that even though it is broadly diagnosed that intelligence rankings do range to some extent, they're surprisingly stable. Jones and Bayley (1941) set up the Berkeley increase study wherein they tested a sample of one hundred and twenty-eight children yearly for the duration of their adolescence on their intelligence and that they recorded their IQ scores. The findings of this look showed that the kids' IQ ratings at the age of eighteen have been positively correlated with the IQ rankings which have been recorded once they were twelve years antique. This helps the argument that intelligence ratings are solid to a point. However, it can be argued that Jones and Bayley's (1941) Berkeley growth study does have some troubles while accounting for a correlation among IQ scores at one-of-a-kind a while. The individuals of their look at were all American kids, and so one may also question whether those results have high ecological validity, that is whether or not those effects may be carried out to youngsters from different cultures. Additionally, all individuals were examined as toddlers, but most effective seventy were accompanied up later in lifestyles. Therefore, the findings were simplest primarily based on twenty-nine children. Support for Jones and Bayley's (1941) take a look at does exist inside the form of a follow-up study of intelligence and correlation between IQ scores conducted via Deary, Whalley, Lemmon, Crawford, and Starr (2000). The mental Survey Committee in Scotland had measured intelligence in Scottish kids who were born in 1921 and attended school in 1932. Those human beings have been followed up, then aged seventy-seven, and consequences confirmed that IQ scores on assessments from early life to past due in life have been enormously strong. Therefore, the correlations among IQ ratings on intelligence tests are putting, but they may be no longer ideal. Inner consistency is every other shape of reliability and involves the consistency of measurement inside the intelligence take a look at itself. An instance of that is given by way of Gregory (1998) who argues that if a Weschler subtest has internal consistency, all the gadgets in the test would be measuring the same skill. Evidence of this would come from excessive correlations between the number of objects. The second query that emerges from the take a look at intelligence is whether or not or not a test measures what it's designed to measures. This is referred to as validity. The query placed forth is whether an intelligence check does in reality measure one's intelligence. But, it needs to be acknowledged that there are one-of-a-kind forms of validity, namely assemble validity, content validity, and criterion-related capacity. As intelligence is regarded as a concept or intellectual assemble, an intelligence check is visible to have assembled validity whilst it effectively assesses the mental concept that it is designed to a degree, specifically intelligence. This will be indicated through hyperlinks among IQ scores and other behaviors that it ought to be related to. Consequently, one may also argue that if intelligence tests had excessive assemble validity, then the person variations in IQ rankings would be the sole result of variations in intelligence. Perfect construct validity can never be attained, as formerly cited, different elements along with motivation and academic history also have a power on IQ ratings. Content validity is likewise visible to make contributions to construct validity. Content validity is the diploma to which gadgets on a take a look at measure all the skills which can be seen to underpin the assembling of interest. If an intelligence check inclusive of the Wechsler person Intelligence Scale became to be analyzed, it'd display that subsets of the check are measuring different intelligence abilities that they have been designed to a degree. Additionally, researchers who increase these intelligence exams strive to have high validity for all components of their take a look at and so if no validity changed into proven in improvement, then the researchers could be obliged to improve the intelligence degree until it had full validity. If an intelligence takes a look at is n reality measuring what it is designed to measure, the IQ rankings it produces ought to permit behaviors that might be considered to be laid low with intelligence to be expected. These predictions are known as criterion measures, and so criterion-associated validity is the capacity of IQ scores to correlate with criterion measures. One grievance of intelligence measures is the diploma to which they predict the forms of effects we count on intelligence to persuade, which includes academic and career attainment.

The very last question which emerges from the size of intelligence is whether their usefulness is exaggerated. Intelligence assessments are criticized similarly in that their capacity to expect intellectual performance in special cultures is overemphasized. It's widely recognized that intelligence check rankings greatly expect one's educational and work overall performance. People who are against intelligence testing argue that fluctuations exist inside the predictive electricity of intelligence tests. For example, while different situations or obligations alternate or while extraordinary demographics such as age, race, or gender are taken into consideration. Benson (2003) argues that unique education is one place wherein those issues are obvious and that's concerned with human beings laid low with unique wishes. This issue emerges from the use of intelligence tests to categories learning disabilities using the IQ-achievement discrepancy model. The model is used to compare kids' instructional success to their IQ score. If a child's success rating is a popular deviation or extra under their IQ score, they're taken into consideration to have a learning difficulty. Two research spotlight the issues of the usefulness of the IQ-success discrepancy model. Each research determined insignificant typical effect size variations between IQ-discrepant and non-discrepant terrible readers, with insignificant variations on most measures of phonological capacity and studying. Other research which as compared humans with poor reading skills with and without large IQ-achievement discrepancies did no longer discover any difference in prognosis. These problems show that the usage of intelligence measuring is certainly exaggerated and that they do not support the technique of identifying getting to know disabilities based on a discrepancy among fulfillment and IQ rankings. moreover, Benson (2003) claims that figuring out individuals as having getting to know disabilities the use of the IQ-fulfillment discrepancy version does now not assist others to apprehend what they need to to help the individual learn or provide any indication to the academic software that a person may also enroll in to enhance themselves. Possibly a better indicator would be to assess the individual's behaviors inside the domestic or social settings. Intelligence researchers have been taking into consideration methods to lessen the issues related to measuring intelligence through the use of an IQ-fulfillment discrepancy model. Kaufman and Kaufman (2001) counseled that intelligence checks ought to be administered by trained educational practitioners with an understanding of the baby getting to know. As opposed to simply getting an IQ rating, these human beings might work closely with the child and make unique recommendations. Kaufman and Kaufman (2001) argue that in this context, there may be no cause to abolish the only use of intelligence checks; rather these exams ought to be used at the side of other academic equipment. In conclusion, both implicit and explicit theories have been advanced in a try and outline the idea of intelligence; but, all theories have limitations that have to be considered. Both varieties of theories can be taken into consideration connected in some manner as implicit theories provide a basis for express theories. The three questions which have been discussed in terms of the dimension of intelligence – validity, reliability, and the usefulness of such measures – display elements that must be addressed so as for the measurement of intelligence to be accurate.

The pros and Cons of Intelligence

Intelligence Redefined It's a vivid, stunning day outside. Birds are cawing, dogs are barking, and kids are yelling as they chase each different around. My pal KC, but, isn't always outside taking part in this climate, however, rather is inside playing video games. Why is that this? Is he lazy? Perhaps it's too warm for him. Maybe the insects eat him up whilst he goes outdoor. While requested approximately his choice of staying inner and playing video games as opposed to going outdoor, he wryly spoke back, "that is what I'm correct at and I experience it." Therein lies the essence of intelligence: spotting what you're proficient at and the usage of those proficiencies in a way that advantages you in some way. Not every person can paint or create a song. a few revels in rock-mountaineering or jogging lengthy…display more content material…

All of us are one-of-a-kind, with various levels and forms of intelligence. In well-known, intelligence isn't merely a measure of one's scalability with a certain talent; it is usually being capable of observe expertise toward actual-lifestyles situations in this kind of way as to be helpful for the man or woman involved. IQ exams degree positive forms of intelligence, but they can't paint a complete photo of someone with just more than a few. Jason Garver also mentions how IQs can trade overtime in his article "Intelligence: shifting past IQ." someone with a low IQ rating could without difficulty be one of the exceptional musicians of our era, or vice-versa. KC possesses well-known intelligence due to the fact he makes use of his earlier knowledge and studies, alongside his diverse competencies so that you can similarly his understanding of the world. the focal point of this paper, but, can be to interrupt down trendy intelligence into Howard Gardner's theory of more than one Intelligence and use KC's reviews and abilities to narrate every kind of intelligence again to every different. Professor of education at Harvard College. It suggests that the traditional perception of intelligence, primarily based on I.Q. trying out is far too limited. Instead, Dr. Gardner proposes 8 distinctive bits of intelligence to account for a broader variety of human capability in kids and adults. This intelligence is:

- Linguistic intelligence ("word smart")
- Logical-mathematical intelligence ("number/reasoning clever")
- Spatial intelligence ("photo smart")
- Physical-Kinesthetic intelligence ("frame smart")

- Musical intelligence ("song clever")
- Interpersonal intelligence ("people smart")
- Intrapersonal intelligence ("self-clever")
- Naturalist intelligence ("nature clever")

Dr. Gardner says that our schools and lifestyle cognizance most in their attention on linguistic and logical-mathematical intelligence. We esteem the exceedingly articulate or logical human beings of our subculture. But, Dr. Gardner says that we have to additionally place equal interest on folks who show gifts in the other intelligence: the artists, architects, musicians, naturalists, designers, dancers, therapists, entrepreneurs, and others who enrich the world wherein we stay. Alas, many kids who have these presents don't acquire a great deal of reinforcement for them in faculty. Many of these children, in reality, become being categorized as "mastering disabled," "upload (attention deficit disorder," or virtually underachievers, whilst their precise methods of thinking and mastering aren't addressed by way of a heavily linguistic or logical-mathematical lecture room. The idea of multiple intelligences proposes a primary transformation within the way our colleges are run. It indicates that teachers study to offer their training in a wide variety of methods the use of song, cooperative mastering, artwork sports, role play, multimedia, discipline journeys, internal mirrored image, and plenty extra. The good information is that the principle of multiple intelligences has grabbed the eye of many educators across the US, and loads of colleges are presently the use of its philosophy to remodel the way it educates youngsters. The awful information is that there are heaps of faculties nevertheless out there that train within the identical antique dull way, through dry lectures, and boring worksheets and textbooks. The venture is to get this data out to many greater teachers, faculty directors, and others who work with kids so that every child has the possibility to examine in approaches harmonious with their unique minds (see of their personal manner). The principle of more than one intelligence also has robust implications for adult studying and improvement. Many adults find themselves in jobs that don't make most fulfilling use in their most notably developed intelligence (for instance, the tremendously physical-kinesthetic character who's caught in a linguistic or logical table-process whilst he or she would be much happier in a task in which they could circulate, consisting of a recreational leader, a forest ranger, or physical therapist). The theory of multiple intelligences offers adults a whole new way to have a look at their lives, analyzing potentials that they left in the back of their formative years (such as a love for artwork or drama) however now have the opportunity to expand through guides, pursuits, or other packages of self-development.

A way to train or research whatever eight one of a kind approaches

One of the most exceptional features of the concept of more than one intelligence is the way it provides eight distinctive potential pathways to gaining knowledge. If an instructor is having an issue achieving a student inside the more traditional linguistic or logical approaches of training, the principle of more than one intelligence suggests numerous different ways wherein the cloth might be offered to facilitate powerful learning. Whether you are a kindergarten instructor, a graduate school trainer, or an adult learner searching for higher methods of pursuing self-take a look at any difficulty of hobby, the same fundamental recommendations follow. Something you are teaching or mastering, see how you may connect it with

- Phrases (linguistic intelligence)
- Numbers or good judgment (logical-mathematical intelligence)
- Images (spatial intelligence)
- Track (musical intelligence)
- Self-mirrored image (intrapersonal intelligence)
- A physical enjoy (bodily-kinesthetic intelligence)
- A social enjoy (interpersonal intelligence), and/or
- A revel in within the natural world. (naturalist intelligence)

as an example, if you're teaching or getting to know approximately the regulation of supply and call for in economics, you may examine approximately it (linguistic), take a look at a mathematical formulation that specific it (logical-mathematical), study a photo chart that illustrates the principle (spatial), study the regulation in the herbal world (naturalist) or in the human world of commerce (interpersonal); look at the regulation in terms of your very own body [e.g. whilst you supply your frame with lots of food, the starvation call for is going down; whilst there's very little deliver, your belly's demand for meals is going way up and also you get hungry] (bodily-kinesthetic and intrapersonal); and/or write a song that demonstrates the law. You don't have to teach or study something in all eight approaches, just see what the possibilities are, and then determine which particular pathways interest you the most, or seem to be the best coaching or mastering gear.

The concept of multiple intelligences is so interesting because it expands our horizon of available coaching/gaining knowledge of tools past the conventional linguistic and logical methods used in maximum faculties. To get began, but the topic of anything you're inquisitive about coaching or getting to know about inside the middle of a blank sheet of paper and draw eight immediately strains or "spokes" radiating out from this topic. Label each line with extraordinary intelligence. Then start brainstorming ideas for coaching or learning that topic and write down ideas next to every intelligence (this is a spatial-linguistic method of brainstorming; you may need to try this in different methods as properly, the use of a tape-recorder, having a set brainstorming session, and many others.). Having the ability to distinguish among what kinds of intelligence humans have is a step toward acceptance on a big scale for any and every person. There are numerous scales among those categories, starting from having a superb deal of said intelligence to having very little. Intelligence isn't black and white as some consider, but as an alternative, a large, interlocking mechanism of our skills and abilities, carried out to actual global situations. all of us are born with a certain level of base intelligence, however, what they do with that intelligence and the way tough they work on their competencies or abilities determines how plenty of a positive intelligence kind that man or woman possesses. a few humans are greater willing towards certain intelligence types than others. Again, this is something they may be born with, but that doesn't mean that they couldn't enhance their different intelligence types through tough work and accumulation of knowledge. The intelligence listed above is not comprehensive, although they provide a solid framework with which we must study intelligence in the way it is.

Educational and intelligence

Although psychologists and laypeople regularly think of intelligence as a unitary entity, diverse aspects of intelligence (e.g., intelligence validated in a schoolroom and intelligence proven in everyday life) may be fairly wonderful. One of the earliest psychologists to make this factor became an experimental psychologist, Thorndike (1924), who argued that social intelligence is wonderful from the sort of intelligence measured by using traditional intelligence tests. Many others ultimately have made this declaration as well as approximately social and realistic intelligence. A related claim becomes made by using a famous psychometrician, who separated behavioral content material from more typical styles of check-like content material in his concept of the shape of mind. Greater currently, Gardner (1983, 1999) has argued that interpersonal and intrapersonal intelligence are wonderful from the more instructional ones and similarly burdened the multidimensionality of intelligence, mentioning the separateness of emotional intelligence. Talking commonly, Neisser (1976) said that the traditional understanding as it should be reflects two distinctive sorts of intelligence, instructional and practical. Implicit theories of intelligence, within the United States of America and elsewhere additionally suggest a few separations of instructional and practical aspects of intelligence. even though specifics of definitions of academic and realistic intelligence range between studies and cultures, the thrust of those notions stays the same: the idea of academic (analytical) intelligence is used to indicate the character's potential to clear up problems in academic (lecture room-like) settings, while the concept of realistic intelligence is used to signify the individual's capability to resolve issues in everyday settings (sensible existence problems). For kids, components of classroom-like settings may additionally invoke practical intelligence. For instance, knowing the information for a take a look at invokes largely educational intelligence, however understanding a way to study for the check invokes a terrific deal of realistic intelligence. The psychological idea underlying the prevailing research makes a similar declare, particularly, for a difference between analytical intelligence (or what Neisser refers to as "instructional intelligence") and practical intelligence. In line with Sternberg's triarchic theory of a success intelligence, the primary data-processing additives underlying abstract analytical and applied practical intelligence are equal (e.g., defining problems, formulating strategies, inferring relations, and so on.). however, differences in obligations and conditions requiring the two sorts of intelligence, and consequently in the concrete contexts in which they're used, can render the correlations between ratings on exams of the 2 sorts of intelligence superb, trivial, or, in precept, negative. From the factor of view of individual variations, individuals who nicely follow a set of techniques in a single context won't be people who niccly observe them in some other context. The issue in this article isn't always over whether analytical (academic) intelligence subjects at all. We consider there's stable proof that the kind of analytical intelligence measured via conventional forms of intelligence assessments predicts performance, at least to a few diplomae, in an expansion of conditions. Therefore, we would not want to check for regular-life intelligence instead, we might need to test for the practical form of intelligence in addition to the especially academic form of intelligence, due to the fact each may predict diverse types of overall performance highly independently. Our argument in this article is that each sort of intelligence can be important in a spread of situations. A developing body of empirical records suggests that there indeed may be a true mental difference between instructional and realistic intelligence. If there are, then conventional capability checks standing by myself may additionally inform us notably less than we preferably would want to recognize approximately human beings' performance inside the realistic situations they come upon in their day by day lives. We cite some of this evidence right here, although greater nearly complete critiques can be discovered. Denney and Palmer (1981) in comparison the performance of adults of various a long time on two styles of reasoning issues: a conventional cognitive measure and a trouble-solving challenge regarding actual-lifestyles situations. The maximum interesting result of this have a look at for our gift motive changed into that performance at the conventional cognitive (instructional) measure reduced linearly after age 20 whereas performance on the sensible hassle-fixing assignment elevated to a height within the 40- and 50-year-antique age groups, and best then declined. Practical intelligence as a result confirmed a developmental function over age greater similar to crystallized than to fluid intelligence. A comparable result became located with the aid of

Cornelius and Caspi (1987), who explicitly looked at measures of fluid, crystallized, and practical intelligence. (The sensible measures worried duties, such as coping with a landlord who might now not make repairs, getting a pal to go to one more frequently, and what to do while one has been exceeded over for promotion.) Fluid talents showed increases from about age twenty or thirty to age fifty and then declined. Crystallized and sensible abilities improved till about age seventy before declining. However, the measures of sensible abilities confirmed most effective modest correlations with each of the fluid and crystallized capacity measures, suggesting that the realistic measures were assessing an awesome assemble. Scribner (1984) investigated techniques used by milk-processing plant workers to fill orders. She observed that in place of using typical mathematical algorithms found out within the lecture room, skilled assemblers used complex strategies for combining partly crammed cases in a way that minimized the range of movements required to finish an order. Even though the assemblers had been the least educated workers within the plant, they had been capable of calculating their heads portions expressed in distinctive base range systems, and that they routinely outperformed the more distinctly knowledgeable white-collar people who substituted whilst assemblers had been absent. The order-filling performance of the assemblers was unrelated to measures of school overall performance, consisting of intelligence-take a look at rankings, arithmetic-test ratings, and grades. Some other series of studies of regular mathematics worried shoppers in California grocery stores who sought to buy on the most inexpensive cost while the same merchandise had been to be had in extraordinary-sized packing containers. Those studies were accomplished earlier than cost-in keeping with-unit quantity statistics became routinely posted. Lave, Murtaugh, and de la Roche (1984) located that effective shoppers used intellectual shortcuts to get without problems acquired solution accurate (even though no longer continually completely accurate) enough to decide which length to buy. however, when those identical individuals have been given an intellectual–arithmetic take a look at that required them to do a good deal of the equal factor in a paper-and-pencil format, there was no relationship between their ability to do the paper-and-pencil troubles and their ability to pick out the first-rate values within the supermarket and feature studied the performance of Brazilian road kids in mathematical reasoning responsibilities. They located, further to Lave et al., that the identical children who were capable of remedy arithmetical issues within the setting in which they truly had to use those operations of their daily lives had been often not able to E.L. mastering and character variations. A comparable locating emanates from the research of Wagner (1978), who confirmed that while Western adults did better than Moroccan rug dealers on a reasonably abstract memory check, the rug sellers did better on exams of their reminiscence for styles on Oriental rugs. In our own research, we've investigated sensible know-how because it applies in a spread of occupations, together with control, income, coaching, and navy leadership. We have devised exams of an issue of practical intelligence, which is what one desires to realize to reach a context of his or her ordinary existence. Specially, we've constructed eventualities of the types humans stumble upon of their everyday lives wherein the humans face on-the-activity issues that they need to clear up. Members in our research then are usually provided with a variety of options for solving the issues. They're asked to charge the pleasant of every one of the alternatives, commonly on a 1–9 scale. Responses are scored towards those of specialists. The nearer the participant's profile is to the implied profile of the specialists, the higher the rating on the test. In a series of about a dozen studies extending over close to 15 years (see Sternberg et al., 2000), we've got made some observations. maximum applicable right here are the observations that (a) realistic intelligence measures generally tend to correlate significantly with every other (b) they correlate variably with measures of academic intelligence—every so often positively, frequently not at all, and occasionally negatively (c) they generally tend to are expecting standards of process achievement about in addition to or at times even better than do indicators of instructional intelligence, IQ (Sternberg et al., 2000); and (d) they expect job overall performance significantly, even if variables including IQ, persona, and forms of thinking are positioned first right into a hierarchical regression version. Right here, we gift only some of the studies especially applicable to the studies provided in this paper. Sternberg, Nokes, et al. (2001) examined in rural young people of western Kenya the belief that educational and realistic intelligence are separable and comparatively distinct constructs. The principal structured variable of hobby becomes the youth' ratings on a test of their knowledge for natural drugs used to fight illnesses. This type of understanding is viewed with the aid of the villagers as essential in adapting to their surroundings, which's understandable given that the overwhelming majority of the youngsters have, at a given time, parasitic infections which could interfere with their daily functioning. In different phrases, it's far this sort of knowledge this is relevant to the villagers' everyday lifestyles. We discovered that ratings at the checks of realistic intelligence correlated trivially or notably negatively with traditional measures of academic intelligence and success, even after controlling for socioeconomic status. Any such result is probably maximum in all likelihood in society, including that of rural Kenya, wherein implicit theories of intelligence depart substantially from Western explicit theories of intelligence. Indeed, Kenyan implicit theories of intelligence strain everyday abilities a long way extra than they pressure educational ones. Moreover, it's been shown that implicit theories of intelligence can affect the manner humans go about doing duties of their instructional as well as everyday lives. In any other take a look at, Grigorenko and Sternberg (2001) studied a large institution of Russian adults living in a provincial metropolis. We used conventional measures of intelligence as indicators of analytical intelligence and vignettes depicting everyday-existence conditions and self-scores of behavior as signs of sensible intelligence. The signs of analytical and sensible intelligence were used to expect the intellectual and physical health of the various Russian adults. Intellectual fitness became measured by using widely used paper-and-pencil exams of despair and tension and physical fitness was measured by using self-report. The high-quality predictor of mental and physical health becomes the sensible-intelligence measure. Analytical intelligence got here second. 186 E.L. studying and individual variations each contributed to prediction, but. Hence, we once more concluded that theories of intelligence, to offer a higher prediction of fulfillment in existence in a selection of domain names (as opposed to in a single domain of faculty achievement), must encompass abilities critical for regular life as well academic abilities. Any individual or even subsets of those findings might be criticized for one or another cause. But taken together, with their one-of-a-kind strengths and weaknesses, the frame of proof shows that the traditional expertise that educational and realistic intelligence are largely separate constructs may additionally honestly best constitute the records which are present to be had. If this is the case, then the overall factor every so often identified as relevant to intelligence wishes to be viewed uniquely from the way its miles conventionally regarded. Claims of a standard factor of intelligence, relationship back to Spearman (1904) and continuing directly to the modern-day then take on a one-of-a-kind cast. This forge is that the general aspect, to the quantity it exists, might also characterize educational styles of intelligence quite properly, but might not extend as properly past them. Our goal is not to argue whether or not there "truly" is a standard factor in human intelligence, due to the fact from our point of view, the query effortlessly degenerates right into a semantic one. If one defines intelligence quite extra narrowly, a general aspect commonly appears. If one defines intelligence quite extra extensively, then it does not seem, or at the least no longer with the entire generality commonly ascribed to it. Our intention inside the present takes a look at become to provide a further check of the speculation deriving from the triarchic theory of a hit intelligence that instructional and sensible intelligence may be, from a person-variations viewpoint, in large part distinct constructs. Persevering with our try to survey diverse unindustrialized cultures (i.e., unique from those in which the idea of intelligence originated) for the difference between those two styles of intelligence, within the gift examine, we behavior research inside the rural and comparatively urban settlements of Alaska Natives, 1 Yup'ik human beings. The primary goal of this examination become to explain the ratings on Yup'ik-valued developments in the studied teenagers through their performance signs on checks of analytical and realistic intelligence. Yet again, our argument in this article is that each sort of intelligence may be essential for predicting these developments of the hobby. Moreover, designing the examination, we expected to look at better predictive electricity of the everyday understanding of the everyday lifestyle communities.

Chapter Five

Brain Research and Learning

Brain studies research the structure and characteristics of human brains and the anxious device. Knowledge the organic foundation of gaining knowledge of, memory, conduct, belief, and cognizance is taken into consideration the "closing undertaking" of behavioral brain research. It is also the call of a peer-reviewed clinical journal that specializes in neuroscience. The magazine has nine subsections that specialize in special specialties within neuroscience. Brain studies' effect aspect, reflecting the number of citations to the latest articles posted, is envisioned to be 3.one hundred twenty-five. Brain studies examine multiple disciplines of biology to recognize brain function and that of the nerves and neural circuits. Many neuroscientists observe research questions that span more than one subfield of mind and conduct studies. There are at least twenty-five fundamental branches of this type of study. Some branches observe the molecular and cell foundation of the apprehensive machine, neurons, and brain areas. Different branches discover the cultural and behavioral foundation for brain interest and gaining knowledge of, which includes brain improvement research. Early brain improvement research examines how cells remodel and migrate to their roles in the fearful gadget. Research into neurological disorders draws on findings from these other subfields. The brain and nervous machine take part in important body features like breathing and produce mind, feelings, and behavior. Studying the brain and anxious device advances our information of basic biology and body function. This know-how facilitates doctors to locate methods to save you or deal with issues that affect the mind, worried device, and body. There are a couple of thousand disorders of the brain and frightening system. That variety from neurological disorders to cancers to musculoskeletal issues. Mind studies, including brain injury studies, research dysfunctions that affect the worried machine, its feature, and improvement. There are numerous distinct brain study techniques for understanding mind interest. They include reviewing the effects of mind damage and the consequences of electrical, chemical (and these days magnetic) stimulation of the mind. Researchers additionally evaluate measures of electrical and chemical activity of the brain. Measuring electrical hobby may include recordings from the scalp thru electroencephalography (EEG). Recordings from the brain itself are taken by placing very thin twine or glass tube electrodes. PC-based totally mind scans can show the shape or characteristic of the mind thru the intact cranium. Modern neuroimaging is increasingly more used as a mind studies method, in particular within the improvement of researchers' information of issues. Positron Emission Tomography (pet) and functional magnetic resonance imaging (fMRI) are two advanced imaging strategies. They are each used to apprehend molecular techniques within the mind. fMRI is likewise used to estimate cognitive activities. Magnetoencephalography (MEG) and electroencephalography (EEG) are different varieties of purposeful neuroimaging techniques used to map mind pastimes. Some neuroimaging researchers integrate statistics from more than one neuroimaging mode to create a greater complete evaluation of the patient's mind. Examples include combining MEG and EEG to get one mind map.

Mind studies and schooling

Experimental mind studies is a peer-reviewed scientific magazine. The magazine publishes findings from experimental research of the crucial and peripheral anxious structures. Brain improvement studies are a key cognizance of articles posted inside the journal. Different regions consist of molecular, body structure, behavior, neurochemistry, and neurobiology. Experimental mind studies reviews experimental pathology applicable to general troubles of cerebral function as nicely. The mind & conduct research basis is a nonprofit basis that budgets intellectual fitness research. The inspiration is America's pinnacle non-governmental funder of brain studies and mental health studies presents. Most research offers discover intellectual infection, mental disorders, and a few investigate more than one issue. Mind computer interface research explores the user or sufferers' ability to control their brain waves, with ascending to send instructions to a brain laptop interface. The computer interfaces with electroencephalogram (EEG) indicators. This protocol is useful for sufferers experiencing paralysis, and for gaming and different futuristic uses. Contemporary mind studies combine findings from research fine practices to help instructors apprehend students' needs for great mastering surroundings. Neuroimaging and mind-mapping research provide insights which educators can use to understand mind hobby and the mastering environment which provides ideal results for students. Numerous country-wide foundations promote mind-based totally research in schooling to help educators with their knowledge of getting to know psychology. EMOTIV gives many solutions for the imagery which assists brain studies. Mind research strategies thru EEG or electroencephalography are price-powerful with EMOTIV's mind put on. A studies team can get entry to a vast array of statistics-amassing and imaging systems on a price range-friendly scale. EMOTIV's solutions were proven in studies and scientific literature for neuroscience, place of business well-being and safety, cognitive performance, neuroimaging, and brain-controlled technology packages. The award-triumphing EMOTIV EPOC+ headset presents professional-grade brain statistics for brain studies in educational and industrial use. The EMOTIV insight headset boasts minimal set-up time and electronics optimized to provide smooth signals from everywhere, making it perfect for overall performance and well-being monitoring. The EMOTIV EPOC FLEX cap gives high-density insurance and moveable electroencephalogram sensors most desirable for research specialists. EmotivPRO is an incorporated research software program solution for neuroscience research and schooling, built for EPOC+, EPOC Flex, and insight headsets.

The mind and consciousness

Recognition is something that the mind learns to do in preference to an intrinsic property of positive neural states and no longer others. Beginning from the concept that neural activity is inherently unconscious, the query, therefore, turns into: How does the mind learn how to be conscious? I advocate that awareness arises because of the mind's non-stop attempts at predicting no longer handiest the effects of its actions on the sector and different marketers, but also the results of activity in a single cerebral area on the hobby in different areas. Using this account, the mind continuously and unconsciously learns to describe its personal interest to itself, so developing systems of meta-representations that represent and qualify the goal first-order representations. Such discovered descriptions, enriched by using the emotional cost related to them, form the idea of conscious experience. mastering and plasticity are hence crucial to consciousness, to the quantity that reports handiest arise in experiencers which have found out to know they own certain first-order states and which have found out to care greater about positive states than about others. That is what I name the "Radical Plasticity Thesis." In a sense as a consequence, this is the inactive attitude, however grew to become both inwards and (in addition) outwards. Consciousness includes "sign detection on the thoughts"; conscious thoughts are the mind's (non-conceptual, implicit) principle about itself. I illustrate these thoughts through neural community models that simulate the relationships among overall performance and attention in one-of-a-kind responsibilities.

Don't forget the standard but proverbial thermostat. A thermostat is an casy device that can flip a furnace on or off depending on whether the modern-day temperature exceeds a set threshold. For this reason, the thermostat can appropriately be said to be touchy to temperature. But is there some feel wherein the thermostat can be characterized as being aware of temperature? Contra Chalmers (1996), I can argue that there's no feel wherein the thermostat can be characterized as being aware of the temperature. There are two critical points that I would love to emphasize in developing this argument. The primary is that there may be no sense in which the thermostat can be characterized as being aware of temperature because it does not understand that it's miles touchy to temperature. the second point is that there's no experience in which the thermostat may be characterized as being aware of temperature as it does no longer care about whether or not its surroundings are warm or cold. I will in addition argue that those two features – information of one's personal inner states and the emotional fee related to such expertise – are constitutive of aware revel in. sooner or later, I will argue that studying (or, greater generally, plasticity) is necessary for each function to emerge in cognitive structures. From this, it follows that attention is something that the mind learns to do thru constantly working mechanisms of neural plasticity. This I name the "Radical Plasticity Thesis. records processing can surely take location without recognition, as abundantly demonstrated not best by way of empirical proof (the satisfactory example of which might be blindsight), however additionally via the very fact that extraordinarily effective facts-processing machines, particularly computers, have now emerged as ubiquitous. only however a few would be willing to provide any quantum of awareness revel in present-day computer systems, yet they're undeniably able to state-of-the-art data processing – from spotting faces to analyzing speech, from winning chess tournaments to helping show theorems. For that reason, cognizance is not records processing; enjoyment is a "more factor" that comes over and beyond mere computation.

With this premise in thoughts – a premise that simply restates Chalmers' (1996) difficult trouble, that is, the question of why it is the case that information processing is followed via revel in humans and different higher animals, there are several approaches in which one can think about the hassle of awareness. One is to truly nation, as in line with Dennett that there's not anything greater to explain. Revel in is simply (a particular kind of) statistics processing in the brain; the contents of experience are just something representations have come to dominate processing at some point in time ("reputation in the mind"); consciousness is only a harmless illusion. From this angle, it is simple to assume that machines could be conscious when they have accrued sufficient complexity; the motive they're not aware of now could be in reality due to the fact they are not state-of-the-art enough: They lack the proper architecture perhaps, they lack sufficiently wide and various statistics-processing competencies, and so forth. No matter what's lacking, the fundamental point right here is that there is no purpose to anticipate that aware experience is something special. As an alternative, all that is required is one or numerous yet-to-be-diagnosed practical mechanisms: Recurrence, possibly balance of representation, global availability, integration and differentiation of information, or the involvement of higher-order representations to call just a few.

Every other attitude is to consider that revel in will in no way be amenable to a satisfactory useful explanation. Revel in, in step with a few is exactly what's leftover once all purposeful factors of awareness have been defined. However, the truth that so defined, revel in is actually now not something possible method from a systematic factor of view, this function recognizes that attention is a unique (a tough) hassle in the Cognitive Neurosciences. However, that could be an exceptional factor from announcing that a reductive account isn't viable. A non-reductive account, but, is precisely what Chalmers' Naturalistic Dualism attempts to offer, via featuring that records, as a relying on ontology, has a twin aspect, – a physical thing and an exceptional issue. "Revel in arises with the aid of virtue of its reputation as one element of statistics, when the opposite factor is determined embodied in physical processing". This position leads him to protect the opportunity that revels in is a fundamental thing of truth. As a consequence, even thermostats, as an instance, may be endowed with very simple stories, in virtue of the reality that they can toggle in two distinctive states.

What, however, do we suggest when we communicate of "subjective enjoy" or of "quale"? The best definition of those concepts is going proper to the coronary heart of the problem: "revel in" is what it looks like for a conscious organism to be that organism. There is something it's far like for a bat to be a bat; there's nothing it is like for a stone to be a stone. As Chalmers places it: "while we see, for instance, we enjoy visual sensations: The felt pleasant of redness, the experience of darkish and light, and the satisfactory of intensity in a sight view". Allow us to try to interact in a few phenomenological analyses at this point to try to capture what it means for each people to have and revel in. consider you see a patch of crimson. You currently have a red experience – something that a digital camera recording the identical patch of red will most simply not have. What is the difference between you and the camera? Tononi (2007), from whom I borrow this easy concept experiment, points out that one key difference is that when you see the patch of purple, the nation you find yourself in is but certainly one of the billions, whereas, for a simple mild-sensitive device, it is perhaps certainly one of best feasible states – therefore the kingdom conveys a lot more differentiated information for you than for a mild-sensitive diode. A further distinction is that you can integrate the information conveyed with the aid of many one-of-a-kind inputs, while the chip on a digital camera can be the concept of a trifling array of independent sensors amongst which there is no interaction.

Hoping not to sound presumptuous, it strikes me, however, that both Chalmers' (somewhat sarcastically) and Tononi's analyses leave out essential statistics approximately revel in: each examines it as an alternatively summary measurement or thing of statistics, while revel in – what it seems like – is something however summary. On the opposite, what we mean whilst we are saying that seeing a patch of purple elicits an "experience" is that the seeing does something to us – especially, we might experience one or numerous feelings, and we may accomplice the redness with memories of pink. Perhaps seeing the patch of red makes you do not forget the coloration of the get dressed that your prom nighttime date wore 20 years ago. Possibly it conjures up vague anxiety, which we now recognize is also shared using monkeys. To a synesthetic, possibly seeing the color pink will evoke the variety five. The point is that if consciousness revel in is what it feels like to be in a sure country, then "What it appears like" can simplest mean the specific set of institutions that have been mounted by enjoying between the stimulus or the scenario you now find yourself in, on the one hand, and your memories, on the opposite. that is what one means with the aid of pronouncing that there is something it's far like to be you in this state instead of nobody or somebody else: The set of memories evoked using the stimulus (or using movements you perform, and so forth.), and, crucially, the set of emotional states related to each of those memories. This is essentially the perspective that Damasio (2010) defends. for this reason, a primary point about the very belief of subjective enjoy I would really like to make here is that it is hard to look at what revel in could mean past (1) the emotional fee associated with a situation, and (2) the massive, complex, richly dependent, enjoy-based community of associations that the gadget has learned to associate with that scenario. "What it looks like" for me to see a patch of red at some point seems to be completely exhausted by using those factors. Granted, one ought to nevertheless consider an agent that accesses particular reminiscences, probable related to emotional price, upon seeing a patch of crimson and who fails to "enjoy" something. however, I surmise that this will be mere simulation: One could lay out one of these zombie agent, but any actual agent that is pushed with the aid of self-developed motivation, and that can't assist however be prompted with the aid of his emotional states will surely have experiences just like ours. therefore, there is not anything it's far like for the camera to peer the patch of pink without a doubt as it does no longer care: The stimulus is incomprehensible; the digital camera lacks even the maximum simple equipment that would make it viable to ascribe any interpretation to the patch of red; it's miles as a substitute only a mere recording device for which nothing subjects. there is nothing it is like to be that digital camera at that factor in time virtually because (1) the experience of different colorings do no longer do whatever to the camera; that is, colors aren't related to specific emotional valences; and (2) the digicam has no mind with which to sign in and procedure its own states. It is straightforward to assume how this could be unique. To hint at my impending argument, a camera ought to, for instance, preserve a file of the colors it's miles uncovered to, and are available to "like" some colorations better than others. Through the years, your digital camera would really like exclusive hues than mine, and it'd also recognize that during a few non-trivial experiences. Appropriating one's mental contents for oneself is the start of individuation, and therefore the start of a self. For that reason, a second point approximately revels in what I perceive as crucially essential is that it does now not make any sense to speak of experience without an experienced who reviews the reports. Enjoy is, nearly via definition ("what it feels like"), something that takes place now not in any physical entity however rather best in unique bodily entities, specifically cognitive dealers. Chalmers' (1996) thermostat fails to be aware due to the fact, even though it may discover itself in different inner states, it lacks the capacity to take away itself from the causal chain which it instantiates. In different phrases, it lacks information that it can find itself in exclusive states; it's however an insignificant mechanism that responds to inputs in certain approaches. While there's indeed something to be skilled there (the distinct states the thermostat can locate itself in), there is nobody domestic to be the subject of those studies – the thermostat actually lacks the perfect equipment to do so. The required machinery, I surmise, minimally entails the ability to know that one finds itself in such or this sort of kingdom.

This factor may be illustrated via well-known results inside the connectionist, or artificial neural community modeling literature. Consider as an example Hinton's (1986) famous demonstration that neural networks educated thru associative studying mechanisms can find out about abstract dimensions of the schooling set. Hinton's (1986) network becomes a highly easy returned-propagation community trained to manner linguistic expressions which include an agent, a relationship, and an affected person, including for instance "Maria is the spouse of Roberto." The stimulus material consisted of a sequence of such expressions, which collectively defined some of the relationships that exist in the family timber of an Italian circle of relatives and an English circle of relatives. The community was required to produce the patient of each agent–dating pair it became given as input. For instance, the network has to produce "Roberto" when provided with "Maria" and "spouse." Crucially, everybody and each dating were offered to the network with the aid of activating a single enter unit. For this reason, there was no overlap whatsoever between the enter representations of, say, Maria and Victoria. Yet, notwithstanding this entire absence of surface similarity between schooling exemplars, Hinton (1986) showed that when education, the network should, under sure situations, broaden inner representations that seize applicable summary dimensions of the area, including nationality, intercourse, or age! Hinton's (1986) point becomes to illustrate that such networks had been capable of gaining knowledge of richly dependent inner representations because of merely being required to manner exemplars of the area. Crucially, the structure of the inner representations discovered by the network is decided by the way wherein distinctive exemplars have interaction with each other, that is, by using their useful similarity, as opposed to using their mere bodily similarity expressed, as an example, in phrases of what number of features (enter gadgets) they percentage. Hinton (1986) as a result furnished a striking demonstration of this critical and frequently misunderstood component of associative getting to know tactics with the aid of showing that under some occasions, unique hidden devices of the network had come to behave as detectors for dimensions of the fabric that had by no means been supplied explicitly to the community. These outcomes definitely flesh out the belief that rich, abstract information can honestly become a derivative of processing established domains. It's far-exciting to word that the life of such single-unit "detectors" has recently been proven to exist in the human neocortex. Unmarried-neuron recording of pastime in the hippocampus, as an instance, has shown that some man or woman neurons solely respond to notably summary entities, along with the phrases "bill Clinton" and photographs of the yank president.

Now, the factor I want to make with this situation is as follows: One could simply describe the community as being touchy to nationality, inside the sense that it exhibits differential responding (consequently, behavioral sensitivity) to inputs that involve Italian sellers vs. English marketers. However, manifestly, the community does no longer knows something about nationality. It does not even recognize that it has such and such representations of the inputs, nor does it know whatever approximately it's very own, self-received sensitivity to the applicable dimensions. As an alternative, the rich, abstract, structured representations that the community has acquired over schooling forever continue to be embedded in a causal chain that starts with the entering and ends with the network's responses. As Clark and Karmiloff-Smith (1993) insightfully talked about, such representations are "first-order" representations to the volume that they're representations in the machine in place of representations for the device this is, such representations are not reachable to the network as representations.

In different phrases, any such (first-order) community can by no means realize that it is aware of: It surely lacks the perfect machinery. This points to an essential difference between sensitivity and consciousness. Sensitivity merely includes the capability to respond in specific approaches to certain states of affairs. Sensitivity does not require attention in any feel. A thermostat can as it should be characterized as being sensitive to temperature, simply as the carnivorous plant Dionaea Muscipula may additionally as it should be defined as being touchy to movement at the surface of its leaves. However, our intuitions (as a minimum, my intuitions) tell us that such sensitive structures (thermostats, photodiodes, transistors, cameras, carnivorous flowers) are not aware. They do no longer have "standard stories," they actually have no reports in any way. Sensitivity can contain enormously sophisticated know-how, and even found out expertise, as illustrated through Hinton's (1986) community, but such knowledge is usually first-order understanding, it is always expertise this is necessarily embedded in the very equal causal chain thru which first-order processing happens and that can therefore handiest be expressed thru motion as an immediate result of notion. Recognition, on the other hand, usually appears to minimally entail the capacity of knowing that one knows. This potential, in the end, paperwork the premise for the verbal reports we take to be the most direct indication of cognizance. And when we have a look at the absence of such capability to record the information involved in our decisions, we rightfully finish that the choice turned primarily based on subconscious understanding. Consequently, it is while an agent well-known shows information of the reality that he's sensitive to a few situations that we take this agent to be an aware agent. This 2d-order expertise, I argue, seriously depends on found out systems of Meta representations, and paperwork the basis for aware experience furnished the agent additionally cares about sure states of affairs extra than approximate others. attention as a consequence no longer the handiest requires the ability to learn about the geography of one's very own representations, however, it additionally requires that the resulting information displays the dispositions and alternatives of the agent. That is a vital point, for it might be clean to software a thermostat that is successful now not handiest of performing primarily based on the present-day temperature, but additionally to document on its own states. Such a talking thermostat could constantly document at the current temperature and on its choices. Could that make the thermostat aware?

Simply now not, for its clean that the reporting is however a trifling extra manner tacked on the thermostat's inherent capability to interchange the furnace in keeping with the temperature. What could move a few ways closer to making the thermostat aware is to set it up so that it cares about sure temperatures more than approximate others, and that these preferences turn out to be a result of learning. What wouldn't it take for a community like Hinton's (1986) a good way to get the right of entry to its own representations, and what distinction could that make with recognize to recognition? to answer the first query, the specified machinery is the equipment of agenthood; in a nutshell, the ability to do something no longer simply with outside states of affairs, however instead with one's own representations of such outside states. This crucially calls for that the agent be capable of getting admission to, look into, and otherwise control its personal representations, and this in flip, I surmise, requires mechanisms that make it possible for an agent to describe its personal representations to itself. The final result of this non-stop "representational description" technique is that the agent ends up understanding something approximately the geography of its own internal states: It has, in effect, found out about its very own representations. Minimally, this will be done instead really, for instance via having any other community take each the input (i.e., the outside stimulus as represented proximally) to the primary-order community and its inner representations of that stimulus as inputs themselves and do something with them.

One elementary thing the machine together with the 2 interconnected networks (the first-order, determined community and the second one-order, watching network) could now be able to do is to make selections, for instance, approximately the quantity to which an outside input to the primary-order network elicits an acquainted pattern of activation over its hidden gadgets or no longer. This will in flip allows the machine to distinguish between hallucination and blindness (see Lau, 2008), or to give you judgments approximately the overall performance of the first-order network. To deal with the second query (what difference could representational description make in phrases of awareness), I appeal to Rosenthal's higher-order thought (hot) principle of attention. whilst I do not experience perfectly satisfied with all aspects of the hot idea, I do accept it as true, but, that better-order representation (I'm able to call them meta-representations in what follows) play a critical function in consciousness. An immediate objection to this idea is as follows: If there's not anything intrinsic to the lifestyles of an illustration in a cognitive machine that makes this representation aware, why need things be exceptional for meta-representations? Despite everything, meta-representations are representations also. Sure certainly, but with an important distinction: Meta-representations inform the agent approximately its own inner states, making it viable for it to expand the expertise of its very own workings. And this, I argue, paperwork the idea for the contents of conscious revel in, furnished of direction – which can't be the case in a contemporary synthetic gadget – that the system has discovered about its representations via itself, over its improvement, and provided that it cares about what occurs to it, this is, furnished its behavior is rooted in emotion-laden motivation (to survive, to mate, to find meals, etc.).

Conscious revel in occurs if and most effective if a records-processing system has found out about its personal representations of the world in such a manner that these representations have acquired price for it. To place this declare even more provocatively: consciousness is the mind's (emphatically non-conceptual) concept approximately itself, won through revel in interacting with the sector, with different retailers, and, crucially, with itself. It's vital to understand the middle of a framework that characterizes how gaining knowledge of shapes availability to recognition. It's vital to preserve it in thoughts that the framework is based on the connectionist framework. It's consequently based on many valuable thoughts that signify the connectionist approach, together with the truth that statistics processing is graded and non-stop, and that it takes location over many interconnected modules such as processing devices. In such structures, lengthy-term information is embodied within the pattern of connectivity between the processing devices of each module and among the modules themselves, at the same time as the temporary styles of activation over the gadgets of each module capture the temporary results of statistics processing. This being stated, a first crucial assumption is that representations are graded, dynamic, energetic, and continuously causally efficacious. Patterns of activation in neural networks and within the brain are typically dispensed and may therefore vary on several dimensions, which includes their balance in time, their power. Or their forte. Balance in time refers to how long a representation can be maintained lively at some stage in processing. There are numerous warning signs that distinctive neural structures contain representations that fluctuate alongside this measurement. For example, the prefrontal cortex, which performs a primary position in working memory, is widely assumed to involve circuits specialized in the formation of the long-lasting representations wanted for the lively upkeep of project-applicable information. The energy of illustration virtually refers to what number of processing units are involved in the representation, and to how strongly the spark of these devices is. Ordinarily, sturdy activation styles will exert more impact on ongoing processing than weak styles. Sooner or later, the uniqueness of representation is inversely related to the extent of overlap that exists between representations of comparable times. Forte has been hypothesized as the primary dimension through which cortical and hippocampal representations range with the latter becoming energetic best whilst the particular conjunctions of functions that they code for are active themselves. The most vital perception that underpins these specific dimensions is that representations, in comparison to the all-or-none propositional representations usually utilized in classical theories, alternatively have a graded character that permits any precise representation to carry the quantity to which what it refers to is certainly present. Some other essential issue of this characterization of representational structures in the mind is that a ways from being static propositions waiting to be accessed with the aid of a few methods, representations instead constantly have an impact on processing irrespective of their nice. This assumption takes its roots in McClelland's (1979) evaluation of cascaded processing which, by displaying how modules interacting with every other need not "wait" for different modules to have finished their processing before starting their very own, tested how degree-like overall performance should emerge out of such non-stop, non-linear systems. For that reason, even susceptible, bad-great strains can influence processing, as an instance through associative priming mechanisms, that is, together with different sources of stimulation. Strong, top-notch lines, in comparison, have the generative capacity, inside the sense that they can influence performance independently of the impact of other constraints, this is, and each time their desired stimulus is a gift. A second crucial assumption is that gaining knowledge is an obligatory outcome of records processing. certainly, each form of neural data-processing produces adaptive changes inside the connectivity of the machine, through mechanisms inclusive of long-time period potentiation (LTP) or lengthy-term despair (LTD) in neural structures, or Hebbian studying in connectionist systems. A critical factor of these mechanisms is that they may be mandatory in the sense that they take place each time the sending and receiving gadgets or processing modules are co-active. O'Reilly and Munakata (2000) have defined Hebbian studying as instantiating what they name version getting to know. The fundamental computational objective of such unsupervised studying mechanisms is to enable the cognitive device to broaden useful, informative fashions of the world by way of taking pictures of its correlational shape. As such, they stand in comparison with mission gaining knowledge of mechanisms, which instantiate the exclusive computational goal of studying specific enter-output mappings (i.e., achieving unique dreams) within the context of precise duties via errors-correcting studying procedures.

Stability, electricity, or forte may be completed especially. Over quick time scales, they could result, for instance, from accelerated stimulus length, from the simultaneous top-down and backside-up activation involved in so-called "reentrant processing", from approaches of "adaptive resonance" from procedures of "integration and differentiation", or from touch with the neural workspace, added about by way of "dynamic mobilization". It is vital to recognize that the final effect of any of these putative mechanisms is to make the target representations strong, robust, and specific. These properties can in addition be envisioned as involving graded or dichotomous dimensions. Over longer time scales, but, first-rate representations arise due to gaining knowledge of or cognitive improvement. Susceptible, fragile representations grow to be progressively more potent and better-high-quality. As a result, they exert more of a power on conduct. In maximum instances, this is a great outcome because the more potent an illustration is, the less it will require aware manipulate and monitoring. Therefore, in any area of enjoyment (from being capable of arising to wine-tasting, from recognizing faces to analyzing) we begin with susceptible representations, which might be a feature of implicit cognition and do not require manipulation because they handiest exert susceptible effects on conduct. Such representations, because of their bad quality, also are most effective weakly to be had to form the contents of recognition. As studying progresses, the relevant representations become more potent, but no longer so sturdy that they may be "depended on" to do their task properly. This is whilst cognitive control is maximum necessary. This is also the factor where such explicit representations are most likely to shape the contents of recognition. Subsequently, with similar education, the applicable representations become even more potent and sooner or later fully tailored. As such, these extraordinary representations feature of automaticity now not require cognitive manipulate both, but this is so for completely special motives than the function of the vulnerable representations of implicit cognition. therefore, when I reply faster to a target stimulus in distinctive feature of the reality that the target changed into preceded through a congruent subliminal prime, I'm able to properly say that there exists a state c such that its existence made me reply quicker, however via assumption I am not sensitive to the truth that this nation c is different from the country I wherein the target stimulus turned into preceded with the aid of an incongruent prime. States c and I are accordingly not conscious states – they merely exert their outcomes on conduct, so reflecting the agent's sensitivity to their lifestyles, however crucially now not its attention of their lifestyles. The cause such states are not aware states need to do with the properties of the corresponding first-order states: It isn't a lot that there is a failure of a better-order system to target these states, but rather that the first-order states are too susceptible to be suitable targets. You cannot recognize what isn't (sufficiently) there. Likewise, but perhaps more controversially so, recurring, automatic conduct is often described as related to unconscious information: The conduct unfolds whether you want to or not, it can unfold with attention engaged someplace else, and so forth. In such instances, behavior is pushed through very remarkable representations that have turn out to be, thru enjoy, optimally tuned to force conduct. Whilst such very splendid representations are appropriate objects for description, the descriptions either do not play a useful function or are prevented from taking region (for instance due to the fact the agent's attention is engaged some other place). Computerized behavior is as a result now not in reality subconscious behavior. As an alternative, it's far conduct for which awareness has to emerge as optional. you may be flawlessly privy to conduct that takes place robotically – you just seldom achieve this for it's far neither important nor acceptable to be able to end up aware of such behavior. This is precisely why the conduct has become automatic: because it is so adapted that it could unfold without the want for aware monitoring.

As a result, a primary critical computational precept through which to distinguish between aware and subconscious representations is subsequent: Availability to focus depends on high-quality representation, in which first-rate of representation is a graded size defined over stability in time, energy, and forte. While being notable for this reason seems to be a necessary situation for a representation's availability to attention, one has to ask, however, whether or not it is enough to condition. Instances together with hemineglect or blindsight genuinely propose that fine representation on my own does not suffice, for even robust stimuli can fail to go into aware consciousness in such situations. In regular participants, the attentional blink, as well as in attentional and alternate blindness, are all suggestive that high-quality stimuli can sincerely fail to be experienced except attended to. Likewise, simply attaining strong representations in an artificial neural network, for instance, will now not make this community-conscious in any experience – that is the trouble pointed out using Clark and Karmiloff-Smith (1993) about the restrictions of what they known as first-order networks: In such networks, even express information (e.g., a stable pattern of activation over the hidden gadgets of a widespread returned-propagation network that has come to feature as a "face detector") remains understanding that is within the network in preference to know-how for the community. In other phrases, such networks might have learned to be informationally touchy to some relevant facts, but they never recognize that they own such knowledge. For this reason, the expertise may be deployed efficaciously via action, however handiest in the context of doing a little particular task. as a result, it may be argued that it is a defining feature of cognizance that when one is aware of something, one is also, as a minimum doubtlessly so, aware that one is aware of being in that kingdom. this is the gist of so-referred to as hot theories of cognizance, in line with which a mental state is aware while the agent entertains, in a non-inferential manner, mind to the effect that it presently is in that mental kingdom. Importantly, for Rosenthal, it's far in distinctive feature of occurrent HOTs that the goal first-order representations emerge as aware. Dienes and Perner (1999) have advanced this idea with the aid of reading the implicit-explicit difference as reflecting a hierarchy of different manners in which the illustration can be express. For this reason, a representation can explicitly imply a property (e.g., "yellow"), predication to a person (the flower is yellow), factivity (it is a reality and not only an opportunity that the flower is yellow), and mindset (I understand that the flower is yellow). Completely conscious knowledge is hence the information that is "mind-set-specific." This analysis suggests that a further vital principle that differentiates between conscious and subconscious cognition is the quantity to which a given illustration endowed with the proper homes (balance, strength, and forte) is itself the goal of meta-representations. For this reason, a second essential computational principle through which to differentiate between aware and subconscious representations is subsequent: Availability to consciousness depends on the extent to which an illustration is itself an item of representation for further structures of representation. It's far thrilling to bear in mind below which conditions a representation will remain unconscious primarily based on combining these two ideas. There are at least 4 opportunities. First, understanding that is embedded inside the connection weights inside and among processing modules can never be without delay available to aware cognizance and control. This is absolutely an effect of the truth that consciousness, by assumption, necessarily entails representations (patterns of activation over processing gadgets). The expertise embedded in connection weights will, but, form the representations that depend on it, and its outcomes will consequently detectable – however most effective in a roundabout way, and only to the volume that these results are sufficiently marked inside the corresponding representations. This is equivalent to Dehaene and Changeux's (2004) precept of "lively firing." second, to enter aware recognition, an illustration desires to be sufficiently brilliant in terms of energy, balance in time, or area of expertise. Vulnerable representations are consequently terrible applicants to enter conscious recognition. This, however, does not always imply that they continue to be causally inert, for they can affect in addition processing in different modules, even if simplest weakly so. This bureaucracy the idea for several sub-threshold effects, together with, especially, subliminal priming. 1/3, a representation may be sturdy enough to enter aware cognizance, however didn't be associated with relevant meta-representations. There are as a consequence many possibilities for a specific conscious content to stay, in a way, implicit, now not because its representational automobile does no longer have the appropriate houses, but as it fails to be integrated with other aware contents.

The Effectiveness of brain Use

Why must college students get out of their seats at some point of getting to know? Ought college students be allowed to get common beverages at the same time as in faculty? Is it okay for students to be running in small corporations, on occasion carrying out loud pupil-directed conversations? Advocates for "brain-based totally" guidance have addressed each sort of question. The concept of "brain-based totally" preparation has been used for many years and is still being researched these days. Information on how the mind approaches information keeps eluding our complete expertise. As instructors, we are not taught to match freshmen' characteristics and mastering patterns with the challenge be counted or our method of presentation. We are taught to get the information across to the scholars but we sense vital. Via examining theories of education making use of brain-based mastering theories; we might also locate progressed strategies of teaching every individual toddler. We need to more absolutely understand how the mind processes data and what techniques will permit this information to be greater without difficulty retained. As mentioned in greater element later, many theorists had been exploring the concepts associated with "brain primarily based" training. Eric Jensen has written extensively explaining his theories. Anne Westwater and Pat Wolfe have contributed their thoughts approximately "connecting records" to this method to instruction as well. Pierce J. Howard has also contributed a few surprises about ideas and practical techniques to be used in the study room. There are even a few theorists like Bloom, as an example, whose contributions date lower back to the 1500s. Bloom developed a category machine this is nevertheless used nowadays. Concept "brain-based totally" techniques are instructional techniques to be used all through study room education. What makes this method specific and exceptional from conventional direct instruction mastering, is how the instructions are applied. at some stage in "mind primarily based" preparation, lots attempt is located on teaching so the information can be related to previous information or reports. This technique utilizes the concept that records that are not made relevant becomes lost or discarded with the aid of the brain's automated "hunting down" procedure. The brain does no longer sees this fact as being critical, consequently discarding them. Through enforcing those strategies, youngsters need to be capable of keep greater of the learned data. When humans speak JQ, they may be generally relating to how clever someone is. Three well-known psychologists, Steinberg, Gardner, and Eysenck have each formulated their personal particular definition of intelligence. "Steinberg defines intelligence as the ability for mental self-management" (Howard, 1994). He feels intelligence is composed of greater than just quantity, word, and~ area troubles, which represent traditional exams. Gardner has evolved a content definition of intelligence and believes that one-of-a-kind kinds of intelligence are present within someone. A character may also own distinctive levels of capability inside each of this intelligence. Hans Eysenck takes a one-of-a-kind approach to intelligence. He believes in measuring intelligence using reaction time, inspection time, and age evoked capability. He feels that people who've better IQs take a far shorter amount of time to react to complex stimuli. So that you can maximize the efficacy of educational transport, it must be tailored to reflect what research has mounted as a powerful practice for mind-well matched studying. The rapidly increasing field of mind-based research has clearly hooked up that the method of gaining knowledge of changes each the shape and functional organization of the mind. Modern-day educators must approach teaching inside the confines of a biologically pushed instructional framework to help this shape and feature regarding how college students learn high-quality. Know-how each the foundational practices and the motives in the back of each exercise will allow instructors to offer the best training possible to assist students to actualize their ability for success. Statement of the problem no matter satisfactory, practice is limited by the student's capacity to retain and keep in mind the statistics being taught. For training to be effective, it ought to be adjusted to reflect research-primarily based best practices regarding how students receive and process new statistics. This enables educators' transition their emphasis from the coaching aspect to the getting to know the side of the coaching/mastering cycle to better consciousness on a measurable stop product. Instructors want to become essential consumers of techniques so one can apprehend, layout, and put in force mind-primarily based education. They must be encouraged to develop foundational know-how of strategies which might be 1 supported by way of real research so that studies-based totally practices can grow to be the basis for classroom instruction. As scientists and researchers are continually unfolding the mysteries of the human mind and discovering how we learn exceptionally, teachers have to hone their capabilities to sift via this mountain of studies and advice to pick key elements that they can use to improve their coaching. At the same time as mind research may in no way be able to dictate precisely what instructors should do within the schoolroom, "If educators do no longer broaden a functional expertise of the mind and its procedures, we can be susceptible to pseudoscientific fads, irrelevant generalizations, and doubtful applications". In current years, electrophysiological studies, neuropsychological assessments, and the use of imaging strategies have created possibilities for researchers in the structural and practical research of the human brain which have furnished clues resulting in big changes for the field of education. By using understanding how the mind works, mind-based totally learning supports studying by using discovering the ways of most mastering. This method associates mastering with the brain and the manner it really works and mentions the fantastic consequences of the brain's features and its enhancing performance on learning. Consequently, it's far particularly interested in the improvement of the mind. Via neuroscience, investigating the relationship between the brain, the neural gadget, and our cognitive behaviors, mind-based getting to know is an increasing number of support with the aid of research, mainly with the development of MRI, puppy, and MEG technologies. These days, checks are completed with the use of this new technology. The location of neurons in a dwelling human mind can be coloration-imaged by way of the impact of mind primarily based on getting to know on academic achievement: A Meta-analytical examine systems consisting of the positron emission tomography and Nuclear Magnetic Resonance Imaging (NMRI). In this way, numerous variables like reminiscence, emotion, interest, mapping, and their outcomes on studying are studied. These studies, each in our USA and around the arena, offer us interesting records. As an instance, it is revealed that cell clusters examined by imaging strategies don't have systematic systems as intended, or that the linguistic part of a person isn't in the identical place as that of some other person. The crucial point of mind-based totally studying is meaningful getting to know. Mapping is needed to maintain meaningful learning. Mapping means that new know-how is connected to previous expertise and the new understanding is positioned into the cutting-edge device. The terms of brain-primarily based studying are the ones that make learning meaningful and everlasting. Those phrases are secure alertness, orchestrated immersion, and active processing. Caine and Caine (1990) explain those: at ease Alertness: It method to create the most appropriate emotional and social climate for studying. A hard learning environment with minimum threats ought to be supplied. When someone is interested in something, s/he's open to analyze, or vice versa. A comfortable and open mind can research more effortlessly. Findings display that some gaining knowledge of is inspired positively in comfortable surroundings, but it is suppressed while chance and tiredness are felt. Orchestrated Immersion: It refers to a college students' attention to the contents they come upon. They'll have to use their memory to discover the content whilst wholeness and correlativity are available. Energetic Processing: A studying mind is actively processing. For instance, to make an enjoyable meaningful, memory certainly reacts to new objects incompatible with the previous maps. Accordingly, the mind checks the studies which are contrary to the recognized. Caine and Caine (1990), who have many books and articles on brain-based totally mastering, have said the center principles of brain-primarily based getting to know. Wolfe (2001), an academic counselor, has carried out mind studies that include its application in the schoolroom. Intensely analyzing mind-based totally learning, brain well-suited techniques, and awesome gaining knowledge of, after thinking about the brain researches, brought beneficial techniques and strategies that may be implemented in school rooms. Nunly (2002), a biology instructor, includes out mind-based totally gaining knowledge of researches and curriculum improvement research at the University of Utah. But, no meta-analytical study has been performed either in our US or in any other US to show the effectiveness of brain-primarily based learning on academic success from a broader point of view. In regards to learning and coaching, evidently, brain research has a long manner to go. Whilst it turns into without a doubt described how understanding is fashioned, organized, and saved in the mind, it's positive that there could be fundamental adjustments. To investigate the impact of mind-based mastering, thirty-one research studies (forty-two outcomes) had been diagnosed and the main study questions that guided the evaluation turned into 'to what quantity does mind-primarily based learning impact college students' instructional success?'. further, it becomes analyzed to look if there's a vast, measurable distinction among the effect sizes of mind-primarily based mastering research in terms of problem count number, training stage, sampling, and the nations in which the studies have been done.

Chapter Six

Autobiographical Memory

Memory` is a label for various sets of cognitive capacities with the aid of which people and perhaps different animals keep information and reconstruct beyond studies, typically for present purposes. Autobiographical memory is a complex and multiplies determined talent, which includes neurological, social, cognitive, and linguistic additives. At the most primary stage, autobiographical recollections confer with personally experienced past occasions. over the last decade, the studies into autobiographical memory have caused an account of human reminiscence wherein private dreams to play a first-rate function inside the formation, get entry to and creation of precise memories. Autobiographical recollections are those enduring memories of events and private reports that are drawn from in the creation of a person's life tale. The non-public and social meanings connected to one's recollections provide us and people we relate our tale to, with an experience of ways we have become who we're. The improvement of an inner autobiographical expertise base starts with the onset of the cognitive self and social interaction plays an important function in shaping and maintaining our reminiscences. This essay will describe three kinds of social interaction and the way these affect the development, employer, and maintenance of autobiographical memory early in lifestyles. The interplay paperwork defined attention on gender development, persona improvement, and distancing from the terrible emotions of an occasion. There may be a debate in psychology over the time frame wherein autobiographical memories start to develop. The sociolinguistic argument states that the acquisition of language is vital to the formative year's development of autobiographical memories which can be created inside the creation of our non-public narrative. Proponents of the cognitive angle but, have located empirical aid for their argument that the development of the cognitive self, recognition of self as a separate man or woman, all through the second one year is of more significance than the onset of language. Howe et al. record the period of amnesia in babies' ends with the ability to recognize oneself and self-consciously contact a purple spot surreptitiously located on one's nose through an experimenter. There is consensus but, that social interaction performs a vital position in the maintenance of reminiscences and how those recollections are stated. Cross-cultural research has proven that culturally pushed kinds of interaction lead youngsters to create their tale from culturally shaped recollections. Investigation of Yankee and Asian mother and child reminiscence reveals the promotion of independence and private actualization valued in the American way of life and interdependence and modesty valued in Asian tradition arise at some point of mother-baby interaction. Comparisons of Chinese and American pupil reminiscences, in reality, show these culturally formed practices influence how occasions are encoded into autobiographical reminiscence. American college students consider certain activities which emphasize the independent, confident self, whilst Chinese language college students are much more likely to keep in mind much less designated occasions with institution orientation and private humility. Research shows that parent and caregiver reminiscence style and content aids the improvement of culturally decided gender norms, values, and ideals. Fivush (1994) discovered at some stage in observations that white middle magnificence mothers tended to be greater elaborative in their talk about individually applicable beyond with girls than boys, whose language skills were now not developed sufficiently to steer or affect the conversation. Greater person reminiscence elaboration and encouragement to construct their very own narrative aids a toddler's autobiographical take into account and solidifies the reminiscences. Similarly, mother's sincerely outstanding among boys and ladies whilst leading talk approximately the emotional content material of events. Girls tended to take delivery of the message that they ought to are seeking for out a person to solve worry or unhappiness and were recommended to locate a resolution to war within their own relationships. Talk with boys protected extra emphasis on independence and attribution and clarification of anger with much less speak of resolution. These styles propose that western children are socialized to understand that anger is greater tolerable in boys than ladies, and girls have greater obligation closer to others emotions in relationships. Studies with adults verify that western men and women recollect differently, girls do not forget extra activities which might be relationship-targeted. The studies mentioned indicate that gender identities are encouraged in early social interplay and autobiographical memories will expand to reflect the gendered values of one's culture. Any other form of memory between adult and young child serves to enhance desirable components of the kid's growing character and discourage less proper elements. Discussion of an infant's memories builds self-attention but can elicit anxiety, for example,, disapproval with regards to an episode when the child becomes especially stubborn. The anxiety lies among the kid's perfect self (loveable) real self (stubborn) and ought self (co-operative). Conway and Pleydell-Pearce (2000) devised the Self reminiscence system to explain how autobiographical reminiscence is organized in terms of the complex hierarchical intention structure of the 'running self which interacts with the autobiographical understanding base. The onset of self-focus, the cognitive self is essential for the corporation of memories. The running-self desires of a younger toddler, i.e. to be loved and regularly occurring, are inspired using needs together with, to boom fine effect and reduce the terrible effect. Conway et al. (2004) advise that self-defining reminiscences have the electricity to include private scripts into enduring autobiographical expertise. Scripts, as an example, cussed behaviors, the related emotion and outcome, turn out to be cues and hyperlink collectively related autobiographical reminiscences into themes. If being loved and prevalent is a child's aim the subject matter stubbornness, will prompt relevant memories from cues inside the state of affairs and assist the child to expect if being cussed in a context will elicit a loving parental reaction or the other. In this way, recollections are prepared to be drawn on as equipment to assess how conceivable and accessible desires are. However, memories are malleable and might emerge as distorted across time and in interplay. Researchers have found that the employer of autobiographical recollections, linked collectively by issues activated by contextual cues, is the rules of character. Memory among caregivers and children can characteristic to equip the kid with the talent to step again from the bad have an effect related to an original occasion. Alternatively, adults will encourage children to have fun with the high-quality effect tagged to an occasion. A frame of research has validated that people normally enjoy the fading affect bias, wherein occasion high quality have an effect on is plenty more potent at remember than equal occasion bad. The extra a reminiscence is talked over the better the renovation of the memory and the more potent the fading affect bias. From approximately and a 1/2 years kids begin to recognize reasoning and regularly become fixated on 'why' questions. Once this wondering is realized caregivers can incorporate knowledge of why occasions came about of their memory with the kid. Reduction of negative effects is the result of conscious self-distancing from the effect and taking note of why they feel negative as opposed to focusing on what they are skilled in. Kross et al. (2005) determined that terrible effects do no longer fade if the character makes use of a cognitive immersion approach at the same time as reflecting on the unpleasant memory. Cognitive distancing from bad has an effect on and savoring nice have an effect on maybe abilities learned in childhood, and will be contributing to the fading have an effect on bias in autobiographical reminiscence observed in grownup populations.

The man or woman's lifestyles tale begins to develop in early formative years with the improvement of the cognitive self. The particular production of the story could be closely influenced through adult-led conversations fashioned by the circle of relatives and cultural values the kid is born into. Lifestyle testimonies bring who we're, as an instance our beliefs approximately gender norms, and are constructed selectively from autobiographical memories. someone will be prompted by way of their modern-day dreams to emphasize factors to their records and persona through the reconstruction of the beyond that maximize effective effect in that particular context. Adult toddler reminiscence aids the organization of those reminiscences which are related collectively by issues and activated by using cues within the surroundings. Adults also have the capability to teach children to experience the effective emotions related to reminiscences and to distance themselves from negative emotions connected to reminiscence by stepping return and asking why an event is unpleasant. Autobiographical reminiscence is characterized by way of person and gender differences because of vast social interchanges and cultural milieus experienced at some stage in the early-developmental and mature phases of lifestyles. The look at is designed to explore the theoretical ideas encompassing the differing types, neural foundation, and several theoretical dimensions referring to the autobiographical memory.

Autobiographical reminiscence may be described as an explicit memory of the beyond events contributed through various positive nostalgic factors including individual's mental understanding, complex spoken or signal language, remembrance of interplay with parents and others, the particular fashion of speaking, self-illustration, non-public views, and narrative comprehension and manufacturing.

Several episodic memories or recollected events belonging to a character's past existence are referred to as autobiographical reminiscences, which have been recognized as an extra complex form of mummeries in comparison to the laboratory memories by several research performed through several cognitive psychologists. The episodic memory experiment conducted in a laboratory is usually concerned with a brief set of reminiscence comprising of events which might be based totally on sure words which are provided on a laptop display screen which generally contain the use of an unmarried sensory modality; showing a diminutive variant in spatial, temporal, emotional, and narrative content material or context that is in my view irrelevant to the concern. alternatively, in autobiographical memories occasions are recalled through regarding multimodal senses as an instance, flavor, smell, touch, hearing, imaginative and prescient and kinesthesis which can be supposed to exhibit widespread version in content material and context of spatial, temporal, emotional, and narrative cause and also reveal non-public relevance. Autobiographical reminiscences contain real-world stimuli and are extraordinarily complicated, therefore, necessitating supplementary theoretical and methodological considerations that are generally no longer required in a laboratory observation related to simplified stimuli.

The primary objective of this examination is to explore the theoretical underpinnings of cognitive psychology related to autobiographical memory. The systemic requirements concerning autobiographical memories contain individual senses as an example visualization, listening to, and smell; a multimodal spatial machine which reminds approximately the location concerning the gadgets and people; emotional device; linguistic gadget; a narrative system concerning informal interactions which does no longer always contain the usage of language and an explicit memory device which enables in coordinating data with the rest. Depending upon a man or woman's reminiscence, each of those structures tends to technique, prepare and assign roles which can be exhibited through precise cognitive behaviors. Some instrumental research is hired to file the evidence proffered by way of every system which includes cognitive-behavioral studies, character differences studies, neuro-anatomy, neuropsychology, and neuroimaging research which might be all beneficial in figuring out the lines of occasions amassed inside the autobiographical memory of a person. it has been studied that autobiographical memory itself, does now not represents an unmarried entity as a substitute it's far complemented by using multiple sys (items; each demonstrating various roles, agency, and processing of the applicable records. The permanence of the autobiographical memory appreciably relies on the continuity of those individual structures and their interaction with every different exactly just like the truth how the recollected memories of a character are shared cultural expertise obtained in the course of the existence span which eventually attributes cultural expectancies rather than individual's autobiographical memory. Long term reminiscence is mainly divided into 3 essential structures together with implicit reminiscence characterized through the reminiscences referring to the overall performance of a mission inside the absence of conscious recollection; semantic memory characterized using genuine memory of events, and episodic reminiscence characterized by the reminiscences of facts inside unique time and area devices. Autobiographical memory is predominantly involved with each of the episodic and semantic recollections which are similarly classified into three sub-kinds inclusive of real reminiscence, self-schemata, conventional reminiscence, and particular recollections which can be explicated as follows:

•   Actual memory-The concept of factual memory has not been extensively appraised inside the theoretical paradigm of autobiographical memory. Factual memory is on the whole worried with the instantaneous statistics and present happenings.

•   Self-Schemata-Self-schemata because the name shows, is the primary idea inside cognitive remedy and is characterized with the aid of self-information or facts approximately one's very own persona, nature, or temperament; that's a way extra complex and contextualized as compared to the regarded facts but is tons generalized compared to precise or everyday recollections. Self-schemata are not simply restricted to particular self-knowledge are the accumulated facts connected to unique self-realization which can be corresponded as information or statements. The method includes a low-priced corporation of statistics associated with abstracted actual-lifestyles reports which greatly differs from the schematic information and this divergence among unique experiences and schematic understanding transpires because the cognitive processes are likely to be encouraged by using the pre-hooked up schemata much like the encoding of revel in.

• Accepted memories-usual recollections are plenty precise in contrast with the self-schemata as concerning the recollections of repeated and similar reviews, however; specific memories are less abstracted compared to widespread memories. The mechanism of conventional memories significantly resembles self-schemata because it entails the stacking of analogous reviews. The most crucial issue of the familiar memories is the sensory and visual-spatial components which substantially limits the stacking of studies making it lots extra precise than self-schemata. Some of the problems specifically melancholy are related to a more probability of recalling universal recollections based on slightly indistinct reminiscence of reviews.

Particular recollections-sturdy sensory and visual-spatial additives are the important thing traits of precise memories which facilitate in the recollection episodic occasions from a person's beyond lifestyles encompassing positive canonical categories of statistics together with ongoing interest, place, individuals, differing's effect and very own affect on. there's a vast distinction among specific and lengthy-term specific reminiscences because the maximum latest happenings can be recollected by way of maximum people preserving specific recollections of the latest past but, the retention of lengthy-term recollections of that unique event, using everybody, is vitally dubious because it has been a have a look at of the specific memories of new past belong to a unique reminiscence device than long time specific recollections. The system of autobiographical reasoning stressing the temporal, causal, and thematic dating and cultural interchanges increase narrative-like structures which are supposed to shape explicit linkage between numerous unique memories. The concept suggests that the reminiscences of the latest beyond aren't subjected to schemata-pushed reconstruction approaches and consequently, particular reminiscences may be considered as an awful lot correct and much less biased. The theoretical underpinnings touching on the neural origins of autobiographical reminiscence are briefly explicated as follows:

Prospection-mental simulation of likely future occasions can extensively assist a person to strategies and plan for the capacity opportunities in pursuit of private goals and thereby, probabilities of failures may be minimized thru constant efforts. it's been studied that prospection is the concept of imagining oneself in the future which finally allows a person to engage in prepared strategic behaviors to obtain pre-deliberate private targets. Remembering beyond occasions and futuristic thinking are both hypothesized to reflect the parallel course of movement which has been explicated with the aid of the sequential distribution of self-generated probable future occasions that have been determined to copy the distribution of recollected past events of several individuals at some stage in their existence cycle. there's an opportunity that the recollection of beyond reminiscences and prospection of futuristic occasions would possibly percentage neural substrate and comparable mechanism as research endorse that, a decreasing style of phenomenological richness and episodic specificity with age has been observed, within the past and destiny occasions.

Navigation-in accordance with the cognitive theory each of the ego-centric and allocentric perspectives facilitates imagining the modern status of a person and the preferred targets followed through unique routes to navigate spatial environments via topographical orientation. Lesser emphasis is interested in a man or woman's stance as consistent with the allocentric angle which is meant to perceive the relation among landmarks with the assist of engaging one's mind to find out the future possibilities which can be appreciably indifferent to the on the spot surroundings or to visualize or map the surroundings.

The idea of thoughts-theory of mind helps in comprehending the social navigation system indicating that the communal interchanges between people are primarily based on a character's perspectives that are significantly encouraged by way of the pre-conceived notions and that allows you to expect the motion and reaction of others, it's imperative to apprehend their perspective. It's been studied that to recognize others' perspectives, individuals make efforts to self-assignment themselves through simulating the mindset of others.

Default Mode-capabilities of the brain studied at some point of the resting phase of a man or woman are typically referred to as default mode that is characterized by using the unprepared mind or thoughts wandering circumstance wherein the mind is will become stimulus-unbiased and maybe irrational at instances. each the outside or inner surroundings has no big have an effect on the brain functioning of an individual in a resting section but, an internal model of cognition may additionally end up activated which allows a person to self-projection or believe one-self in a favored situation without being stimulated using the respective environment.

Theories of Autobiographical reminiscence development-The theoretical underpinnings of autobiographical memory improvement have skilled considerable progression in the context of explaining infantile amnesia which reflects the failure of adults to remember events from their early stages of lifestyles. it's miles quite a thriller that youngsters seem to keep in mind plenty from their long-time period memory financial institution, however; as they develop vintage and reach adulthood it becomes particularly tough for them to remember their past recollections mainly relating to their early formative years.

Number one impact Theories-throughout the beginning of pre-faculty duration there may be a lack of a cognitive and social-cognitive framework that's accountable for encoding memories which ultimately fails in retrieving self-applicable recollections in later stages of lifestyles. The replicate venture of self-reputation (MSR) has been diagnosed because of the most vital device for the encoding and garage of autobiographical memories. however, it's been hypothesized that self-popularity performs a quintessential position in retrieving autobiographical memories but, kids in early a long time do no longer poses the capability to recognize the basics of nature, personality, and person makes it difficult for them to advantage not on time self-popularity. studies advise that the reminiscence financial institution will become actively responses as soon as a child develops information of one-self and achieves sizeable representational focus agreeing to this, the cognitive-motivational idea of adults autobiographical reminiscence presented by way of Conway and Pleydell-Pearce 2000, who recommend that self-grounding is an essential a part of retrieving the memories but, they further emphasized on the identification of dreams and argued that the lack of ability to reconstruct the reminiscences in later degrees of existence has a completely near hyperlink with the incongruity of self-desires with the encoding and retrieving duration.

A couple of affect theories-a number of research concur with the previous idea of the insufficient cognitive or social-cognitive framework in the course of early preschool years, is the important purpose interfering with the encoding and retrieval of autobiographical memories but; they similarly attempted to analyses the essential talents of a man or woman to encode and retrieve the memories, in the larger social and linguistic realm for the kid. Children are unable to recognize the causal-temporal collection of events and can't set up the order of self-applicable activities right into a chronological narrative which allows a frequent encoding and retrieval of autobiographical recollections as the representational device in large part depends upon linguistic abilities which subsequently broaden after four-five years. several theories also propose that social interaction is every other huge detail to retrieve autobiographical memories and further argue that children increase their important cognitive capacities thru social interactions and reminiscing practices. Furthermore, parental cooperation in discussing, evaluating, and elaborating the past activities additionally facilitates in providing rich information which therefore develops within the retrieval of autobiographical reminiscences. It has additionally been studied, that other than linguistic aid children additionally necessitate a reason to examine and bear in mind past activities which could be robust social bonds and near relationships which significantly enables them in self-popularity method and the greater they recognize themselves in their early childhood, the greater it becomes simpler to reminisce their autobiographical memories.

Social Cultural Developmental Theories-There is three full-size arguments encompassing the social and cultural developmental theories referring to autobiographical memories such as (i) gradual emergence of autobiographical reminiscence throughout the preschool years; (ii) autobiographical reminiscence gadget is pretty reliant upon the language that is the essential tool for social interchanges; and (iii) autobiographical memory is characterized by cultural, gender, and person variations across lifestyles that need significant explanation. It has been studied that the remembrance of events from a lifespan of youngsters and person may additionally considerably range and it's pretty evident that everybody isn't always capable of remembering greater of events with identical detailing and in a similar narrative manner as expressed through others. This shows that variations in each route and time of emergence of the autobiographical recollections and their eventual outcomes significantly range relying upon age, intercourse, gender, non-public reports, social interactions, and cultural variations. The improvement system starts with the beginning observed by toddler memories which are instituted through social interactions with mother and father, siblings, and relatives, throughout which nascent conceptions are built in a character's thoughts which might be unconsciously penetrated inside the reminiscence financial institution. Studies additionally advocate that toddlers are very much aware of their surroundings and still have a concept of core self which has been basically related to intentionality. It's been studied that babies as consistent with their core self have decided goals and actions that are fuelled by the infusion of positive skills, rising principles, and social experiences. The later section after four-5 years whilst the kids respond to what they hear and begin speaking through the use of linguistic aids outcomes within the upkeep of a sound reminiscence bank which can be encoded and retrieved later in lifestyles relying upon a man or woman's capability to reminisce the autobiographical reminiscences. The key additives of the development machine facilitating the early development of reminiscence base are characterized through the initiation of recollections being stored inside the memory bank of an unborn baby. it has been studied that the unborn infant is capable of differentiating and discriminating between the incoming statistics and is also capable to keep the facts over time. Children have been studied to have implicit reminiscences which have been accumulated all through the first trimester of pregnancy, however; the remembrance of such reminiscence can be extraordinarily quick. Then again, it has been studied that the time period wherein a baby emits a previously conditioned response can be extended with the usage of reminders as a consequence, strengthening their memory base. The position of language is extraordinarily full-size inside the retrieval and narration of autobiographical reminiscences. it has been studied that language is vast within the retrieval of autobiographical reminiscence in three precise ways including (i) its miles concerned in supplying the organizational and evaluative characteristic of autobiographical reminiscence; (ii) it notably allows in developing and preserve social interactions which sooner or later results inside the organized representation of past studies specifically for youngsters; and (iii) it enables in growing the awareness of younger kids to maintain memory as an illustration of past revel in which may be evaluated from a couple of subjective. adult memory communication is the 1/3 essential component of the developmental system in which mothers play an indispensable function in developing the memory system of their kids as they may be the initial point of contact to kids, permitting them to apprehend their external surroundings and educating them to reply. There's an extensive difference between number one focus and symbolic awareness however, it has been studied that the attention of the past is greatly accountable within the developmental machine as it helps in defining the idea of the present, past, and destiny in the autobiographical reminiscence. Sooner or later, the self-reputation or self-in-time is a closely related idea contributing inside the developmental machine and it has been studied that to relate oneself inside the beyond or inside the gift necessitates the simple mapping of two wonderful representations. The recollections related to early levels of life can significantly assist in gaining an insight into oneself hence, offering them opportunities for emotional boom and improvement. similarly to this, self-popularity and self-expertise distinctly help in improving the overall character and temperament of a man or woman as the autobiographical memories can facilitate in defining non-public lacking subsequently, enabling the man or woman to convert right into a better human being. The observation has efficaciously set up the grounds for expertise differing types and neural origins of the autobiographical memory and finally opened up various factors of theoretical paradigms associated with the subject place indicating that the memory bank may be evolved with growing age. Moreover, the take a look at additionally exhibits that social interchanges and cultural influences in the early stages of life have enormous influences on the memory development system. It could be instituted that cognitive psychology is an extensive challenge having an extensive variety of theories associated with autobiographical memory, and this examination inside its restricted scope tried to address several speculative areas of the concerned subject.

Theories of autobiographical reminiscence

Autobiographical reminiscence is characterized through individual and gender differences as a result of sizeable social interchanges and cultural milieus experienced at some stage in the early-developmental and mature phases of lifestyles. They have a look at is designed to discover the theoretical concepts encompassing the different types, neural basis, and numerous theoretical dimensions bearing on the autobiographical memory. Autobiographical memory can be described as a specific reminiscence of the beyond activities contributed through various sure nostalgic elements inclusive of individual's psychological understanding, complicated spoken or sign language, remembrance of interplay with mother and father and others, the particular fashion of speaking, self-illustration, private perspectives and narrative comprehension and production. several episodic memories or recollected activities belonging to a character's beyond existence are referred to as autobiographical memories, that have been recognized as an extra complex form of mummeries compared to the laboratory recollections according to numerous studies carried out by using several cognitive psychologists. The episodic reminiscence test conducted in a laboratory is typically concerned with a quick set of reminiscence comprising of activities that are primarily based on certain phrases which are offered on a computer display which basically involve the use of an unmarried sensory modality; displaying a diminutive version in spatial, temporal, emotional, and narrative content or context this is individually inappropriate to the problem. on the other hand, in autobiographical memories events are recalled by related to multimodal senses as, taste, scent, touch, hearing, imaginative and prescient, and kinesthesis that are meant to show off massive variation in content and context of spatial, temporal, emotional, and narrative purpose and also display personal relevance. Autobiographical memories contain actual-international stimuli and are extremely complicated hence, necessitating supplementary theoretical and methodological issues that are usually no longer required in a laboratory study involving simplified stimuli. The main goal of this study is to explore the theoretical underpinnings of cognitive psychology related to autobiographical reminiscence. The initial section of the study ambitions to identify special types of autobiographical memory which extends to the center phase which is supposed to assess its neural foundation. The later phase of the examination explicates the exclusive theories of the problem remember main to the very last end. The systemic requirements about autobiographical recollections involve character senses as an instance visualization, hearing, and smell; a multimodal spatial machine which reminds about the vicinity concerning the items and those; emotional device; linguistic system; a story system regarding informal interactions which does now not necessarily involve using language. Relying upon a character's memory, each of these structures tends to process, arrange and assign roles that might be exhibited with the aid of specific cognitive behaviors. Some the instrumental studies are hired to file the evidence proffered with the aid of every system which includes cognitive-behavioral research, man or woman variations research, neuro-anatomy, neuropsychology, and neuroimaging studies that are all helpful in figuring out the traces of occasions amassed within the autobiographical memory of a man or woman. it's been studied that autobiographical memory itself, does not represent a single entity rather it's far complemented with the aid of a couple of structures; every demonstrating various roles, employers, and processing of the applicable information. The permanence of the autobiographical memory drastically is based on the continuity of these character structures and their interplay with each other precisely much like the fact how the recollected reminiscences of a character is a shared cultural knowledge acquired throughout the life span which eventually attributes cultural expectancies as opposed to person's autobiographical memory. Long time memory is principally divided into three primary structures consisting of implicit memory characterized using the reminiscences referring to the performance of an undertaking within the absence of conscious recollection; semantic memory characterized through genuine memory of activities, and episodic reminiscence characterized by way of the recollections of records inside precise time and space units. Autobiographical memory is predominantly worried about both the episodic and semantic reminiscences which can be further categorized into three sub-types together with authentic reminiscence, self-schemata, regularly occurring memory, and unique memories which might be explicated as follows:

Real memory-The concept of real reminiscence has not been widely appraised within the theoretical paradigm of autobiographical memory. real memory is in most cases concerned with instantaneous information and present happenings.

Self-Schemata-Self-schemata because the name shows, is the principal conception within the cognitive remedy and is characterized by way of self-knowledge or information approximately one's very own character, nature, or temperament; that is a long way more complex and contextualized in comparison to the known information but is a great deal generalized compared to specific or ordinary reminiscences. Self-schemata aren't just confined to selected self-knowledge are the accumulated information linked to particular self-consciousness which can be corresponded as information or statements. The manner involves low-cost enterprise of data related to abstracted actual-life reports which substantially differs from the schematic expertise and this divergence among authentic reports and schematic information transpires as the cognitive techniques are probably to be motivated by the pre-installed schemata similar to the encoding of an experience. It's been studied that the insistence and distortion of self-schemata can also considerably vary depending upon a person's.

Everyday recollections-time-honored memories are a lot particular in assessment with the self-schemata as concerning the memories of repeated and comparable reports however, precise reminiscences are less abstracted in comparison to popular reminiscences. The mechanism of universal reminiscences significantly resembles self-schemata as it entails the stacking of analogous reports. The maximum critical aspect of the well-known reminiscences is the sensory and visible-spatial components which substantially limits the stacking of experiences making it plenty more precise than self-schemata. Some of the disorders in particular melancholy are related to a greater likelihood of recalling regularly occurring memories based on a slightly vague memory of experiences.

Precise reminiscences-sturdy sensory and visible-spatial additives are the important thing characteristics of particular reminiscences which facilitate inside the recollection episodic activities from a character's beyond existence encompassing sure canonical classes of data which includes ongoing interest, region, humans, other's effect and very own effect. there's a considerable difference between unique and lengthy-term precise reminiscences because the maximum recent happenings can be recollected by maximum people maintaining precise reminiscences of the recent beyond but, the retention of lengthy-time period memories of that precise occasion, by anyone is vitally dubious. After all, it has been studied that the specific recollections of the recent past belong to a distinctive memory gadget than long-term specific memories. The manner of autobiographical reasoning stressing the temporal, causal, and thematic dating and cultural interchanges increase narrative-like structures which are supposed to form explicit linkage among numerous specific memories. The principle indicates that the memories of recent beyond are not subjected to schemata-pushed reconstruction methods and therefore, unique memories can be taken into consideration as a good deal correct and less biased.

Prospection-mental simulation of probably future events can substantially help a man or woman to techniques and plan for the capability possibilities in pursuit of private objectives and thereby, chances of disasters may be minimized via consistent efforts. It's been studied that prospection is the concept of imagining oneself in the future which eventually allows a man or woman to have interaction in prepared strategic behaviors to acquire pre-planned private targets. Remembering past events and futuristic questioning are each hypothesized to reflect the parallel direction of motion which has been explicated via the sequential distribution of self-generated possibly future activities which have been found to copy the distribution of recollected beyond occasions of numerous people at some point of their life cycle. there may be a possibility that the recollection of past recollections and prospection of futuristic occasions may proportion neural substrate and similar mechanism as studies propose that, a reducing style of phenomenological richness and episodic specificity with age has been found, inside the beyond and future activities. According to the cognitive theory, both the egocentric and allocentric perspectives facilitate imagining the modern status of a person and the desired objectives accompanied with the aid of particular routes to navigate spatial environments via topographical orientation. Lesser emphasis is interested in a character's stance as per the allocentric attitude which is meant to identify the relation between landmarks with the help of engaging one's thoughts to find out the future potentialities which are extensively indifferent to the instantaneous environment or to visualize or map the surroundings.

The concept of mind-principle of thoughts allows in comprehending the social navigation system indicating that the communal interchanges between human beings are based on a person's views that are greatly encouraged through the pre-conceived notions and on the way to predict the movement and reaction of others, it's imperative to understand their perspective. It's been studied that to understand others' views, individuals make efforts to self-mission themselves using simulating the attitude of others. Default Mode-features of mind studied all through the resting segment of a man or woman are commonly referred to as default mode which is characterized by the unprepared thoughts or thoughts wandering condition wherein the mind is will become stimulus-unbiased and can be irrational at times. each the external or inner surroundings has no good-sized influence on the brain functioning of an individual in a resting section however, an internal model of cognition might also become activated which permits an individual to self-projection or imagine oneself in a preferred condition without being influenced with the aid of the respective surroundings. The theoretical underpinnings of autobiographical memory development have skilled widespread progression in the context of explaining childish amnesia which displays the failure of adults to consider activities from their early degrees of existence. It's far pretty a mystery that children appear to keep in mind plenty from their long-time period reminiscence bank, however; as they develop antique and reach maturity it will become distinctly hard for them to recall their past reminiscences especially touching on their early childhood. During the start of the pre-college period, there's a loss of cognitive and social-cognitive framework which is chargeable for encoding reminiscences which ultimately fails in retrieving self-applicable reminiscences in later tiers of existence. Replicate mission of self-recognition (MSR) has been identified because the maximum important instrument for the encoding and storage of autobiographical memories. on the other hand, it has been hypothesized that self-popularity plays a crucial position in retrieving autobiographical recollections but, youngsters in early a while do no longer poses the potential to understand the basics of nature, persona, and individual which makes it difficult for them to advantage behind schedule self-reputation. research endorse that the reminiscence bank becomes actively responses as soon as a child develops a knowledge of one-self and achieves considerable representational recognition agreeing to this, the cognitive-motivational theory of adults autobiographical memory presented using advocate that self-grounding is an important a part of retrieving the recollections, however, they further emphasized on the identity of goals and argued that the inability to reconstruct the memories in later levels of existence has a completely close link with the incongruity of self-desires with the encoding and retrieving period. some of the research concur with the previous concept of the inadequate cognitive or social-cognitive framework at some stage in early preschool years, is the vital cause interfering with the encoding and retrieval of autobiographical reminiscences but; they, in addition, attempted to analyses the essential skills of a person to encode and retrieve the reminiscences, within the large social and linguistic realm for the child. kids are not able to recognize with the causal-temporal collection of occasions and cannot establish the order of self-relevant events into a chronological narrative which permits a frequent encoding and retrieval of autobiographical recollections as the representational gadget largely relies upon linguistic abilities which in the end increase after four to five years. Several theories also endorse that social interplay is every other vast element to retrieve autobiographical memories and further argue that kids broaden their critical cognitive capacities via social interactions and reminiscing practices. Furthermore, parental cooperation in discussing, evaluating, and elaborating the past occasions also allows in supplying rich information which consequently develops in the retrieval of autobiographical memories. It has also been studied, that other than linguistic aid youngsters additionally necessitate a purpose to learn and do not forget beyond events which can be strong social bonds and near relationships which substantially helps them in self-reputation method and the extra they recognize oneself in their early childhood, the greater it becomes simpler to reminisce their autobiographical reminiscences.

Social Cultural Developmental Theories

Three large arguments are encompassing the social and cultural developmental theories about autobiographical recollections which include (i) gradual emergence of autobiographical memory across the preschool years; (ii) autobiographical reminiscence device is pretty reliant upon the language that's the vital tool for social interchanges; and (iii) autobiographical memory is characterized through cultural, gender, and individual variations across life that want great clarification. it has been studied that the remembrance of events from a lifespan of children and person can also significantly range and it's miles quite obtrusive that everyone isn't always able to remember more of occasions with identical detailing and in a comparable narrative manner as expressed by others. This indicates that differences in both the route and time of emergence of the autobiographical memories and their eventual effects drastically vary relying upon age, sex, gender, non-public reports, social interactions, and cultural variations. The development machine starts with the start accompanied with the aid of infant reminiscences which are instituted thru social interactions with dad and mom, siblings and spouse, and children, during which nascent conceptions are built in a man or woman's mind might be unconsciously penetrated in the memory financial institution. Research additionally advises that toddlers are very much aware of their environment and now have a concept of middle self which has been basically related to intentionality. It has been studied that infants as in step with their core self-have decided goals and moves that are fuelled by the infusion of sure competencies, emerging standards, and social studies. The later phase after four-five years when the youngsters respond to what they listen to and start speaking by using the use of linguistic aids consequences within the upkeep of a valid reminiscence bank which can be encoded and retrieved later in life depending upon a character's capability to reminisce the autobiographical memories. The important thing components of the improvement gadget facilitating the early development of reminiscence base are characterized by using the initiation of memories being saved in the memory financial institution of an unborn baby. It has been studied that the unborn child can differentiate and discriminating among the incoming facts and also is successful to save the information through the years. Kids were studied to have implicit reminiscences that have been gathered for the duration of the primary trimester of pregnancy however, the remembrance of such reminiscence can be extraordinarily short. Alternatively, it has been studied that the time period wherein a child emits a formerly conditioned reaction may be extended with the use of reminders accordingly, strengthening their reminiscence base. The role of language is extraordinarily significant inside the retrieval and narration of autobiographical recollections. it's been studied that language is large within the retrieval of autobiographical memory in 3 unique methods including (i) it's far concerned in imparting the organizational and evaluative characteristic of autobiographical memory; (ii) it substantially enables in growing and maintain social interactions which eventually consequences inside the prepared representation of past reports in particular for kids; and (iii) it allows in developing the awareness of younger kids to maintain reminiscence as an illustration of beyond enjoying which may be evaluated from multiple subjective views. Grownup reminiscence talk is the third important component of developmental gadget in which mothers play a critical function in developing the reminiscence gadget of their youngsters as they are the initial factor of touch to children, permitting them to recognize their outside surroundings and educating them to respond. There is a huge distinction between number one recognition and symbolic attention but, it's been studied that the recognition of the past is substantially responsible within the developmental gadget because it allows in defining the idea of a gift, beyond and destiny inside the autobiographical memory. Sooner or later, the self-reputation or self-in-time is a closely associated idea contributing to the developmental machine and it has been studied that to narrate oneself within the beyond or inside the gift necessitates the clear-cut mapping of two wonderful representations. The memories related to the early ranges of life can appreciably help in gaining an insight into oneself, for this reason, imparting the possibilities for emotional growth and improvement. Further to this, self-popularity and self-know-how relatively help in improving the general character and temperament of a character because the autobiographical memories can facilitate in defining personal lacking hence, enabling the character to convert into a better man or woman. The take a look at has efficiently hooked up the grounds for know-how different sorts and neural origins of the autobiographical memory and sooner or later unfolded various components of theoretical paradigms associated with the challenge location indicating that the reminiscence financial institution may be advanced with growing age. Moreover, the study also famous that social interchanges and cultural influences in early ranges of existence have good-sized effects on the memory development machine. To conclude, it may be instituted that cognitive psychology is a great subject having huge-variety of theories related to autobiographical memory; and this has a look at inside its restricted scope attempted to cope with several speculative regions of the worrying theme.

Poor effects of Autobiographical reminiscence

First-year university students are prone to traumatic environments. Being far away from domestic for the primary time would regularly elicit bad emotions, especially loneliness and disappointment. But what happens while one's temper is always negative? In step with the DSM-five, symptoms of medical depression consist of feeling unhappy, or hopeless, having dwindled delight, and having emotions of worthlessness and guilt, almost every day for at least two weeks. In easier words, melancholy is a regular revel in negative emotion. This mindset could bias personal studies, especially, autobiographical memory. Autobiographical memory errors episodic reminiscence represents reminiscences of reports and particular events in time in a serial form, from which you can actually reconstruct the real events that occurred at any given point in your lives. It's the reminiscence of autobiographical occasions (instances, places, related emotions, and different contextual knowledge) that may be explicitly said. Individuals tend to peer themselves as actors in those activities, and the emotional charge and the complete context surrounding an occasion is usually part of the memory, not simply the bare information of the occasion itself. The brain is in the middle of the recollections, and it receives data about reviews randomly till the facts are delivered returned up or a particular reminiscence itself. Reminiscence is the 'glue', in effect, that holds highbrow tactics together, from perception, interest, and language, to reasoning, choice-making, and hassle fixing. Memory also performs an important position in social and emotional functioning, because it is a sense of whom one is and different humans are from factual and autobiographical records in reminiscences. Forgetting is also a part of reminiscence. Quick-term retention is a vital stage for the solid acquisition of recent facts in long-term memory. Since the reminiscences of the event that came about have been over a year ago the elements of long-term reminiscence loss want to be considered in addition to reminiscence errors.

Autobiographical reminiscence is basically a system that includes episodic recollections from people's lives, autobiographical reminiscence is what makes each person specific to every other, and essentially what paperwork the self, connecting us to others, records, and the future. "Autobiographical memories from the mundane to the profound, assist form the self, they offer personal historic context or personal biography for who we're now: they're in essence a 'database' of the self." The idea that shiny memories are associated with a better level of emotion or arousal inside the player and consequently more easily available, via displaying a photograph in place of a verbal cue contributors show a higher degree of connection to the cue. studies carried out once more concerned with the hyperlinks between gender variations and bear in mind within autobiographical reminiscence, the distinction inside this examine is that contributors had been scaled on the melancholy and anxiety scale from a questionnaire completed and then categorized into dysphoric or non-dysphoric agencies to look if more exact or trendy responses have been provided to a hard and fast of tremendous, neutral and negative cue words. Research right here was being performed to peer if unique genders, genetics, or childhood reviews are more at risk of depression. Speculation here being examined changed into to peer if patients with depressive and dysphoric signs had issues gaining access to autobiographical reminiscences and whether or not it might be viable to decide among the two agencies. It turned into cautioned that patients who scored high on the dimensions for depressive signs and symptoms might offer greater trendy descriptions from autobiographical reminiscence whilst referring to emotions. Discussion of gender variations here suggested that ladies are extra regularly identified with melancholy than men and that guys had been more likely to engage.

Capabilities of Autobiographical memory

Functional technique to autobiographical memory (AM) posits its three vast features: directive, self, and social. Even though these capabilities are probably familiar, existence degree and gender variations are expected. Autobiographical memory (AM) research is frequently targeted at the quantity and accuracy of remembering. In comparison to know-how how AM works, literature on why we keep in mind non-public lifestyle activities over long durations is pretty understudied. From the theoretical factor of view, some of the thoughts on the features of AM were positioned forth, yet not as regularly have these ideas been empirically established. Whilst tapping into the capability of AM we speak either its use or its adaptivity. Even though the use and adaptivity of memory are most certainly intertwined, the right study direction seems to be: (1) to pick out the approaches in which AM is used, and (2) to problematic on its (mal) adaptivity in everyday existence. This concept is mirrored within the current improvements in AM research resulting in concept-based totally questionnaires of AM capabilities (e.g., considering lifestyles experience Scale—story; "matters about memory" questionnaire. (3) primary theory-driven features of AM, nested in those scales, are directive (planning for present and destiny behaviors), self (self-continuity, self-expression), and social (communique, dating maintenance) function. Although AM may additionally serve different features beyond the ones advised by the tripartite model, maximum researchers agree upon the three principal features.

The Directive feature

This characteristic of AM describes using past studies to direct or manual modern-day and future actions, minds, and behaviors. To date, research has mentioned numerous approaches in which the directive nature of AM is evident. Statistics saved in AM supports normal decision-making by retrieving past stories to enable the fixing of contemporary problems and expect future occasions. Robinson and Swanson (1990) take this assumption a step further using suggesting that AM enables us to create fashions of encountered activities and those which permit higher expertise of differing's internal worlds. Such models also facilitate the prediction of different human beings' behavior. Cohen (1998) complements these assumptions by arguing that AM also can result in the development of private opinions and attitudes. Empirical statistics fits properly with these thoughts: private reports approximately reminiscence of beyond events are inwrought with morals on the significance of instructions learned for our future behavior.

The Self function

AM serves as a repository of self-facts that play an essential position in growing strong and enduring illustrations of ourselves over the years. The self-function refers to the usage of non-public facts to maintain an experience of being the equal man or woman in the course of one's lifetime or to replace the self even as keeping continuity. Autobiographical narratives mutually form a solid identity, starting in youth, and persevering with for the duration of the existence span. This experience of identification is then conveyed to others through the expression and sharing of AM. Basic, information of the self in the beyond and its echo projected into the future is viewed as a crucial kind of self-information and its adequacy relies upon its ability to reinforce continuity and improvement of the self. Empirical work reveals support for self-characteristic found that people with low self-concept clarity (i.e., with poorly defined and internally inconsistent self-concept) are much more likely to use and do not forget the beyond for self-continuity functions, suggesting that reminiscences may be used to "remind" an individual of the sense of identification.

The Social characteristic

Numerous authors have argued that social bonding thru retrieving and sharing personal memories is the number one function of AM. Autobiographical reminiscences are viewed as vignettes used to provoke, broaden, foster, and hold social bonds and members of the family. Most normally, private memories function as a medium for sharing of reports, accordingly facilitating understanding and empathy in social interactions. Sharing of AM can also foster intimacy function regarding the conversational companion due to the fact people tend to feel toward the listener after sharing an AM because of self-disclosure procedures. But, AM may also involve memories about loved ones, which aren't necessarily shared with others. The social feature obviously serves a myriad of functions. It might be first-class viewed as an umbrella dimension, which is differentiated into particular but complementing, sub-capabilities. Empirical research is granting proofs for any such attitude. For instance, the use of AM to bypass valuable existence classes, the so-called educate/inform feature, has additionally been suggested as a part of the AM's social characteristic. Additionally, the initial evaluation of social features turned split into two elements addressing the nurturing of existent relationships and the improvement of new ones, although authors have argued that these two capabilities are a mirrored image of different phases of the connections throughout generations.

Chapter Seven

Cognitive Science and Problem Solving

Cognitive science is the interdisciplinary study of mind and intelligence, embracing philosophy, psychology, artificial intelligence, neuroscience, linguistics, and anthropology. Its highbrow origins are inside the mid-1950s while researchers in numerous fields started to broaden theories of thoughts based totally on complicated representations and computational strategies. Its organizational origins are inside the mid-Seventies whilst the Cognitive technological know-how Society changed into formed and the journal Cognitive science commenced. Given that then, multiple hundred universities in North the United States, Europe, Asia, and Australia have established cognitive science programs, and lots of others have instituted guides in cognitive technological know-how. Attempts to recognize the thoughts and their operation go returned at the least to the historical Greeks, while philosophers which include Plato and Aristotle attempted to explain the character of human expertise. The look at mind remained the province of philosophy till the nineteenth century when experimental psychology evolved. Wilhelm Wundt and his students initiated laboratory techniques for analyzing intellectual operations extra systematically. Within a few a long time, however, experimental psychology has become dominated by way of behaviorism, a view that virtually denied the existence of thoughts. Psychology has to restrict itself from inspecting the relation between observable stimuli and observable behavioral responses. Talk of consciousness and mental representations became banished from the respectable scientific dialogue. Mainly in North America, behaviorism ruled the mental scene via the 1950s. Around 1956, the highbrow panorama started to alternate dramatically. George Miller summarized numerous studies which showed that the potential of human thinking is restrained, with quick-term reminiscence, for example, restricted to round seven gadgets. He proposed that reminiscence limitations can be conquered through recoding data into chunks, mental representations that require intellectual tactics for encoding and interpreting the statistics. Presently, primitive computers had been around for only some years, but pioneers including John McCarthy, Marvin Minsky, Allen Newell, and Herbert Simon had been founding the field of artificial intelligence. Further, Noam Chomsky rejected behaviorist assumptions approximately language as a discovered dependency and proposed alternatively to explain language comprehension in phrases of intellectual grammar inclusive of guidelines. The six thinkers cited in this paragraph can be considered because of the founders of cognitive technology. Cognitive technology has unifying theoretical thoughts, however, we need to recognize the range of outlooks and strategies that researchers in extraordinary fields bring to the examination of thoughts and intelligence. Although cognitive psychologists nowadays often engage in theorizing and computational modeling, their primary approach is experimentation with human participants. People, often undergraduates' pleasurable direction requirements, are added into the laboratory so that distinctive styles of thinking can be studied underneath managed situations. For instance, psychologists have experimentally tested the varieties of errors people make in deductive reasoning, the ways that people shape and follow concepts, the velocity of people questioning with intellectual pics, and the overall performance of human beings fixing troubles the use of analogies. Our conclusions approximately how the mind works need to be primarily based on more than "common feel" and introspection, for the reason that these can deliver a deceptive photograph of mental operations, a lot of which aren't consciously handy. an increasing number of, psychologists draw their experimental contributors from Amazon's Mechanical Turk and culturally numerous sources. Psychological experiments that cautiously method intellectual operations from numerous guidelines are consequently essential for cognitive science to be medical. Experimentation is also a method hired by using experimental philosophy. Even though theory without experiment is empty, experiment without theory is blind. To address the crucial questions on the character of thoughts, the mental experiments want to be interpretable inside a theoretical framework that postulates mental representations and techniques. One of the satisfactory ways of growing theoretical frameworks is via forming and checking out computational fashions intended to be analogous to mental operations. To supplement psychological experiments on deductive reasoning, concept formation, intellectual imagery, and analogical hassle fixing, researchers have advanced computational fashions that simulate factors of human overall performance. Designing, building, and experimenting with computational fashions is the critical approach of artificial intelligence (AI), the department of laptop technology involved with shrewd systems. Preferably in cognitive technology, computational fashions and psychological experimentation cross hand in hand, but an awful lot of crucial work in AI has examined the strength of various strategies to information representation in relative isolation from experimental psychology. Even as a few linguists do mental experiments or increase computational fashions, maximum presently use special methods. For linguists inside the Chomskian lifestyle, the principle theoretical mission is to perceive grammatical standards that offer the primary structure of human languages. Identity takes place through noticing diffused variations among grammatical and ungrammatical utterances. In English, as an instance, the sentences "She hit the ball" and "What do you like?" are grammatical, however "She the hit ball" and "What do you like?" aren't. A grammar of English will explain why the previous are desirable however no longer the latter. An opportunity technique, cognitive linguistics, places much less emphasis on syntax and extra on semantics and ideas. Like cognitive psychologists, neuroscientists regularly carry out controlled experiments, however, their observations are very distinct, because neuroscientists are concerned at once with the character of the mind. With nonhuman topics, researchers can insert electrodes and report the firing of character neurons. With humans for whom this method might be too invasive, it is now common to use magnetic and positron scanning devices to look at what's occurring in special elements of the mind whilst people are doing diverse intellectual duties. For instance, brain scans have diagnosed the areas of the brain concerned with intellectual imagery and word interpretation. Additional evidence approximately brain functioning is collected by looking at the performance of human beings whose brains had been damaged in identifiable ways. A stroke, as an instance, in part of the mind devoted to language can produce deficits together with the incapacity to utter sentences. Like cognitive psychology, neuroscience is often theoretical in addition to experimental, and concept development is often aided by growing computational fashions of the conduct of businesses of neurons. Cognitive anthropology expands the examination of human wondering to remember how notion works in special cultural settings. The examination of thoughts should manifestly now not be restrained to how English speakers suppose but should recollect viable differences in modes of wondering throughout cultures. Cognitive technological know-how is becoming increasingly aware of the want to view the operations of the mind specifically physical and social environments. For cultural anthropologists, the main approach is ethnography, which requires dwelling and interacting with individuals of a subculture to a sufficient quantity that their social and cognitive structures turn out to be obvious. Cognitive anthropologists have investigated, as an example, the similarities and variations throughout cultures in words for colors.

Traditionally, philosophers do now not perform systematic empirical observations or construct computational models, although there has been the latest rise in work in experimental philosophy. However, philosophy remains vital to cognitive science because it deals with essential problems that underlie the experimental and computational techniques to mind. Abstract questions which include the nature of illustration and computation want not to be addressed in the regular exercise of psychology or synthetic intelligence, however, they unavoidably arise when researchers assume deeply about what they're doing. Philosophy additionally offers well-known questions together with the relation of thoughts and body and with methodological questions along with the nature of explanations located in cognitive technological know-how. Similarly, philosophy worries itself with normative questions about how people have to suppose as well as with descriptive ones approximately how they do. Except for the theoretical goal of know-how human thinking, cognitive technological know-how can have the real purpose of improving it, which calls for a normative mirrored image on what we want questions to be. Philosophy of mind does not have a wonderful technique but needs to proportion with the quality theoretical work in different fields a challenge with empirical effects. In its weakest shape, cognitive technological know-how is just the sum of the fields noted: psychology, synthetic intelligence, linguistics, neuroscience, anthropology, and philosophy. Interdisciplinary work will become an awful lot extra interesting when there is theoretical and experimental convergence on conclusions approximately the nature of mind. As an instance, psychology and synthetic intelligence may be combined through computational fashions of the way people behave in experiments. The fine way to understand the complexity of human questioning is to apply multiple techniques, especially mental and neurological experiments, and computational fashions. Theoretically, the maximum fertile technique has been to recognize the mind in terms of illustration and computation.

Cognitive technology studies the fundamental processes of cognition, regularly mirroring the easy informational environments for which our mind is customized. Even though our brain is tailored for simple environments, we live in a technology in which we've to get entry to extra records and are surrounded with the aid of multiple distractions vying for our interest. This "interest economy" has redefined essential questions in cognitive technology. The work of cognitive technology needs to be translated to the modern surroundings. This bankruptcy examines how cognition works or fails to work in an interest financial system across quite a several phenomena from safety and strength of mind to the appreciation of artwork and the potential to suppose creatively. The costs of a divided cognition and the way cognitive technology can also assist us to understand what has long past incorrect are provided, with a look to the future to examine how the generation underlying an interesting economy may additionally help improve cognitive characteristic. The bankruptcy concludes with a dialogue of the increasing relevance of cognitive technology and a name for cognitive technology to study and understand the issues of our distraction-rich international. Cognitive technology is the look at thoughts, consisting of their structure and the whole thing it does. It consists of a selection of research sciences, including:

- Schooling, the have a look at of the way humans study
- Philosophy, the have a look at of information, reality, and lifestyles
- Synthetic intelligence, the study of questioning machines and systems
- Psychology, the observation of conduct and the mind

- Neuroscience, the study of the fearful device
- Linguistics, the observation of language
- Anthropology, the general observations of the human society and way of life

By using taking a more popular method to the mind's intricacies, cognitive scientists are beginning to look beyond each subject's possibilities and biases, seeing the human thoughts for the complex shape and entity that it is. Guy has attempted to understand his own thoughts for the reason that the start of time. The earliest writers talked about awareness, foolishness, and the marvel of concept. Biblical authors spoke of each the clever and the clever, along with aspects of training, psychology, philosophy, linguistics, and anthropology. Early Greek thinkers, consisting of Plato and Aristotle, attempted to explain how human knowledge works whilst speaking of the mind and its functions.

As the technology of psychology commenced to develop inside the 1800s, mainly experimental psychology, researchers started to search for specific characteristics that were not unusual for the human mind. In pursuit of consistency and knowledge, the medical network adopted the concept of behaviorism, a factor-of-view that handled the human mind as little extra than an array of programmed behaviors, taking place absolutely as biological reactions to stimuli. In other phrases, the behaviorists did not view you plenty differently than they did a canine or a single-celled creature. They noticed humans as simply extra advanced versions of 'cause and effect,' stimulus and response. In extra latest instances, starting early within the 1900s, scientists started projecting the idea that there's much greater to human thoughts than merely programmed responses. As pc models were being built that simulated tiers of human thought, scientists commenced understanding greater about the reasoning technique, becoming aware of the complexity of the operations that pass on inside the mind. As the expertise of the neural networks, the trails of nerve signals that produce and guide wondering operations within the mind, developed within the Nineteen Eighties and 1990s, the complexity of the bodily structure of the mind grew greater obvious. Via numerous approaches of taking snapshots of the mind, neuroscientists were able to see the gadget change, adapting to experiences and becoming a distinctive gadget on an everyday foundation. Every day, your reports regulate the person who you are by way of remapping your mind. also, scientists commenced conflicting with the huge range of viable human mind as opposed to the narrow range of opportunities dictated with the aid of the regulations of an in basic terms genetic (based totally on the chemical building blocks that make up the layout of the human frame) approach to human construction. You are greater than your constructing blocks and extra than the background your dad and mom gave you. Your daily picks reason your thoughts to continually adapt and evolve, inflicting you to change, continuously and dynamically.

Cognitive technology has additionally targeted fashionable principles of problem-solving and studying that are probably relevant for physics training research. This paper examines three selected troubles that have relevance for the issue of switch in hassle solving domains: specialized structures of memory and reasoning, the significance of content material in wondering, and characterization of reminiscence retrieval in problem-solving. One of the fundamental human cognitive approaches is trouble fixing. As a higher-layer cognitive process, problem fixing interacts with many different cognitive approaches along with abstraction, searching, gaining knowledge of, selection making, inference, evaluation, and synthesis on the idea of internal information representation by way of the object–characteristic-relation (OAR) model. Problem fixing is a cognitive system of the brain that searches for a solution for a given problem or reveals a direction to attain a given aim. whilst a problem object is recognized, problem-solving can be perceived as a search procedure in the memory space for locating a dating among a hard and fast of answer dreams and a fixed of opportunity paths. This paper presents each a cognitive version and a mathematical model of the problem-fixing manner. The cognitive structures of the mind and the mechanisms of internal expertise representation in the back of the cognitive procedure of problem fixing are explained. The cognitive procedure has officially described the usage of real-time process algebra (RTPA) and concept algebra. This work is part of the cognitive computing task that designed to show and simulate the essential mechanisms and strategies of the brain consistent with Wang's layered reference model of the mind (LRMB), which's anticipated to cause the development of destiny era methodologies for cognitive computing and novel cognitive computer systems which are capable of supposing, study, and understand.

Problem solving

Research on problem fixing has a protracted and sundry background. Most of the early psychologists at Würzburg together with Oswald okülpe, Karl Bühler, and Otto Selz investigated the mental techniques which can be engaged in during complex reasoning and problem fixing. Even as they made some interesting discoveries on the nature of questioning and trouble solving, which had a huge effect at the later Gestalt school of Psychology, their studies have been nearly forgotten by using cutting-edge researchers. The Gestalt psychologists overlapped with and persevered studies on complicated questioning and hassle fixing. Inside the 1940s and Nineteen Fifties, gestalt psychologists investigated how humans resolve hard problems. These studies resulted in some of the traditional issues which have been used extensively in trouble solving studies. as an example, Karl Dunker's radiation hassle in which subjects were requested to discover a manner to wreck a stomach tumor without destroying the encircling tissue. The types of problems that the Gestalt psychologists used frequently were troubles wherein topics need to find out critical detail and once this detail is located all the other factors fall into the area and the hassle is solved. Those are perception troubles. Gestalt psychologists argued that in preference to problems being solved through trial and mistakes (because the behaviorists argued), trouble solvers advantage "perception" into the trouble. The Gestalt psychologists often noted the special degrees that someone might undergo in solving a hassle (coaching, incubation, perception, and verification). What perception is, and the mechanisms underlying insight needed to wait until extra designated bills of problem fixing and languages for capturing trouble solving were invented. One similar technique to trouble solving is the one taken through Sir Fredrick Bartlett in his 1958 e-book thinking. In this e-book, Bartlett characterizes hassle solving as a shape of exploration. It turned into no longer until the 1960s while Herbert Simon and his colleagues started out investigating human subjects fixing difficult issues that problem-solving studies took their current form. There have been numerous extraordinary and influential functions that characterized Simon's method: First, he used complex problems in which there was nobody key detail that caused the answer of a hassle, and consequently the point of interest become no longer on perception, however on characterizing the procedures underlying all problem-solving. Second, Simon used concurrent verbalizations (in place of introspections) acquired from topics to discover the intellectual operations, representations, and techniques that people use once they resolve problems. 0.33, Simon and his colleagues constructed a chain of PC packages that simulate human hassle solving. With the use of both protocols and computational modeling, Newell, and Simon (1972) were able to propose a complete theory of problem-solving that remains at the heart of cutting-edge theorizing approximately problem fixing. Because the 1970's researchers in trouble solving have tended to use the techniques of Simon, or have used a more descriptive method of hassle solving within the Gestalt tradition. One key aspect of research on hassle solving has been the use of verbal protocols. With the usage of this technique, subjects are asked to kingdom out loud what they had been wondering whilst they're fixing a hassle. These "think aloud protocols" turn out to be the records for formulating models of problem-solving. The researchers use the protocols, and actions the subjects took, to construct a model of the trouble solving techniques that the topics used. The early work on problem fixing was worried about troubles that have been puzzles or games along with the Tower of Hanoi challenge. Later studies have tended to the cognizance of extra complicated 'actual international' responsibilities taken from the domains consisting of technological know-how and writing. Knowledge hassle fixing: looking at problem areas Newell and Simon (1972) proposed that trouble solving consists of seeking in a troubled space. A hassle area has an initial kingdom, a goal country, and a hard and fast of operators that can be implemented on the way to flow the solver from one country to every other. Thus, the hassle area adds the belief of an operator to the definition of trouble fixing supplied earlier. The whole set of states that may arise while the operators are carried out is referred to as the trouble space. A classic venture that has been used to analyze problem-solving is the Tower of Hanoi venture. The initial states and purpose states for this task are proven in discern 1. in this task, a topic is given a board with three rods on it. Three disks of reducing size are located at the leftmost rod. The aim of the problem is to vicinity all the five disks at the rightmost rod. There are two rules for shifting the disks -best one disk can be moved at a time and a larger disk can never be positioned on a smaller disk. The trouble solver will carry out many moves (both bodily actions, and intellectual operations) to get from the preliminary kingdom to the goal state. in the Tower of Hanoi instance, the simplest operation that a solver can carry out is to transport disks. Humans often use heuristics for looking at hassle areas. In problem-solving studies, a heuristic is a rule of thumb as a way to commonly get one at an appropriate answer, however does now not assure the ideal solution. An example of a heuristic might be that "If I begin gambling tic-tac-toe through setting an X within the middle square, I can win. This heuristic does not always work; once in a while I lose regardless of this strategy! Heuristics may be contrasted with algorithms, in which the utility of the algorithm usually ensures the correct answer (e.g., the regulations of addition). I can speak a number of the distinctive heuristics for looking at a trouble area in order of growing complexity. The maximum simple search method is to randomly select a subsequent step. Frequently humans will use this approach once they don't have any concept of what will lead them to the goal country. A barely more complex approach is to transport to the country that appears most just like the intention state. In this case, the solver simply seems one pass in advance and chooses the state that maximum closely approximates the aim country. This is called a hill hiking method. This strategy may be useful if it's not possible to appearance multiple passes ahead, but can lead subjects off target. that is, a pass that locally may also appear to be it's bringing the solver toward the goal kingdom, might also in reality be taking the solver similarly away from the purpose kingdom. As an example, within the Tower of Hanoi task, transferring from kingdom to country may additionally appear like the first-rate pass as the country extra carefully resembles the aim country than the nation. However, a country could lead the hassle solver quicker to the purpose nation than a state. For troubles together with this, a greater powerful method is method-ends-analysis. In the use of this approach, a solver looks at what the goal nation is and sees what the distinction is between the contemporary nation and the intention kingdom. If the solver cannot practice an operator so one can get to the aim kingdom, due to the fact the operation is blocked or cannot be done, then the solver units a sub-goal of doing away with the block. With the usage of means-ends analysis, the trouble solver then decomposes the distinction between the modern-day nation and the aim kingdom into any other sub-problem and sets an intention of solving that trouble. In this situation, getting rid of the blocked kingdom becomes a brand new purpose. If that sub-problem cannot be solved by the usage of the present-day operators, the hassle is further decomposed until an operator can be applied. This method may be carried out recursively until the trouble is solved. While the solver can clear up one of the sub-problems the solver can then remedy the better degree problem, and in the end, attain the purpose state. Way-ends- analysis is a mainly beneficial approach for fixing the Tower of Hanoi trouble. A preliminary aim is probably to get the largest disk onto the rightmost rod, but this aim is blocked by the medium-sized disk. A sub-goal is ready to get the medium-sized disk out of the way, however, this is additionally blocked, so a new sub-goal is set of doing away with the smallest disk. This aim may be achieved, and the solver can then reap the goal of eliminating the medium-sized disk. Strategies that include hill climbing and manner-ends analysis involve an incremental search of a problem area. As an example, the hassle solver moves from country to state via the opposite states inside the Tower of Hanoi trouble. No longer all seek heuristics are like this. For sure issues, it is possible to leap from one part of a problem space to another component bypassing most of the intermediate states. One heuristic for leaping from one part of a hassle area to every other is to purpose analogically. If the hassle solver has solved comparable trouble within the beyond, he or she can move at once to the solution by way of mapping the solution to the antique problem onto the present-day problem. An amazing example of that is the way that subjects clear up Duncker's radiation trouble (referred to above) after they had been pre-uncovered to a problem with a comparable answer. Keith Holyoak and Mary Gick (1983) advised topics about a problem in which an army is attacking a fortress. All the roads main to the fort have landmines to be able to explode when a load of a whole navy walks on it. Overall break up the army into smaller corporations to avoid putting off landmines. Each small organization takes a different avenue to the fort and they converge at the fort. Subjects had been then given Duncker's radiation problem to solve. Subjects that have been uncovered to the fortress trouble map the army onto the radiation and will remedy the radiation trouble by providing to break up the radiation right into a converging set of rays. We can interpret the Holyoak and Gick results from a hassle-fixing attitude. In their undertaking, subjects are proven an appropriate path thru the hassle space using being given the solution to the castle trouble. The subjects can then use a preceding hassle (the castle hassle) to resolve brand new trouble (Duncker's radiation problem) and bypass engaging in an incremental seek of the hassle area. Consequently, analogical reasoning may be visible as an effective approach for making a more efficient seek of massive trouble areas. 8 the use of analogies to look huge trouble spaces is very green and is frequently utilized in technological know-how. Kinds of problems Researchers have prominent among important styles of problems; properly defined and ill defined. Well-described issues have a specific initial country and the dreams and operators are known. Examples of properly defined trouble might be fixing an equation or the addition of numbers. Unwell-described problems are ones wherein the solver does not recognize the operators, the goal, or maybe the modern country. Examples of a sick-defined problem might be locating a cure for cancer, or writing the first exquisite twenty-first-century novel. For unwell-defined troubles, the solver should discover operators, define greater specific purpose states, or possibly even the preliminary state. Maximum studies have been conducted using well-defined issues. Researchers including Simon have argued that a few of the heuristics which might be used in nicely-described issues may also be used in ill-defined problems and that the distinctions between the two sorts of issues won't be as important as they seem before everything glance. Is trouble solving restricted to fixing puzzles? even as a good deal of the early work on trouble fixing turned into worried with fixing puzzles, a whole lot of human thinking and reasoning may seem as a shape of problem fixing. Hassle solving strategies can be used in lots of special domain names, regardless of what the domain names are. Tons of studies in hassle solving have intended to identify those domain popular heuristics, as they are true of splendid significance and can be used to apprehend hassle fixing in popular. Domain popular techniques are contrasted with area-specific techniques which can be relevant only to a very particular domain including chess or designing a test using a particular hormone in endocrinology. Herbert Simon and his colleagues have characterized clinical questioning and idea acquisition as forms of problem-solving and feature diagnosed some of domain general techniques including "finding a consistent" that can be carried out in a large number of different domains. The hassle fixing framework has been applied to many domain names ranging from structure to scientific nine reasoning to medical Reasoning. The motive that it's been viable to regard those distinctive activities as a shape of trouble solving is due to the idea of searching a hassle area. Hence, Simon and Lea have argued that a lot of concept acquisition and medical thinking maybe the notion of a search in two trouble spaces: A space of hypotheses and a space of Experiments. What researchers have performed is to identify the shape of those areas and the heuristics which are used to go looking those spaces. Trouble solving and representation. One of the key factors to fixing trouble is locating an excellent way of representing the trouble. When trouble is represented, the solver will forefront positive capabilities of the trouble and uses these capabilities to pick what to do when searching a hassle area. That is often the case in politics. Often, rival political events will shape exceptional representations of what is the cause of economic trouble, and recommend very special operators to use while solving the problem. For this reason, tax cuts might be a solution supplied through one birthday celebration and tax increases may be the solution supplied via the rival birthday celebration. What's at the root of those extraordinary answers is an underlying distinction within the way that the problem is represented. What this means is that the same problem may have some distinct representations and that some representations can be greater useful to solving trouble than other representations. This frequently happens in technology. For example, molecular biologists these days determined the breast cancer gene (BRCA1). while exceptional laboratories have been in search of the breast most cancers gene, every laboratory represented the trouble in extraordinary methods, and it became out that one way of representing the hassle turned into the maximum efficiency in coming across the gene. Therefore, rival laboratories having extraordinary representations of the trouble space that they had been looking in resulted in the use of different techniques for locating the breast cancer gene. How do trouble solvers discover an illustration? In experiments using pretty simple problems inclusive of the Tower of Hanoi, the subjects assemble their illustration primarily based upon the hassle statement and capabilities of the task surroundings. The solver isolates what she or he thinks are the applicable capabilities of the trouble after which constructs a representation of the problem the use of the ones' capabilities. By using varying the types of commands given and monitoring their impact on problem-solving behavior, it is possible to find out the outcomes of different sorts of illustrations on solving a problem. as an instance, inside the Tower of Hanoi problem, researchers have used exclusive isomorphs of the problem. One version might be the disk version discussed above. Any other version that has been used is the tea rite problem. On this problem, 3 human beings need to perform an oriental tea ritual. There are a fixed of regulations that specify what order the steps can be completed in, and the hassle solver should find out the series of steps that can be used to finish the ritual. The underlying shape of the tea ceremony trouble and the Tower of Hanoi hassle is identical; however, the cover story and project environments are special.

What researchers have discovered is that the duvet story may have a very massive effect on the way that someone will constitute trouble; even minor differences in the wording of a hassle can lead hassle solvers to very distinctive styles of representations of a hassle. Trendy models of problem-solving Researchers have proposed many unique fashions of ways unique issues are solved; however, there were few well-known fashions of the hassle-solving manner. The overall models of trouble fixing that have been proposed had been based upon the trouble space hypothesis and were instantiated as production systems. Information is represented in those fashions as symbols, and the production structures operate on the symbols to produce new knowledge and resolve problems. The primary location that problem-solving takes place is in "working memory." operating reminiscence is the part of memory wherein computations on the currently active symbols take location. What occurs is that manufacturing (i.e. a rule) will update one symbol with some other, and could incrementally search thru the hassle space. While fixing trouble the production structures assemble many transient representations in working reminiscence as a hassle area is searched. One of the maximum influential early models was the GPS model of Newell, Shaw, and Simon. On this model, they proposed a comprehensive version of hassle solving that carries many one-of-a-kind search techniques and may remedy problems from many exceptional domain names. One principal element of GPS is means-ends evaluation. While the GPS application is given a Tower of Hanoi hassle to resolve, it's going to use approach-ends evaluation to remedy the trouble. In 1990 Newell proposed a Unified theory of Cognition using the leap structure, in which all human behavior can be the concept of seeking in a problem space. Newell and his colleagues have implemented the leap architecture to an extensive kind of domains, and feature proven how to seek in a hassle space may be used to apprehend many different components of cognition. John Anderson (1983, 1993) has proposed the ACT family of fashions that he has used to account for cognition in trendy and trouble solving especially. Other approaches to problem solving. Two different computational procedures to modeling trouble solving were the connectionist method and a hybrid method that is a combination of a symbolic device and a connectionist machine. There are few connectionist models of hassle-solving approaches, extra than probable because trouble-solving regularly involves the use of many brief representations. Those forms of techniques have proved somewhat tough to the version in connectionist structures, even though it is a critical topic of contemporary research. While connectionism has been used to version problem fixing, it has been used in hybrid models wherein there is a symbolic stage this is connected to a connectionist layer. The Barnden and Holyoak (1991) e-book have an interesting series of hybrid models. This could also be a place of hassle fixing studies as a way to hastily alternate over the following few years. Lately, there was a lot of debate in the hassle fixing literature concerning the position of the undertaking environment in problem-solving. a few researchers, inclusive of Jim Greeno and Lucy Suchman, have argued that one of the maximum vital elements in hassle solving is the assignment environment and that the task surroundings are the major determinant of ways someone will remedy the trouble. This "located" viewpoint stresses the function of the objects and bodily capabilities of the surroundings and how the environment constrains what a hassle solver can and could do. A precise of different perspectives on this subject matter can be observed in a unique version of the journal Cognitive technological know-how edited through Norman. latest trends in hassle fixing studies One essential difficulty in problem fixing hassle solving is how preceding enjoy with a problem, or related issues influences present-day overall performance on a problem. Gestalt psychologists proposed the idea of practical fixedness to account for the terrible consequences of preceding enjoy with trouble. However, it is simplest these days that the results of revel in had been included into a trouble area view of problem fixing. Marsha Lovett and John Anderson (1996) have checked out how preceding revel in with a specific elegance of troubles may have an impact on performance at the current hassle. They've proven that trouble solvers will use each the current kingdom of the problem and their previous records of achievement at using unique operators when finding out what to do subsequent while fixing a hassle. For instance, if making use of an operator, including moving a chunk in chess, theoretically leads one towards the aim country, however past enjoy with that unique operator leads to failure, a hassle solver ought to include these assets of expertise while trying to solve the problem. They have developed a version in ACT-R that mixes both stories with the unique operators and the current kingdom of the problem in an additive manner to predict overall performance on problem-fixing challenges. This mixture of previous enjoy and kingdom of the hassle is a consequence of the cognitive architecture and not necessarily available to awareness. Indeed, Schunn and Dunbar (1996) have investigated how answers to problems may be primed via fixing a comparable hassle, and have shown that subjects are regularly unaware that in advance experience on trouble is having a predictable effect on their cutting-edge hassle solving efforts. a great deal of cognitive research on hassle solving has targeted the methods that a man or woman trouble solver sets about solving a problem. Furthermore, a whole lot of work on hassle solving has thirteen involved using puzzles in very artificial domains. Recently, some researchers have commenced analyzing more complex real-world troubles and trouble solving in corporations (e.g., software program layout, engineering, and technology). These researchers have found that a good deal of actual-international hassle solving takes location in groups -instead of individuals. Work on hassle fixing in companies shows that businesses inspire the generation of trade representations of a hassle. Whilst fixing trouble, a set can doubtlessly look at some of the feasible representations of a hassle and decide which representation appears to be high-quality. Furthermore, in organization hassle solving, steps such as inductions, deductions, and causal reasoning may be distributed among individuals. Therefore, an important component of group hassle fixing is shipped reasoning. Organization problem fixing isn't always continually a hit. If all the members of a set are from an equal history, they generally tend to symbolize the problem identically. If their illustration is inaccurate, they fail to remedy the problem. If, however, the individuals of the group are from distinct backgrounds, however additionally share similar desires and have overlapping knowledge bases, many representations of a problem are generated. Studies on trouble solving have tended to take the area impartial of research on different better-degree cognitive activities, including standards, choice-making, induction, deduction, and causal reasoning. However, each of these regions might be appeared as a shape of trouble solving. whilst some of the models consisting of John Anderson's and Allan Newell's have integrated trouble solving right into a widespread account of cognition, hassle solving and search in trouble spaces has been regarded as best applicable to properly defined troubles together with puzzles. Consequently, a mission for researchers in trouble solving is integrating problem-solving with different cognitive activities along with memory, reasoning, and selection making. General, research on problem-solving has centered on the notion of the representation of know-how and the concept of operating in a troubled space. Early studies centered on puzzles, and more recent studies have focused on extra complicated domain names. The shift to greater complex domains has necessitated the postulation that hassle solvers seek in a couple of hassle areas, as opposed to one trouble area, and has pressured researchers to present a good deal 14 greater express debts of the role of the challenging environment in hassle fixing. As a result, one of the desires of present-day research is to decide how humans generate new representations and trouble spaces as they work on trouble. The next decade of research must-see models of hassle solving on the way to incorporate theoretical constructs from other aspects of cognition. Finally, researchers in problem-solving at the moment are beginning to address the question of what's the role of the mind in trouble fixing and what different parts of the mind mediate what aspects of hassle solving. Many discoveries look forward to researchers within this field.

Philosophy and Cognition

Developments in psychological concept practice regularly parallel advances made in era. for instance, Robins et al. have documented the (successive) "digital demise" of psychoanalysis, the upward thrust and intense decline of behaviourism, the emergence and big ascent of cognitive psychology (the "cognitive revolution") and the beginning of the upward push in neuroscience in the remaining century inside the field of scientific psychology by myself – which may be visible to mirror technological advances. particularly, as Tracy et al. (2003) acknowledge, the cognitive revolution of the 1970s become driven largely through the computer revolution – moving its foundational theories of successive/linear records processing and practical modularity from device to brain. The metaphor of brain as information processor first passed off in the Fifties to sooner or later develop into cognitive science and then, with the emergence of neuroscience, and the arrival of neuro-imaging technologies, got here the anticipated go-reducing of the taxonomies of neuroscience and cognitive technological know-how to ultimately provide upward thrust to cognitive neuroscience within the eighties – worried with how cerebral methods underlie cognitive programmes. With the 90s got here the "decade of the brain" and with the beginning of the 21st century, there might simply appear to be a preoccupation with neuroanatomy – where the majority of cognition-based studies emerges coupled with a few shapes of neuroanatomical reference. Indeed this will be seen to reflect the advent of neuroimaging technologies together with fMRI; arguably the most prominent tool in cognitive neuroscience invented in 1990. on account that then fMRI studies on my own have explosively elevated, from just being posted in 1991 to two,224 being posted in 2003 on my own; with there now being at least 30-forty fMRI research emerging weekly. indeed, wherein Kuhn (1970) has mentioned how clinical paradigms compete with one another until the restrained ability capabilities of 1 succumbs to the riper possibilities of every other, Rand & Ilardi (2005) have emphasized that technological advancements function fortifications for the growth and maturation of specific paradigms and their replacement of others. for example, Galileo's implementation of the telescope facilitated the appearance of a brand new technology within an equal manner the improvement of the computer functioned in cognitive science's overtaking of behaviourismbehaviorismthe major paradigm in psychology. Likewise, the appearance of neuroimaging and its coupling with cognitive technology can be seen as supplying the force which inaugurated the cognitive neuroscience paradigm that is presently predominant. Cognitivism' arose in reaction to the insufficiencies of behaviourism. Behaviourism – itself a response to in advance schools which hired introspectionist (deemed too unreliable due to its subjectivity), treated the thoughts as a 'black field'; handiest accounting for input stimuli and output, observable behaviors. The cognitive sciences as such emerged to cope with this 'black field' difficulty through the implementation of a computational approach. The roots of this approach, says some authors (lies in the 18th-century work with the aid of LaMettrie ('guy as machine') from which the fundamental characterization of guy as being similar to a clockwork mechanism become drawn. no matter the several different metaphors LaMettrie used, it turned into this guy-as-mechanism that caught; providing impetus for the Enlightenment-era idea that underlying human behaviors had been undying laws and policies. while taking metaphors rooted in technological advances can be beneficial; facilitating new insight, an inherent chance lies in taking such metaphors actually. particularly there is a twofold threat: reification (taking the summary to be a concrete fact) and assuming isomorphism among both referents of the metaphor (i.e. that each one quality of each referent are the same e.g. man = system). certainly with that is the priority that should we class laptop as thinking machine (i.e. artificially shrewd) we not directly infer thinking-man as a computer – as such, dehumanizing man even as personifying system. as an alternative astoundingly, however, a few authors have definitely endorsed taking the computational metaphor actually claiming that treating it as a simple heuristic metaphor lets in too many perspectives and thereby obstructs development. What Plyshyn right here overlooks is that treating a metaphorical affiliation literally can also hinder progress – as being overly zealous in a single specific paradigmatic method can near one-off to new opportunities or avenues of research. Arguably, however, the computer metaphor is taken actually in lots of sensible time's i.e. biological psychiatry, precluding many intrinsically crucial sides of what having thought involves – i.e. subjectivity, intentionality, and so forth. As such, we will see that due to such inadequacies of the staunch cognitive scientific approach; and the way it's branched into cognitive neuroscience and turn out to be increasingly more enmeshed with neuro-anatomical research, numerous authors are calling for a go back to phenomenology to be able to address the issues the cognitive neurosciences have resurrected. indeed, as Mishara et al. (1998) have mentioned, debates inside the philosophy of mind and cognitive sciences have started to enchantment theories of focus as a method of highlighting the insufficiencies of the greater popular fashions of mind (i.e. mind as PC). 'Embodied' and/or 'enactive' cognition, in particular, has to turn out to be an important attitude on this reconciliation of consciousness and cognition. As such, we can define 3 major approaches to cognition – symbolicism (or classical computationalism), connectionism, and dynamics that have been informing neuroscientific studies. The rest of this essay intends to define how several criticisms fuelled with the aid of troubles in the philosophy of mind & science highlight the warning that ought to be taken while the usage of the computational metaphor and similarly integrating experimental consequences from cognitive neuroscience into theories of mind. in the first example criticisms of the major computational version of thoughts might be sampled. For problems of space, dialogue concerning connectionism and dynamism-based approaches will now not be undertaken. The preferential treatment of computationalism is justified insomuch that it is nevertheless one of the greater predominantly used models of cognition. Following this, the complex issues regarding the implementation of neuroimaging 'proof' to espouse paradigms inside the discipline of technology will be highlighted. Therefore it is going to be concluded that while cognitive neuroscience has an incredible capacity for unifying the sector of psychology it can also be applied to propound particular viewpoints, running the hazard of undermining others and the lived experience of the human character.

The 'classical' computational approach involved the convergence of 3 essential fields of studies; synthetic intelligence (AI), cognitive psychology and linguistics. Namely, the fundamental principles of AI studies: claiming that intelligence was the coping with/manipulation of symbol strings, cognitive psychology: modelling human cognitive procedures at the operation of computer systems, and linguistics: which informed that units of rules govern (semantic) operations in the brain, had been assimilated to broaden a "computer among ears" or "representational-computational" view of the mind. This 'classical' view of the thoughts changed into summated by Fodor who offered the language of thought hypothesis which claimed that we think inside the language of thought – a machine of symbols with semantic and syntactic houses, manifested in accordance with the structural design of the brain. Such symbols are intrinsically representational neural activities. while the computational method isn't explicitly reductionistic, insomuch that questioning + brain feature combine to instantiate computation, as hardware and software do; as I'm able to presently allude to, this technique re-introduces a Cartesian dualism which itself causes problems. The computational machine is characterized as constituted by way of units of tokens for which sets of policies govern arrangement and/or transfiguration into different sets of tokens. Of the number one criticisms levelled at the classical approach were the symbol grounding trouble and the Chinese language Room argument. The essence of both those arguments refers back to the inherent hassle of unique ranges of reductionism in operation within the computational paradigm which inherently throw away intentionality but resultantly re-introduce the Cartesian dichotomy and the 'tough' hassle of attention. Explicitly, it is hard to envision how the computational machine knows and learns at an extrinsic level. The enter-procedure-output gadget, says Searle, simply cannot be "empirically aware". different criticisms of computationalism is that its processing is based on linear mechanisms – a dramatic quandary considering the complexity of certain obligations- and that malfunction on the image-degree involves whole abrupt disruption of techniques – not like the "sleek degradation" that virtually appears to arise inside the brain. Is also the inadequacy of advanced AI to collect and maintain "not unusual-experience" information (i.e. the body hassle). Eventually is that its emphasis on rule-ruled image manipulation virtually isn't biologically viable. Therefore, even as paradigmatic packages of computational principles frequently "fit" with the brain (explaining their persisted popularity in spite of criticisms) they unavoidably dismiss the ones additives of intellectual lifestyles which can be "non-computable". It's far these components which pose the most important venture to (cognitive-) neuroscientific based totally principle/studies today. The "hard" problem of thoughts/attention plagues the inflexible cognitive (neuro-) sciences insomuch that there exists a subjective element of recognition which goes past any materialist clarification of capabilities. Although this has been critically debated somewhere else, it might appear that any tries to exclude subjectivity genuinely result in its surreptitious re-entrance thru the again door. as an example, the ones money owed which approach thoughts and mind in simply reductionistic/eliminativist phrases (i.e. wherein subjective revel in is a trifling byproduct of mind mechanisms in movement) in a feel customize cerebral additives with the aid of granting them features normally indicative of complete human skills i.e. "studying" "perceiving" etc. Stapp (2008) comprehensively decomposes the problem insomuch that the difference among intrinsic and extrinsic description renders it inadequate. In particular, must the brain be a system of parallel laptop processors (or the mixture general of a number uniquely purposeful organic components), an intrinsic description information each processor as generating a selected unit of records (i.e. like a television set producing pixels). The extrinsic description, conversely, is likened to that which an outside viewer of the TV set sees – i.e. no longer character pixels but a sum general image. The laptop version cannot account for both intrinsic and extrinsic levels of description without implicit appeal to meta-representational "ghosts within the machine" or homunculi and consequently implicitly re-introduce a Cartesian break up. one of the most powerful re-interpretations of this latter hassle has been supplied by

Dennett (1978) who espouses an "army of homunculi" technique, wherein a hierarchy of homunculi of decreasing complexity/intelligence exist with the most basic processes at the lowest. That is corresponding to a connectionist or 'Parallel allotted Processing' technique and suffice it to say has been criticized itself. similarly to this charges of reductionism and/or dualism, with cognitive psychology's convergence with neuroscience to become cognitive neuroscience; a secondary source of rivalry arises — specifically, within cognitive neuroscience is the tendency to map cognitive methods immediately onto mind states or, even more problematically, localize them to precise brain areas. The latter authors have attributed this "taking of phrenology in the head" to three precise moves inside psychology basically: 1) the impetus evolutionary psychology and its concept of modular functioning provided for neurosciences to discover modules of unique function in the mind 2) renewed interest in mechanistic explanations of thoughts and mind and (3) the emergence of cognitive neuroscience and the implementation of neuro-imaging strategies. The biggest problem with localization of processes, say the authors, is brain plasticity and the concordant multi-functionality it provides neural components. Certainly looking for the characteristic of any person cerebral region seems needless considering that the equal location may carry out a number of things depending on what else is taking vicinity within the mind. On an associated point, the computational approach has been criticized insomuch that it can function best in phrases of static, discrete entities (i.e. symbols) which could best reliably to applied to static, discrete realities and, by way of quantity, static, discrete cerebral 'hardware'. Whilst it offers nicely with systematicity and productiveness, its 'crude' input-process-output formulization belies difficulty in accounting for the unendingly interactive and reciprocal nature of the relationship between cognition, the frame and the environment. Similarly, as referenced above, the mind is anything but a static organ – as a substitute it's far dynamic, with multitudes of overlapping neural networks, and high levels of plasticity.

Notwithstanding the criticisms that have been levelled at these strategies to cognitive tactics, results from neuro-imaging technology have the propensity to be used as means of aid for the reductionistic-computational bills of free will, autonomy, self and everything such standards entail (i.e. cognizance, lived experience and so on.). The use of neuroimaging technology as proof for localization, however, or reductionism, isn't as valid as might be first notion. certainly, outcomes from neuroimaging are frequently handled as if they may be "pix of the mind", and are treated as objective sources of proof regarding how the mind operates with reference to overall performance in cognitive duties have proven that mind pix have a significantly powerful effect on judgments of the validity of scientific evidence. Specifically they observed that presence of a brain photo (i.e. over a bar chart) significantly accelerated individuals' willingness to believe the conclusions of the item. in this feel we will get a touch of ways such a method is probably implicated, perhaps unintentionally, to propound goal validation of a specific paradigm, frequently undermining the totality of lived experience. To explore this point similarly i can now in short define a number of the criticisms of this belief of neuro-imaging as capable of providing objective proof.

Thinking about neuroimages as "photos of the brain" is a as a substitute inapt analogy as Roskies (2007) discusses. Specially, treating neuro-pics as an 'evidential medium' inside the way we deal with photos is an analogical misnomer in that they best circuitously degree brain interest – they measure "the timescale of the de-phasing of water molecules within the brain, [and no longer neural interest]". The very last photos which are carried out in studies and articles, which display parts of the brain as "lighting fixtures-up"/activating, are in reality computer reconstructions of the actual records generated through the fMRI test and associated null hypothesis importance checks (NHSTs) executed on each area of the mind (voxels) – which facilitate the technology of "statistical parametric maps" (SPM) superb- imposed at the obtained images of the brain. In the manner wherein the strategies are oblique measures, epistemic challenges can be posed. On the realistic level, as Bechtel & Stufflebeam (2001) outline, a number of the epistemic demanding situations (i.e. are consequences artifacts of the technique itself or true portions of freestanding, reliable facts?) may be summated to consist of a lack of ecological validity and an assumption of faith within the cognitive decomposition-project. The former regards the novelty of the state of affairs – lying horizontal & ultimate motionless in a darkened, constrained area. This means an issue in reliably judging the relevance of neuroimaging facts to real-life cognition – in which it's miles enormously fantastic that such regulations might exist.

The latter of Bechtel & Stufflebeam's challenges regards the faith the experimenter locations in the cognitive task applied within the experimental putting. Particularly it should be ensured that the venture sincerely draws upon the techniques which one wishes to investigate. Certainly, the modelling of many such procedures and obligations comes from cognitive psychology and its essential computational model; which itself is extensively debated and contested (as previously outlined), especially through the ones fashions of cognition which draw on dynamic systems theory and non-linear processing paradigms. As such, as the authors contend, any imaging take a look at is best as good as the ones assumptions which it is primarily based upon. at the same time as questions have also been raised regarding the poor reliability of neuroimaging throughout studies more problematically are those theoretical and conceptual issues which lie at the center of the technology itself and no longer simply merely in its realistic utility. Klein's (2009) exegesis of the underpinnings of how fMRI technology operates is a clear expression of how inherently intricate the use of neuroimages as evidential data is. mainly, the reality that fMRIs do no longer display conveniently interpretable images of sign variations within the brain however as an alternative they show an amalgamation of the areas for which there has been located to be a statistically enormous distinction in sign between mission conditions illustrates a supply of rivalry. Specifically, inasmuch as neuroimaging records are the end result of heaps of simultaneous null speculation checks they inherit the many conceptual troubles inherent in the NHST methodology. Certainly, one of the essential troubles with neuroimaging effects is the result of the 'causal density of the brain. Any and every mission may have tremendous consequences on the mind – but fMRI will not display these as, for a large element, these consequences will be small and functionally insignificant (within the statistical feel). Nevertheless, the fact that they occur is an important factor – they might be important for the cognitive procedure' instantiation. That is somewhat much like the problems of arbitrary thresholds and vague alternatives Klein (2009) similarly describes. in particular, with regards to the former point, the "activation" of cerebral places that we see in neuroimages are primarily based on the selection of an alpha stage of significance but this desire is rather arbitrary; need to we be conservative in our choice then very few areas will appear to "prompt". Meanwhile, a more liberal preference of alpha degree will bring about a great deal more activation obvious throughout the mind. a far mentioned examine has shown that prediction of item elegance being perceived i.e. a house or a face, maybe reliably ascertained thru evaluation of patterns of activation that arise beneath the threshold for significance with exclusion of those areas showing extensive activation (i.e. the Fusiform Face place in face belief). As such, many areas no longer discovered through neuroimages can be playing a vital useful role inside the strategies under research. Further so far is that high activation in a place does no longer equate to a crucial useful function it might truly be a by-product of the cognitive procedure and now not particularly indicative of a important and enough condition for said precise cognitive method. as an example, studies have shown that at the same time as extensive hippocampal activation occurs for the duration of delay classical conditioning methods, hippocampal lesions do no longer disrupt this function. Moreover, one of the most basic points is that imaging research aren't based totally on causal connections – alternatively they may handiest display probabilistic covariance, an elicitation of the nicely-worn adage "correlation does not suggest causation". As such, even as cognitive neuroscience has outstanding potential to reconcile the various factions of a disjointed psychology – linking biology to principle, it conversely may be used to propound positive paradigms over others, inappropriately so. The techniques of neuroimaging are not infallible assets of goal 'finalists' proof; alternatively they inherit a diploma of interpretation and feature several practical and conceptual barriers.

Hassle solving

Humans face problems each day, normally, multiple issues at some stage in the day. Now and again those troubles are trustworthy: To double a recipe for pizza dough, for example, all this is required is that each factor within the recipe be doubled. On occasion, but, the issues we come upon are more complex. For instance, say you have got a work closing date, and also you need to mail a broadcast replica of a file on your supervisor via the end of the enterprise day. The file is time-sensitive and have to be sent overnight. You finished the file last night, however your printer will now not work these days. What should you do? First, you need to identify the trouble and then apply a method for solving the trouble. Cognitive processing aimed at identifying a way to obtain a goal is referred to as hassle solving. In hassle fixing, the trouble solver seeks to devise a way for transforming a trouble from its contemporary kingdom right into a preferred kingdom when an answer isn't always at once apparent to the trouble solver. Thus, the hallmark of trouble solving is the invention of a new method for addressing a hassle. This definition has three components: (1) trouble solving is cognitive–this is, it occurs internally within the thoughts (or cognitive machine) and ought to be inferred not directly from conduct; (2) problem fixing is a procedure–it includes the manipulation of information representations (or wearing out mental computations); and (3) trouble solving is directed–it is guided by the dreams of the problem solver. A problem takes place whilst a hassle solver has a aim but to begin with does no longer know a way to achieve the goal. This definition has 3 components: (1) the present-day nation–the hassle starts in a given state; (2) the intention kingdom–the hassle solver wishes the problem to be in a distinctive country, and hassle solving is required to convert the trouble from the modern (or given) kingdom into the intention nation, and (3) barriers–the hassle solver does no longer understand the correct answer and an powerful solution approach is not apparent to the problem solver. According to this definition a problem is private, in order that a scenario that could be a hassle for one man or woman won't be a problem for any other character. For instance, "3 + 5 = ___" is probably a problem for a six-year-vintage child who motives, "let's have a look at. I'm able to take one from the five and supply it to the three. That makes four plus four, and that I recognize that 4 plus 4 is 8." however, this equation is not a problem for a grownup who knows an appropriate answer.

Sorts of troubles
Routine and non-routine problems: it is standard to

differentiate between routine and non-recurring problems. In a routine problem, the problem solver is aware of a solution approach and best needs to carry it out. As an instance, for maximum adults the trouble "589 × 45 = ___" is a recurring trouble if they understand the system for multicolumn multiplication. Ordinary problems are every so often known as sporting activities, and technically do now not in shape the definition of trouble stated above. While the goal of an educational hobby is to sell all the components of trouble fixing, (including devising a solution plan), then non-routine issues (or sports) are suitable. In a non-routine hassle, the hassle solver does now not to begin with recognize a method for solving the hassle. as an example, the subsequent trouble is non-habitual for the majority: "Water lilies double in area every twenty-four hours. At the beginning of the summer, there's one water lily on the lake. It takes sixty days for the lake to be absolutely blanketed with water lilies. On what day is the lake half of covered?" in this trouble, the hassle solver must invent an answer approach based totally on working backwards from the final day. Based totally on this approach, the hassle solver can ask what the lake might appear to be at the day earlier than the ultimate day, and finish that the lake is half of blanketed at the fifty-ninth day. Well-defined and ill-described problems: it's also commonplace to differentiate between properly-described and sick-defined issues. In a well-described problem, the given country of the problem, the goal state of the hassle, and the allowable operators (or actions) are every surely specified. as an example, the subsequent water-jar problem is an example of nicely-described trouble: "I can give you three empty water jars; you may fill any jar with water and pour water from one jar into some other (until the second one jar is full or the first one is empty); you may fill and pour as commonly as you want. Given water jars of length 21, 127, and 3 devices and an unlimited deliver of water, how can to procure exactly one hundred gadgets of water?" this is a properly-defined trouble because the given state is truly exact (you have got empty jars of length 21, 127, and 3), the goal state is virtually certain (you need to get 100 units of water in one of the jars), and the allowable operators are certainly unique (you may fill and pour in step with unique strategies). nicely-described troubles can be both ordinary or non-ordinary; if you do not have previous revel in with water jar troubles, then finding the answer (i.e., fill the 127, pour out 21 as soon as, and pour out 3 two times) is a non-ordinary hassle. In an ill-described trouble, the given kingdom, purpose state, and/or operations aren't truly specific. as an example, inside the problem, "Write a persuasive essay in prefer of year-spherical schools," the purpose country isn't always clean due to the fact the standards for what constitutes a "persuasive essay" are indistinct and the allowable operators, such as how to access sources of information, are not clean. Best the given kingdom is clear–a clean piece of paper. Ill-defined issues can be routine or non-habitual; if one has giant experience in writing then writing a brief essay like this one is a recurring problem.

Methods in trouble solving

The manner of problem solving may be broken down into essential levels: hassle representation, wherein the problem solver builds a coherent mental representation of the problem, and hassle solution, in which the trouble solver devises and includes out a solution plan. hassle illustration can be broken down in addition into trouble translation, wherein the problem solver interprets each sentence (or photo) into an internal intellectual illustration, and trouble integration, wherein the problem solver integrates the data right into a coherent intellectual illustration of the trouble (i.e., a mental model of the state of affairs defined in the problem). Trouble solution can be damaged down similarly into answer making plans, wherein the hassle solver devises a plan for how to resolve the trouble, and answer execution, in which the hassle solver incorporates out the plan through conducting solution behaviors. Despite the fact that the four procedures of problem fixing are listed sequentially, they may occur in many distinct orderings and with tons generation in the course of fixing a hassle. As an example, do not forget the butter problem described by Mary Hegarty, Richard Mayer, and Christopher Monk: "At lucky, butter expenses sixty five cents in keeping with stick. That is cents less in line with stick than butter at Vons. If you want to shop for four sticks of butter, how much will you pay at Vons?" in the trouble translation phase, the trouble solver may also mentally constitute the primary sentence as "fortunate = 0.65," the second sentence as "fortunate = Vons - 0.02," and the 0.33 sentence as "4 × Vons = ___." In problem integration, the trouble solver might also construct a mental variety line with fortunate at 0.65 and Vons to the right of lucky (at 0.67); or the problem solver might also mentally combine the equations as "four × (fortunate + 0.02) = ___." A key perception in problem integration is to apprehend the right relation between the value of butter at lucky and the fee of butter at Vons, particularly that butter fees extra at Vons (even though the keyword within the problem is "much less"). In solution making plans, the problem solver may additionally destroy the problem into parts, which include: "First upload 0.02 to 0.65, and then multiply the end result with the aid of 4." In answer executing, the problem solver carries out the plan: $0.02 + 0.65 = 0.67$, $0.67 \times 4 = 2.68$. In addition, the hassle solver have to display the hassle-solving process and make changes as needed.

Coaching for hassle solving: An undertaking for educators is to train in methods that foster meaningful gaining knowledge of instead of rote studying. Rote instructional methods sell retention (the potential to remedy troubles which can be identical or particularly just like the ones offered in guidance), however no longer trouble fixing transfer (the ability to apply what turned into found out to novel problems). As an instance, in 1929, Alfred Whitehead used the time period inert information to refer to learning that cannot be used to remedy novel issues. In comparison, meaningful educational techniques promote both retention and transfer. In a conventional instance of the difference among rote and meaningful mastering, the psychologist Max Wertheimer (1959) defined two methods of coaching students to compute the region of a parallelogram. Within the rote method, college students discover ways to degree the base, degree the peak, and then multiply base time's height. College students taught by the $A = b \times h$ approach are capable of discover the place of parallelograms formed just like the ones given in preparation (a retention trouble) but not unusual parallelograms or different shapes (a switch hassle). Wertheimer used the time period reproductive questioning to consult trouble solving in which one blindly incorporates out a formerly found out manner. In comparison, inside the meaningful approach, students analyze by using slicing the triangle from one stop of a cardboard parallelogram and attaching it to the other quit to form a rectangle. As soon as college students have the perception that a parallelogram is only a rectangle in conceal, they are able to compute the region due to the fact they already recognize the process for finding the vicinity of a rectangle. Students taught by means of the perception technique perform well on both retention and transfer problems. Wertheimer used the time period effective thinking to refer to hassle solving wherein one invents a new technique to fixing a singular problem. Educationally relevant Advances in problem solving: current advances in academic psychology point to the function of domain-unique know-how in trouble solving—which include knowledge of unique techniques or trouble kinds that apply to a selected field. Three crucial advances had been: (1) the coaching of problem-fixing approaches, (2) the character of professional trouble solving, and (3) new conceptions of man or woman differences in trouble-solving potential.

Coaching of problem-fixing tactics: An essential develop in educational psychology is cognitive method practice, which includes the coaching of hassle-fixing strategies. As an instance, in task Intelligence, elementary school children efficaciously learned the cognitive processes wanted for fixing troubles just like those found on intelligence tests. In Instrumental Enrichment, college students who were labeled as mentally retarded learned cognitive procedures that allowed them to reveal tremendous improvements on intelligence tests.

Expert hassle solving: every other essential improve in instructional psychology worries variations between what experts and beginners recognize in given fields, consisting of medicinal drug, physics, and PC programming. as an example, expert physicists have a tendency to keep their understanding in huge integrated chunks, whereas beginners tend to save their knowledge as remote fragments; expert physicists generally tend to focus at the underlying structural traits of physics phrase problems, while beginners recognition at the surface functions; and expert physicists tend to work ahead from the givens to the goal, whereas beginners work backwards from the intention to the givens. Research on expertise has implications for expert education as it pinpoints the sorts of area-precise know-how that experts want to study.

Person variations in trouble-solving ability: This 1/3 advance concerns new conceptions of highbrow ability primarily based on variations in the way humans procedure data. As an instance, people may also range in cognitive fashion—such as their alternatives for visible as opposed to verbal representations, or for impulsive versus reflective approaches to hassle solving. Instead, human beings may vary in the speed and performance with which they carry out specific cognitive tactics, including creating an intellectual comparison or retrieving a bit of information from reminiscence. Instead of characterizing highbrow potential as a unmarried, monolithic potential, current conceptions of highbrow ability recognition on the position of a couple of variations in records processing.

Problem-solving strategies

When you are supplied with a trouble whether or not it is a

complicated mathematical trouble or a broken printer, how do you remedy it? Before locating a way to the trouble, the hassle must first be simply diagnosed. After that, one in all many problem-fixing techniques can be applied, with any luck ensuing in a solution. A trouble-fixing strategy is a plan of action used to find a solution. Special techniques have distinctive action plans related to them ([hyperlink]). For example, a famous strategy is trial and errors. The old adage, "If before everything you don't be successful, strive, try again" describes trial and errors. In phrases of your broken printer, you may try checking the ink tiers, and if that doesn't work, you can take a look at to ensure the paper tray isn't jammed. Or perhaps the printer isn't honestly related on your computer. While the usage of trial and error, you'll retain to attempt different answers till you solved your trouble. Despite the fact that trial and errors isn't always commonly one of the maximum time-efficient strategies, it's far a commonly used one.

Technique - Description - instance

- Trial and error   hold attempting distinct answers until the trouble is solved

- Restarting cellphone, turning off Wi-Fi, turning off Bluetooth that allows you to determine why your telephone is malfunctioning

Algorithm   -   Step-through-step   problem-solving formula   instruction guide for putting in new software program to your computer

Heuristic   -   widespread hassle-solving framework   - operating backward; breaking an undertaking into steps

Any other kind of approach is a set of rules. A set of rules is a problem-fixing formula that offers you with step-by-step commands used to gain a preferred final results. You can think about an algorithm as a recipe with quite specific instructions that produce the identical end result whenever they may be finished. Algorithms are used regularly in our ordinary lives, especially in pc science. When you run a search on the internet, search engines like Google like Google use algorithms to decide which entries will appear first on your list of effects. Facebook additionally uses algorithms to decide which posts to show on your newsfeed. Are you able to pick out different situations wherein algorithms are used? A heuristic is any other type of trouble solving method. Whilst an algorithm need to be followed precisely to supply a correct end result, a heuristic is a well-known problem-solving framework. You may suppose those as mental shortcuts which are used to clear up issues. A "rule of thumb" is an instance of a heuristic. Any such rule saves the man or woman time and electricity when making a decision, but in spite of its time-saving traits, it isn't always usually the satisfactory method for creating a rational choice. Exceptional kinds of heuristics are utilized in exceptional kinds of situations, but the impulse to apply a heuristic happens while considered one of five situations is met

• While one is confronted with an excessive amount of information

• While the time to come to a decision is constrained

• While the selection to be made is unimportant

• Whilst there may get entry to little or no information to apply in making the choice

• When an appropriate heuristic takes place to come back to mind in the identical moment

Operating backwards is a beneficial heuristic in which you begin solving the problem by using focusing on the quit result. Take into account this example: You stay in Washington, D.C. and were invited to a wedding at four PM on Saturday in Philadelphia. Understanding that Interstate has a tendency to return up any day of the week, you need to plan your route and time your departure thus. if you need to be at the wedding provider by using 3:30 PM, and it takes 2.5 hours to get to Philadelphia without traffic, what time should you go away your own home? You use the operating backwards heuristic to plot the occasions of your day on a regular foundation, likely without even considering it.

Some other beneficial heuristic is the practice of conducting a massive intention or mission by means of breaking it into a chain of smaller steps. College students regularly use this not unusual approach to finish a massive research mission or lengthy essay for faculty. as an instance, students commonly brainstorm, increase a thesis or main subject matter, research the chosen subject matter, organize their information into a define, write a rough draft, revise and edit the hard draft, develop a final draft, arrange the references list, and proofread their work before turning within the project. The huge project turns into much less overwhelming whilst it's miles damaged down into a series of small steps.

Pitfalls to hassle solving

Now not all troubles are efficaciously solved, however. What demanding situations stop us from correctly solving a problem? Albert Einstein once said, "Madness is doing the equal aspect time and again and waiting for an exclusive result." imagine a person in a room that has 4 doors. One doorway that has always been open inside the beyond is now locked. The character, aware of exiting the room by way of that precise doorway, maintains trying to get out thru the equal doorway despite the fact that the opposite three doorways are open. The individual is stuck however she simply desires to go to some other doorway, in place of looking to get out via the locked doorway. A mental set is where you persist in drawing close a hassle in a manner that has labored inside the past however is virtually now not running now. Practical fixedness is a type of mental set where you can't understand an object getting used for something other than what it become designed for. At some stage in the Apollo 13 venture to the moon, NASA engineers at challenge manage had to overcome useful fixedness to keep the lives of the astronauts aboard the spacecraft. An explosion in a module of the spacecraft broken more than one structures. The astronauts had been in threat of being poisoned with the aid of growing stages of carbon dioxide because of issues with the carbon dioxide filters. The engineers observed a manner for the astronauts to use spare plastic luggage, tape, and air hoses to create a makeshift air filter, which saved the lives of the astronauts. Researchers have investigated whether useful fixedness is affected by lifestyle. In one test, individuals from the Shuar institution in Ecuador have been asked to apply an object for a purpose apart from that for which the object turned into firstly meant. as an instance, the participants have been advised a story approximately a undergo and a rabbit that have been separated by using a river and requested to pick out amongst diverse objects, which include a spoon, a cup, erasers, and so on, to help the animals. The spoon become the best item long enough to span the imaginary river, however if the spoon changed into offered in a manner that contemplated its everyday utilization, it took individuals longer to pick out the spoon to clear up the hassle. The researchers desired to recognize if publicity to notably specialized equipment, as happens with people in industrialized nations, affects their capability to transcend purposeful fixedness. It became determined that practical fixedness is experienced in both industrialized and non-industrialized cultures. In an effort to make proper decisions, we use our information and our reasoning. Regularly, this understanding and reasoning is sound and strong. Every now and then, however, we're swayed by using biases or by way of others manipulating a situation. As an instance, let's say you and three buddies wanted to hire a house and had a mixed target price range of $1,600. The realtor suggests you most effective very run-down homes for $1,600 after which shows you a completely high-quality residence for $2,000. Might you ask absolutely everyone to pay more in rent to get the $2,000 home? Why could the realtor show you the run-down homes and the quality house? The realtor may be challenging your anchoring bias. An anchoring bias takes place while you focus on one piece of statistics while you decide or solving a trouble. In this situation, you're so centered on the amount of cash you are willing to spend that you can no longer understand what forms of houses are available at that charge factor. The affirmation bias is the tendency to consciousness on facts that confirms your existing ideals. For instance, in case you think that your professor is not very excellent, you be aware all of the times of rude behavior exhibited by using the professor whilst ignoring the countless satisfactory interactions he's worried in on a each day foundation. Hindsight bias leads you to accept as true with that the occasion you simply skilled become predictable, although it in reality wasn't. In different phrases, you knew all along that matters might flip out the way they did. representative bias describes a faulty way of wondering, in which you by accident stereotype a person or something; as an instance, you can anticipate that your professors spend their free time analyzing books and engaging in highbrow communication, due to the fact the idea of them spending their time gambling volleyball or visiting an entertainment park does not match in together with your stereotypes of professors.

Purposeful technique to reminiscence officially started with Baddeley's (1988) article that caused researchers to examine reminiscence phenomena in an ordinary context. Nearly thirty years later, some active students have firmly grounded their research in a functional angle. Empirical studies derived from these theoretical views are nonetheless fantastically scarce due to the lack of a preferred dimension device. The maximum distinguished bounce on this studies quarter might be obtrusive within the construction and later psychometric high-quality-tuning and validation of the story questionnaire. The development of the story began with an exploratory component analysis as an initial evaluation, observed by confirmatory issue evaluation, and resulted in a quick 15-item self-file degree tapping into the 3 predominant features of AM.

The story functions items with excessive face validity and research have shown precise inner consistency for every subscale. Empirical studies assessing convergent and discriminant validity of each of its subscales showed first-class results. Bluck and Alea (2011) administered tale to one hundred and fifty-six younger and one hundred fifty older adults showing regular age variations in fundamental cognitive capabilities. Furthermore, a subset of those participants finished the Self-idea readability Scale, the future Orientation Scale, and the big five stock—subscales of Extroversion and Neuroticism, in an try and provide evidence of validity for self, directive, and social features of AM, respectively. As anticipated, this takes a look at showed top convergent validity. Sizable correlations determined for the tale self-function and SCSS confirmed that people with decrease self-idea clarity use AM greater frequently in a try and obtain a clearer self-concept. In phrases of discriminant validity, the tale self-feature did now not correlate with persona or future orientation. Moreover, the frequency of use of one's beyond to serve as a Social-bonding function turned into located to be related to higher extroversion and did not relate to either self-concept readability, or destiny orientation. Ultimately, the Directive function subscale turned into extensively correlated with future orientation indicating that humans with a more secure view of the destiny record the use of AM extra to direct their current and destiny conduct. There has been no relation located between the Directive subscale and other unrelated constructs (self-concept readability, extraversion, neuroticism). Also, studies have shown that tale may be used as a psychologically meaningful tool for inspecting adult age variations in the functional use of AM.

Chapter Eight

Cognitive Styles and Creativity

What makes a person creative? That is one of the questions that researchers inside the subject of creativity have been looking to remedy and apprehend. \in this book, I can compare the two theorists, Teresa Amabile and J.P. Guilford. Everyone has proposed a model of creativity so that you can understand exactly what creativity is and how it works. The wish in doing so is that information on how creativity functions will stimulate more creative wondering and problem-solving. Guilford becomes the first to identify creativity as a type of intelligence and sought to identify common characteristics and cognitive abilities of regarded creative individuals and sell the development of those characteristics so one can assist stimulate innovative wondering. Amabile categorizes those traits and cognitive capabilities as innovative-applicable talents; certainly one of four components in her version of creativity. Amabile believes that even as these talents are wished, they need to work with domain-applicable skills, assignment motivation, and the social surroundings of the trouble-solver. The two fashions have commonalities, in addition, to well as differences. I hope to explain each while comparing the two, and applying this expertise to my very own work. There is an amazing quantity of evidence of the human race, creativity, and that we all have a hobby in training. Schooling is so crucial to us because it's far the most effective thing we will use for this unpredicted destiny. All children have talents, but our schooling gadget crushes our creativity due to the fact we're taught to assume a certain manner. Due to the worry of being wrong children are no longer being innovative that is why many adults lose that "capability" that will be innovative. Few of the children who are allowed to continue using their creativity generally tend to not hate their lives as a lot as different adults who weren't able to pursue passions they truly enjoyed. Picasso said, "All children are born artists, the trouble is to remain an artist as we grow up." Creativity is absolutely just as crucial and literacy there may be many prodigies who discover their gift earlier than they could ever speak sometimes. Literacy enables them to be capable of communicating with others approximately what they're doing and the common sense at the back of their creativity and how their minds assume. Literacy is so pressured down the throats of children we don't allow them to explore themselves and the matters they want to do. We develop out of creativity because of the way schooling is taught. The tale of his son facilitates because youngsters aren't' afraid to be incorrect till they're taught they aren't allowed or purported to be wrong. children don't mind being incorrect due to the fact they don't even recollect themselves as wrong, they're inclined to take a threat to do what they assume.

Cognitive styles or "questioning styles" seek advice from how a person understand, collect, method, and recall statistics. Those patterns illustrate a person's way of questioning, remembering, or problem-solving. It significantly pictures contrasts in people think, see and remember records. the focal point of cognitive psychologists is on the mental procedures that affect conduct while the motive of the Myers-Briggs kind Indicator is to make the theories of C. G. Jung associated with character psychological kinds understandable and useful in human beings' lives. the main purpose of this idea is that the version of human conduct is regular.

Feeling: Thinkers: judgments made intellectually of actual and fake Feelers: judgments made using non-public and subjective values.

• Judgment vs. belief: Judgers: these human beings conclude and act on them easily Perceivers: these people determine hesitantly with flexibility and adaptability Jung identifies dimensions/features on how humans gather and compare records. They may be statistics-gathering and facts-assessment functions.

• ST (Sensor/philosopher). These humans recognition on information, use impersonal evaluation and generally tend to end up realistic, use technical capabilities with statistics and items.

• SF (Sensor/Feeler). These humans attention to statistics, use impersonal analysis, tend to grow to be sympathetic, and select sensible assistance and offerings to people. NT (Intuitive/thinker). Those human beings focus on possibilities, use personal analysis, and tend to become logical, focus on theoretical and technical development.

• NF(Intuitive/Feeler)- this human being's consciousness on possibilities, uses private evaluation, generally tends to end up enthusiastic, and is higher at know-how and speaking with people.

Numerous investigations of chiefs and directors uncover that their dominating character likewise is detecting and judging. They tend to be more dutiful, careful, and focus on credentials and traditions

• SPs are creative arms on trouble solvers. Tend to be laugh-loving, positive. They pride themselves on being unconventional, formidable, and spontaneous. NTs are conceptualizers. They tend to be skeptical, self-contained, and targeted on hassle fixing and evaluation. They frequently can provide understanding into the internal intent and essential standards of frameworks and associations. NFS can see ability outcomes but are centered extra on individuals and foundations than on thoughts and ideas. The enthusiastic; are seeking for their actual self and dream of attaining awareness. They can be nurturing mother and father and inspirational

Dr. Seuss once stated, "it's far better to know how to learn than to simply recognize". The talk over cognitive patterns and their impact on studying has been common for over fifty years and continues to be being researched nowadays. Cognitive styles, additionally known as gaining knowledge of patterns, may be defined as "statistics processing behavior" and are believed to be similar to tendencies of persona in that they stay stable and unchanged over the years. There are three distinctive forms of studying styles which include visual, auditory/verbal, and kinesthetic. A kinesthetic learner may additionally decide upon demonstrations and more palms-on processes which will manner records. The most widespread and debated gaining knowledge of styles are visual and verbal. a visible learner is someone who learns thru images or diagrams at the same time as a verbal learner might also analyze quality thru discussions and speaking out issues. According to Kollofel (2012), there are extraordinary sorts of visual freshmen, folks who learn high-quality through spatial imagery and those who research excellent thru images or item imagery. Gaining knowledge of patterns in colleges is largely debated due to the fact it is regularly hard for teachers to fulfill every scholar's studying wishes. Growing numbers of students mean that there may be extra desired gaining knowledge of patterns. Consistent with Romanelli, bird, and Ryan (2009), learning patterns vary via lifestyle so one form of preparation that may match in the USA may not always work in eastern cultures.

Cognitive fashion, also called wondering style, refers to the commonplace patterns of behaviors which frequently emerge in cognitive technique. Cognitive style isn't appreciably related to the capacity of thinking reasoning among students, often formed by attitude and expression during the technique of belief, reminiscence, and problem fixing. Cognitive style is character differences within the cognitive process with exquisite sorts, together with subject unbiased style and area dependent style, reflective style and impulsive style, and wholist style and analytic fashion. Subject independent fashion and discipline dependent style are personal differences in cognitive style that Herman Witkin, an American psychologist, has located in his studies.

The wholist style tends to respond to cognitive projects through holistic strategy. They're used to perceiving fabric from a holistic angle. There is a long span in reading comprehension. By research, English majors within vocabulary learning, wager phrases in context. The reading fabric affords them with statistics to help them guess the means. With the aid of college students' understanding, revel in, common feel, contrast, and evaluation, they can wager the word's meaning. Within the research, giving English predominant an unknown phrase, at the identical time, permitting them to read materials, therefore, they can bet the means by bearing on the word to the context, sentences, clauses, or paragraphs. This is a powerful strategy to grasp phrases and vocabulary. Analytic style tends to pay greater attention to the information and tactics. They can set up clear and identifiable formation components. This is the typical function of the analytical style. In vocabulary studying, English majors apprehend word elements. For instance, they are given phrases, and that they have to ruin into components. The phrase "manufacturing", English fundamental can rewrite the phrase in elements, production. They can also underline the phrases to show the components pro/duct/ion. Cognitive studies on creativity are both conventional and innovative. It is conventional within the feel that a few of the properly identified tactics, systems, and stores from mainstream cognitive psychology have been used to apprehend innovative questioning. It is revolutionary due to the fact there's a want to recognize approaches that aren't identified unless one is especially interested in creativity. Some of those are inherently subjective, a truth that is regularly left out through the ones hoping for traditionally clinical analysis. still, tons of the interest inside the cognitive sciences issues how new constructs come into being; and all of us interested in this is in fact considering creativity. This is creativity. I evaluate several traditional cognitive topics, inclusive of expertise, memory, category, judgment, and categorization, and describes how each can influence innovative wondering. It also provides an original model of creative wondering with problem locating, ideation, and judgmental tactics as primary additives, and knowledge and motivation as secondary (contributing however not controlling) components. Several troubles are blanketed, along with the relegation of motivation, the difference between declarative and procedural information, and the capacity for understanding to both facilitate and inhibit creative ideation. J.P. Guilford advanced a model for creativity based on the idea that creativity is a shape of intelligence. Till Guilford released his studies, psychologists have been beneath the belief that creativity became a byproduct of intelligence, linking the two in a structured relationship where high IQ way high creativity and vice versa. In his psychological version known as "structure of intellect" Guilford used a factor analytic approach to separate intelligence into types of questioning: divergent and convergent questioning. Divergent questioning is the capacity to get the right of entry to memory, from which you can actually derive numerous precise solutions to a single hassle; convergent thinking is the potential to provide you with 1 accurate answer for each question. (Explaining Creativity, Sawyer) once Guilford evolved this version he commenced to look for ways that he may want to degree divergent questioning in individuals. The take a look at the evolved is now known as Guilford's opportunity makes use of assignment. The challenge is straightforward, or seemingly so: listing as many feasible makes use of for a common object. (I.e. a paperclip) once finished taking a look at takers that had been scored on 4 components: originality, fluency, flexibility, and elaboration. Guilford located that these four additives and some others are usually seen in creative people. Guilford acknowledges that on the way to solve troubles, one has to first be able to articulate the deficiencies in commonplace products or social institutions. Fluency is the ability to assume properly and effortlessly. Fluency may be similarly damaged down into four kinds: phrase, associational, expressional, and ideational fluency. The flexibility of questioning is another characteristic that exists in Guilford's model. Flexibility may be similarly damaged down into classes: spontaneous flexibility and adaptive. Spontaneous flexibility is the ability to supply a super style of thoughts; Adaptive is the ability to generalize the necessities of a problem to find a solution. Originality is the capability to form associations between elements that can be far-flung from one another logically. The capability to complicated is being able to fill in the information given a fashionable scheme. Additionally to those traits, creative sorts frequently show the capacity to redefine makes use of for commonplace items, can be given some uncertainty in conclusions while rigid classes aren't getting used. It is also useful for the man or woman to have an interest in each divergent and convergent wondering. (Measuring Creativity) if you want to try to raise creativity levels individuals undergo schooling programs that teach them to have these traits. However, this does not always mean the individual will become more innovative for having these traits.

Teresa Amabile proposed her very own model of creativity primarily based on underlying assumptions. The first assumption is that there may be a continuum from regular levels of creativity in everyday life to the very best ranges of creativity in the traditionally massive products of the humanities and sciences. The second assumption being that there are special tiers of creativity in the works of any unmarried individual, even within one domain. Within the componential model, there are four portions that each one works together to steer innovative questioning. These components: area-relevant talents, creativity-applicable techniques, task motivation, and the social surroundings of the author are all vital pieces in creative trouble solving. Area- applicable competencies consist of know-how, technical capabilities, intelligence, and expertise in the domain the individual is working in. Creativity- relevant processes encompass cognitive capacity and style as well as take persona characteristics into attention. These personality trends consist of independence, threat taking, flexibility, skills in producing ideas, and disciplined work conduct. One of the most vital components of Amabile's creativity model is intrinsic motivation to finish a venture. In the simplest form, intrinsic motivation is passion and the incentive to adopt a challenge or solve trouble because it's far thrilling, personally challenging, or pleasant.

The final factor of this version is the social surroundings. With a purpose to stimulate creativity, the work environment must encourage creative behavior. Creativity can effortlessly be hindered using bad grievance closer to new thoughts and approaches of wondering. Creativity can also be hindered by using a conservative, low-danger mindset amongst management. Immoderate time strain is likewise a destructive element to the creative system. In Amabile's version, these additives have an impact on the creative method which includes several sub-methods: analyzing and articulating the precise nature of the trouble to hand, collecting and reactivating applicable statistics, generating thoughts, checking out the validity of a delegated answer, and speaking the solution to others. The components work collectively with the creative technique. The procedure itself isn't concrete; these sub-tactics may also arise in any order and can be repeated until one in all outcomes takes place: fulfillment or failure. (Amabile, Componential idea of Creativity). Now that we've taken a study of both Guilford and Amabile's fashions we will see how they're alike. Both Guilford and Amabile characteristic creativity to sure cognitive skills. I experience as though Amabile's model is nearly a variety of Guildford's version. Guildford's version particularly specializes in viewing innovative thinking as a sort of intelligence. Guilford cautioned traits located in recognized innovative people will be used to degree creativity in others. in addition to assisting sell those characteristics in human beings to stimulate more innovative wondering. Amabile's componential model of creativity additionally verifies this as one of the four components that useful resource inside the innovative technique, creativity relevant approaches. It is from here I agree with Amabile has brought to the understanding with the other components of her model. Even as Guilford and Amabile's models have some overlapping traits, there is a whole lot to be said about the differences between them. Guildford theorized that intelligence may be broken up into two types of problem-solving: divergent and convergent questioning. Divergent questioning is the one associated with innovative wondering. Guilford hypothesized that if divergent questioning will be measured and tested, and then one should discover a way to apply this insight to boost creativity stages. Amabile but, breaks creativity down into 4 additives, most effective 3 of which are from inside the man or woman, and one from out of doors the man or woman. Already we start to see a vital difference within the two fashions: Guilford modeling creativity as going on solely due to cognitive abilities and traits a man or woman possesses, even as Amabile indicates that cognitive competencies are important however different additives want to be happening as properly. The additives are now not blanketed in Guilford's version: domain-applicable competencies, task motivation, and the social surroundings. Amabile believes that whilst innovative-applicable approaches are critical to creative questioning, one will no longer generate certainly specific and valuable answers without the others. Amabile is also developing her model below the belief that everybody has the capability to be innovative; it is just a remembrance of spotting your own form of creativity. What makes someone creative? Based on my findings in Guilford and Amabile's fashions I agree with there are numerous elements that result in creative questioning in any character. There is no such issue as a creative character; in truth, all of us possess the capability to be creative. Without even knowing it everybody sporting events creativity in ordinary duties all the time. via searching at those fashions I have reached the realization that those fashions are related. Guilford explores creativity thru the scope of intelligence. From right here it appears as although Amabile tailored and expanded on Guilford's findings. Amabile proposed her componential version of creativity which incorporates some of the traits Guilford talks approximately in his findings. Those traits fall underneath creative-applicable methods inside the componential version. Amabile also talks of three different components that useful resource within the innovative system: area-relevant skills, intrinsic mission motivation, and work surrounding that are nurturing of creative thinking.

The Cognitive-style stock

Lorna P. Martin introduction In companies the amount and nice of cognitive behaviors, the ones associated with the activities of wondering, gaining knowledge of, hassle fixing, and choice-making produce a dramatic impact on productiveness, performance, and potential for increase. The Cognitive style version and its accompanying instrument, The Cognitive-style stock, offer a foundation for identifying the styles of conduct that typify humans' tactics to those vital sports. The instrument identifies cognitive styles that mean favored and constant patterns of responses that are recurring and unconscious as well as planned. Using introducing individuals, companies, and businesses to both the version and the device, the human resource development (HRD) practitioner can accomplish the following:

• Assist human beings to identify their personal cognitive styles and to apprehend the advantages as well as the drawbacks of all cognitive styles

• Train human beings a way to expect their personal behaviors in addition to the ones of others in regards to questioning, learning, and hassle fixing

• Prescribe developmental strategies that people can use

to beautify their personal cognitive patterns and/or to build energy in styles that they do now not commonly use
- Boom people's talent and flexibility in various trouble-solving situations; and
- Facilitate interactions among people and groups.

The Cognitive-fashion version

Theories about cognitive style were developed as a result of early research carried out by using Witkin, Lewis, Hertzman, Machover, Meissner, and Wapner (1954); Witkin, Dyk, Patterson, Goodenough, and Karp (1962); and Bruner (1966). Those and different studies led to theories that generally assumed an unmarried size of cognitive style, with an individual's style falling someplace on a continuum between the extremes of this dimension. A few of the theories assigned a nice fee to one of the extremes and a terrible price to the alternative. The two extremes are described in standard phrases by way of eagerness, the Pfeiffer Library quantity, and the second version. Copyright ©1998 Jossey-Bass/Pfeiffer, (1973), McKenney and keen (1974), and Botkin (1974): the systematic fashion (usually considered as "suitable" when a fee is assigned) is associated with logical, rational conduct that makes use of a step-by way of-step, a sequential method to thinking, mastering, problem fixing, and choice-making; in evaluation, the intuitive fashion (typically regarded as "awful" while a fee is assigned) is associated with a spontaneous, holistic, and visible approach. Ultimately, many research, books, and magazine and magazine articles concerning cognitive styles have regarded, for example, Sargent (1981), Martin (1983),

Buzan (1983), marvel and Donovan (1984), and Latting (1985). Everyone addresses the equal fundamental elements identified in advance because of the systematic and intuitive styles. These theories may be linked with the ones of left-brain/proper-brain questioning, which follow the same bipolarity pattern. Brain research inside the late Nineteen Sixties and early Nineteen Seventies resulted in the discovery that the two aspects of the mind are chargeable for special mental features. Taking brain principle one step similarly and linking it to the idea of cognitive style, surprise, and Donovan (1984, p. 3) state, "because of our unique genetic inheritance, our family life, and our early training, most of us prefer to use one facet of the mind extra than the opposite." The forms of behaviors related to the two aspects are as follows: Left brain: analytical, linear, sequential, concrete, rational, and aim orientated; and a couple of. Right brain: intuitive, spontaneous, holistic, symbolic, emotional, and visible. An overview of the fabric on each cognitive fashion and left-mind/right-mind theory resulted in the following generalizations about cognitive patterns: 1. there are distinct, observable, and measurable variations among people's cognitive styles. 2. Cognitive style can without problems be detected via language and nonverbal behavior patterns. Dialogue between individuals can screen differences and might highlight the want for consciousness and know-how of those variations. 3. Styles are frequently associated with profession selections; therefore, there are connections among behavioral patterns and certain capabilities or divisions within a business enterprise. In truth, style can dominate an agency's tradition. 4. Styles tackle connotations of "right" or "horrific," with one style generally considered being "higher" or "nice" depending on the individual interpreter or machine evaluator. 5. There is a need to apprehend, recognize, and broaden each area of cognitive strong point. 6. Creativity and effectiveness can be elevated whilst the bipolar dimensions are fused. Further, most of the latest research concerning mind functioning and cognitive fashion asserts the need to apply each of the bipolar elements of the systematic and intuitive patterns (either with the aid of combining or alternating among them) to generate greater performance, productiveness, and creativity. even though the systematic and intuitive styles furnished the foundation for The Cognitive fashion version, those two patterns had now not previously been proven to reflect the whole spectrum of people's conduct about wondering, mastering, and particularly trouble fixing and selection making. Therefore, a multidimensional model supposed to reflect the entire spectrum turned into created. This model consisted of continua: 1. Excessive systematic to low systematic and (2) excessive intuitive to low intuitive. Ongoing observational research, alongside efforts to expand dimension gadgets for assessing cognitive conduct, has resulted in a multiplied model of that authentic version. 1. Systematic fashion. A man or woman diagnosed as having a scientific fashion is one who charges high on the systematic scale and low on the intuitive scale. Consistent with findings in the Harvard studies, a character who typically operates with a systematic fashion makes use of a properly-defined, step-through-step technique while fixing trouble; looks for a universal approach or programmatic method; after which makes a normal plan for fixing the trouble. 2. Intuitive style. An individual who charges low on the systematic scale and excessive on the intuitive scale is defined as having an intuitive fashion. A person whose fashion is intuitive makes use of an unpredictable ordering of analytical steps while solving a hassle, is based on revel in styles characterized with the aid of unverbalized cues or hunches, and explores and abandons alternatives quickly. 3. included style. Someone with an integrated fashion costs excessive on both scales and is capable of trade patterns quickly and easily. Such fashion changes seem to be unconscious and take place in a count of seconds. A result of this "rapid-hearth" capability is that it appears to generate strength and a proactive approach to trouble fixing. In reality, integrated humans are frequently called "hassle seekers" due to the fact they consistently try to. 4. Undifferentiated fashion. An individual score low on both the systematic and the intuitive scale is defined as having undifferentiated cognitive conduct. Such someone appears no longer to distinguish or differentiate among the two styles extremes and, consequently, appears no longer to show a fashion. In fact, in a trouble-fixing or getting to know the situation, he or she can also exhibit receptivity to commands or tips from out of doors sources. Undifferentiated individuals tend to be withdrawn, passive, and reflective and regularly appearance to others for hassle-fixing strategies. 5. Break up fashion. A person scores inside the middle range on each system and the intuitive scale is taken into consideration to have a cut-up style concerning pretty equal (average) tiers of systematic and intuitive specialization. At the beginning glance, the cut-up style appears to differ from the included fashion best within the degree of specialization. But, people with a breakup fashion do now not own an included behavioral response; as a substitute, they exhibit each separate dimension is completely special settings, the usage of best one fashion at a time based totally on the nature of their tasks or their work organizations. In other words, they consciously reply to trouble-solving and gaining knowledge of conditions by using selecting the appropriate style. Because an evaluation score figuring out a cut-up fashion commonly indicates an identical degree of both dimensions, it might be assumed that both dimensions could be equally exhibited. But, actual observational findings have now not produced this result. Quite often, in annoying situations, one size appears to dominate, generally due to addiction. it's been full-size that many people exhibiting this precise cognitive fashion have indicated that they have been within the process of a cognitive transition; they were stepping into a new place of cognitive specialization and have been "trying out new behaviors and abilities." There are symptoms that the result of excessive cognitive specialization in one measurement can appreciably impact usual effectiveness in non-public and professional conditions. Severe specialization may restrict a character's or a group's capacity to think, learns, resolve issues, and have interaction with others.

Entrepreneur representative researcher, undifferentiated fashion receptive isn't a problem-fixing professional; does no longer showcase a specific uniqueness Passive, reflective relies closely on guidelines, procedures, commands, guidelines, or hints reacts to the hassle stimulus and does not impose a process on the problem.Has trouble making choices. Procrastinates; delays motion. Passive, mainly nonverbal Reflective Low involvement Confluent waits patiently for specific guidelines Bookkeeper Administrative assistant Clerical employee. Split fashion: Descriptors of style Language styles and nonverbal patterns projected career. Positions have identical degrees of systematic and intuitive fashion that is common/medium in phrases of stages of depth. Patterns are used as absolutely separate entities. Patterns are not at all included and are consciously decided on for every particular situation Out of addiction; one style is used often than the others. Sample adjustments according to the fashion getting used at the time of observation. typically an individual with a cut-up style is inside the method of a cognitive transition related to constructing new strengths and competencies inside the dimension this gives the impression to the weaker of the two (systematic or intuitive). Pattern modifications consistent with the style being used at the time of observation. usually, a man or woman with a breakup style is inside the system of a cognitive transition concerning constructing new strengths and abilities inside the dimension this seems to the weaker of the two (systematic or intuitive) outcomes at the man or woman. Cognitive style specialization especially in systematic, intuitive, and undifferentiated styles appears to restrict one's capability to absolutely characteristic in getting to know and trouble-fixing situations. In many instances, people whose styles are specialized are especially a hit in most endeavors but have a blind spot within the methods wherein they take in information, sort the data, and in the long run respond. The same blind spots seem in conversations and interactions between people or agencies that specialize in one-of-a-kind cognitive patterns. The dialogue regularly turns into stilted and often breaks down.

Boundaries and misunderstandings among individuals occur because of variations in methodologies and language or nonverbal communique styles. Differences in cognitive specialization also can cause bad overall performance opinions, battle situations, and a loss of "task match" or healthy among a man or woman and a business enterprise. Certainly, the fulfillment of the "match" between an individual and a collection or an organization can be anticipated using the degree to which the cognitive patterns match. As soon as a group or an organization will become characterized by way of a specific style, it can start to reward that fashion exclusively; for instance, managers would possibly insist that subordinates use the equal techniques or processes that they use. In such a situation humans whose styles are specific from the businesses may be classified "resistant," "cursed," "bizarre," or maybe "incompetent"; therefore, they'll locate it tough or even impossible to succeed in the agency. When the sort of bias occurs inside an agency, frequently it is in want of the systematic style, which is generally related to the left facet of the brain. Surprise and Donovan (1984) describe this phenomenon as follows: Researchers talk to the left mind because the dominant hemisphere and the right because the non-dominant one because the competencies of the left mind are dominant in our society. Money, generation, efficiency, and power are thought to be the rewards of the left-brain making plans. In a business and incredibly technological society, systematic capability is important; therefore, systematic fashion has grown to be favored. yet innovation is fostered using the intuitive fashion. results on the Work organization variations in style amongst contributors of a workgroup can also create problems in reaching goals. Cognitive-specialization variations in groups often result in the manner and verbal exchange troubles. If extreme sufficient, the problems can motive communication breakdowns, which, in turn, can result in spending an incredible deal of time on the technique of problem-solving as opposed to on accomplishing the assignment with the greatest effectiveness. In a few remote instances whilst the degree of cognitive distinction is extreme, the institution contributors now and then revel in a mental "logjam." The institution turns immobilized and receives caught, surely not able to proceed. If the trouble of differences is severe sufficient and the organization has the option to do so, it could select to terminate its efforts. But, whilst differences and similarities amongst cognitive styles in a collection are diagnosed and taken into attention, a form of synergy can be created. This synergy outcome when the institution honors the efforts of each of its members to use his or her particular cognitive knowledge in those tiers of the problem-fixing process where it's far maximum appropriate. As an instance, systematics and intuitive would possibly work collectively on the first segment of the problem-solving system (problem identity). Then the intuitive would possibly use a divergent technique by way of expanding all the problem possibilities to discover all capacity issues. Ultimately, the systematics may employ a convergent method, the use of the intuitive' listing to become aware of practical problems. In the long run, the focal point of the group's hassle-solving hobby might turn out to be an increasing number of slender and unique till a hassle announcement could be generated. Another kind of synergy is created when a group's participants all percentage the same cognitive style and begin to work on an assignment that calls for a methodology characteristic of that fashion. In this example members easily understand one another's language and comfortably select up on nonverbal cues. As a result, they talk and work well collectively. But, it's far critical to remember the fact that the opposite result additionally could occur while the participant's proportion one fashion. as an example, the group may find it important to complete a project that calls for behaviors feature of an opposite fashion. Consequences at the corporation Organizational structures can from time to time revel in the difficulties brought about via cognitive-fashion specialization of complete divisions. For instance, one young, newly appointed VP of a well-known publishing organization explained that she was having a remarkable deal of issues coping with her work unit. She reported behaviors of resistance, sabotage, and raging battles that she defined as an ongoing battle. She was in charge of coordinating the activities of the manufacturing department (a feature characterized by a systematic fashion) and the marketing and advertising division (a characteristic characterized by way of an intuitive style). Her overall performance evaluation and role were depending on her potential to instill and preserve peace and harmony between the 2 divisions. What she did not understand and become amazed to discover was the belief that these two groups essentially spoke one-of-a-kind languages and thought and acted in distinctly unique methods. As a result, each department perceived the other as "misfits." once she understood the results in their cognitive-fashion variations, she should deal with the hassle. THE instrument The Cognitive-style stock consists of forty statements, half of which pertain to the systematic style and half to the intuitive style. Respondents evaluate each assertion in step with the diploma to which they believe it. Finally, the respondents transfer their responses to the scoring sheet, which yields a scientific score and an intuitive rating. Those ratings are then transferred to the interpretation sheet, which allows them to decide to what degree they specialize in systematic and intuitive patterns. Ultimately, they find their ratings on the scales furnished in the interpretation sheet to discover their very own precise styles. Validity and Reliability the Cognitive-fashion stock has face validity. due to the fact it's far used on the whole as a basis for discussion of the effects of cognitive style on individual, organization, and organizational functioning, no strive has been made to establish validity and reliability past this point. Management; the tool, the scoring sheet, and the translation sheet may be completed using most respondents in about twenty to thirty minutes. it is advisable to observe scoring and interpretation with a lecture and discussion on cognitive styles. If the HRD practitioner prefers, respondents may be told to complete the device, pay attention to the lecture and participate within the discussion, and then predict what their patterns could be before they complete the scoring and interpretation sheets. This paper; cover the contents with the respondents; after which display a videotape of a collection trouble-fixing consultation, asking the respondents to reveal verbal and nonverbal styles and to identify individual patterns. Uses of the tool and the version. The HRD practitioner can play a vital function in supporting an organization to recognize, appreciate, and increase the range of cognitive behaviors utilized by its contributors. To meet this role, the practitioner can administer The Cognitive-style stock and explain the model to organizational contributors for the subsequent purposes: 1. boost humans' attention to the significance of cognitive patterns in general and in their personal in particular. Organizational individuals need to study the benefits and liabilities related to every unique fashion, mainly because it interacts with other styles. Botkin's (1974) take look shows that an individual's focus on his or her personal cognitive style can improve that person's ability to talk and engage with others. 2. Assist humans to broaden the capabilities, attitudes, and behaviors related to styles that they do now not generally use. in keeping with Buzan (1983), studies have shown that a synergistic effect takes region in all intellectual performance while a man or woman develops one intellectual area (both the systematic or the intuitive fashion) that became previously considered to be susceptible. The HRD specialist can offer training and improvement activities to enhance humans' present patterns and/or to construct every person's underutilized or weaker fashion. For example, a seminar on creativity that specializes in lateral wondering and creative trouble-fixing strategies together with brainstorming and visualization might substantially advantage people with a scientific style at the same time as helping those with an intuitive fashion. 3. Teach human beings to be facilitators and/or advisors within the problem-fixing method of a piece institution or a challenging forces. These people might grow to be familiar with both the Cognitive-fashion version and the inventory and could act as interpreters or even negotiators in organizations as wished which will bridge the distance of cognitive variations. This strategy would be mainly useful in assisting corporations to cope with struggles. in addition, these people will be trained in team-building strategies so that they could assist agencies in developing better intragroup relationships. 4. Use individual style similarities and variations in team-building periods to look at interaction "pinch points" and "synergy points" to set up group suggestions. The HRD professional, thru method commentary, should discover whilst and the way cognitive boundaries occur inside the problem-fixing technique and could then offer preventive and prescriptive measures. 5. Form mission forces or product-innovation organizations whose members are identified as professionals in precise cognitive patterns. This method would "champion" creative designs from the inception section to creation within the marketplace. The HRD practitioner ought to help to create such companies throughout a corporation (much like "high-quality circles") in a try to foster a cultural change geared in the direction of modern responses. Development activities may want to construct and integrate systematic and intuitive skills, both of which are wished for creative growth. 6. Decide whether the company as a whole practices a cognitive-style specialization. The HRD professional ought to provide control-development packages to address the problem and build the skill base that is wanted. A single fashion throughout an organization imposes limitations; consequently, the practitioner ought to behavior interventions designed to alter the tradition to foster exchange.

There are many distinctive kinds of people with different methods of thinking so one can give you choices. People use the exclusive wondering patterns of their personal and professional lives. Their reviews that they've discovered because they were kids, each formal and casual method, have significantly fashioned the way they assume. I looked at and analyzed three distinct thinking styles and the way they affect the crucial thinking method. Via being able to recognize the character of these questioning styles, we grow to be greater ready to investigate conditions and be able to make exceptional decisions.

The three thinking styles

 Logical thinking the majority in the enterprise global use the logical manner of wondering. Logical persons analyze situations for you to give you the consequences or solutions to the problems which are possible to arise. Logical thinkers do not forget all eventualities as viable results and this is the purpose why choices made are considered extra informed selections and there may be decreased likelihood that an incorrect end is achieved.

Creative wondering-innovative wondering specializes in growing something this is new or authentic. Its purpose is to stimulate curiosity and divergence is promoted using the use of the abilities of images, flexibility, fluency, pressured relationships, brainstorming, metaphorical thoughts, change, and so forth. While someone starts questioning in a way that expands and includes metaphorical ideas, we can say that he/she is starting to spark the procedure of innovative wondering. Every person can think creatively as absolutely everyone has a large creative capacity. But, they were with us more when we were children. Education has suppressed creativity in adults however while it's reawakened and developed, something specific and original contributes to the achievement in any undertaking.

Creative thinking takes on many bureaucracies and we can see it inside the sort of responses in any given situation. even as creative thinkers use divergent questioning wherein they begin from few thoughts and answers after which provide you with greater, logical thinkers use a convergent way of wondering that's distilling few solutions from many picks. at the same time as innovative wondering deals on opportunities, logical questioning is about reasons and evaluation.

Persuasive thinking-Persuasion is an art and it isn't always an easy challenge. The individual persuading a person must have a strong idea that he/she believes strongly. The persuasive thinking person can strongly argue his/her ideas and ideas to inspire others to assume the identical manner as he/she is and recruit them to consider in his/her thoughts. The skillful persuasive person is characterized by information and rationality coupled with honesty and objectivity, all of which permit the target audience to agree with him/her. It is less complicated to sway others if the persuading man or woman is appreciated by others.

Assessment and evaluation of the thinking styles and how everyone influences the essential thinking method

Consistent with Lane (2009), kingdom psychologist, innovative thinkers use the left aspect of her or his brain even as the logical thinkers use the right aspect of their brain in processing statistics. innovative thinkers have a greater artistic mindset and that they pay much less attention to the organization even as the logical thinker's attention to processing information in a disciplined manner and that they examine and quantify this fact to technique situations and give you choices. To engage the full capability of the creative and logical components of the brain to work together and broaden a sense of open-mindedness, researchers are currently the usage of standards together with the thoughts mapping approach. A rational persuasive thinker convinces human beings using common sense. In the persuasion method, common sense substantially facilitates the persuasive man or woman by rationally conveying the message. Persuasive thinkers "can use examples with inductive reasoning and theories applied in syllogisms; and they could use statistics, analogies, and reason-and-impact relationships to convince.

The thinking styles within the place of work

Each of us is creative in our very own way. But, if a person is afraid that his/her ideas might be rejected or replied negatively in the place of job, his/her ability to assume creatively is affected, and the ordinary ability to give you knew thoughts is hindered. In a fantastic running environment, two techniques can be executed to increase creativity: Brainstorming and big-name bursting. When people work by themselves and their minds are allowed to drift from one thought to every other and stimulating one concept with another, brainstorming is effective in this case. When individuals are allowed to discover his/her creative competencies via asking questions on certain topics in a collection placing, famous person bursting is used. Many businesses have used these strategies in employee training to further enhance the creativity of their personnel. Different techniques used to balance strengths between innovative and logical thinking, organizations administer mind-mapping so that there could be ability gains from the training of the worker, discount of price, and upgrades in the ability-level of employees as a method in justifying these schooling tactics. We will discover many persuasive thinking individuals in one-of-a-kind companies. A shop clerk endorses or sells a product through persuasive techniques. A manager seeks to motivate his workforce rationally using good judgment and his/her emotional attraction. Indeed, the questioning styles: innovative, logical, and persuasion had been witnessed inside the exceptional place of job environments in the course of the arena. A complete review of research in cognitive psychology has indicated that people exhibit significant man or woman variations inside the cognitive processing patterns that they undertake in problem fixing and other comparable decision-making activities. As for individual differences, one-of-a-kind researchers have different definitions and behavior studies from unique perspectives for this reason. But, findings from each qualitative and quantitative study have indicated several constant predominant dimensions of person variations. Of those dimensions, cognitive style is a major one. The construct of cognitive patterns changed initially proposed through Allport (1937), relating to a man or woman's routine or traditional manner of perceiving, remembering, questioning, and hassle fixing. Considering then, mainly in the previous few a long time, there was additional large research on this area. Cognitive style has been broadly investigated by psychologists. Messick (1976) identified as many as 19 cognitive patterns. Smith (1984) also tabulated at least 17 mastering style inventories.

There are many one-of-a-kind definitions of cognitive

fashion. Tennant (1988) defined cognitive patterns as "a person's feature and regular approach to organizing and processing statistics". Driving, Glass, and Douglas (1993) termed cognitive patterns as "a fairly constant characteristic of a person" and "are static and are noticeably in-constructed capabilities of the individual". Primarily based on the above definitions, within the authors' points of view, cognitive/learning patterns talk to the person's regular and characteristic predispositions of perceiving, remembering, organizing, processing, wondering, and trouble fixing. distinct researchers emphasize one-of-a-kind aspects of cognitive patterns. consequently, there are various phrases encountered within the literature associated with this vicinity. these phrases consist of the breadth of categorizing deep-elaborative vs. shallow-reiterative, divergent vs. convergent, area dependence vs. discipline independence, international vs. analytical, impulsive vs. reflectivity, leveler vs. sharpener, want for cognition, goal vs. nonobjective, organizer vs. non-organizer, right- vs. left-brained, risk-taking vs. cautiousness, scanning vs. focusing, sensitizers vs. repressors, sensory modality possibilities, simultaneous vs. successive, verbalizer vs. imager, verbalizer vs. visualizer, visual vs. haptic perceptual kind; holist vs. analytic, holist-analytic vs. verbal-imagery, holist vs. serialist, Kolb's studying style version, as well as the MBTI getting to know style model.

In most situations, cognitive patterns and gaining knowledge of patterns are used interchangeably, as well as in this article. Normally, cognitive styles are more associated with theoretical or academic research, even as studying styles are extra associated with practical packages.

A primary difference between these two terms is the number of style factors worried. Particularly, cognitive patterns are extra associated with a bipolar size at the same time as learning styles aren't necessarily either/or extremes. Cognitive/mastering styles measures conventionally lie someplace between aptitude measures and persona measures. in addition, cognitive/gaining knowledge of patterns inside the literature has been regarded in three important respects—structures, process, or each structure and technique.

Consistent with Schmeck (1988), there are basic types of mastering styles. One is worldwide-holist/field-dependent/proper-brained, the other is targeted-distinctive/subject unbiased/left-brained. Schmeck asserted that, even though each style is equally correct for problem fixing, each style is probably to be related to more performance in specific tasks. The only trouble solvers must exercise strategies connected with each aforementioned pattern. In addition, Ausburn and Ausburn (1978) argued that cognitive styles had been characterized via 3 important properties. The first vital belongings are the generality and balance across tasks and overtime. Consequently, they're proof against schooling and trade. The second important property is the relative independence of cognitive styles from traditional measures of preferred capacity. The 0.33 important property is cognitive patterns' relationships with a few particular competencies, characteristics, and mastering obligations. Cognitive styles have either tremendous or poor relationships with motivation and educational success relying on the character of the learning task. The remainder of this paper involves three sections: (a) an assessment of foremost dimensions of cognitive styles, (b) predominant traits of distance training, and (c) diversifications of design and transport of distance training to college students' cognitive styles.

An evaluation of Cognitive patterns

This segment reviews the characteristics of five primary dimensions of cognitive styles which can be both lengthy-standing and/or well supported inside the literature. Those foremost dimensions encompass field independence-dependence, holist-analytic, sensory choices, hemispheric choices, and Kolb's learning style version.

Field independence vs. discipline Dependence

There was a developing frame of research within the beyond many years for the reason that field dependence-independence dimension becomes first proposed using Witkin (1962; 1979). In keeping with Witkin, field dependence-independence is cost-impartial and is characterized because of the ability to differentiate key elements from a distracting or confusing background. Field dependence-independence has critical implications for a man or woman's cognitive conduct and his/her interpersonal conduct. Mainly, field-independent human beings tend to be greater self-reliant when it comes to the development of cognitive restructuring abilities and less independent with regards to the improvement of interpersonal abilities. Conversely, area-based humans tend to be greater autonomous in terms of the improvement of high interpersonal skills and less self-sustaining on the subject of the development of cognitive restructuring capabilities. Further, in keeping with Witkin, Moore, Goodenough, and Cox (1977), field impartial people tend to be intrinsically motivated and revel in individualized learning, even as field established ones tend to be extrinsically motivated and revel in cooperative mastering. The sphere independence dimension is also related to some other character characteristics, consisting of solving analogical troubles. In line with Antonietti and Gioletta (1995), cognitive styles, rather than widespread competencies, are associated with analogical hassle solving. Antonietti and Violetta found that subject independent participants were more likely to be analogical solvers than area-based ones. Adult males tended to apply analogical answers more regularly than women. In addition, in step with Braune and Wickens (1986), there are three vital dimensions of individual differences in time-sharing—serial processing, parallel processing, and the inner model. Field-independent humans perform better within the parallel processing conditions, while discipline-established ones carry out higher inside the serial processing situations.

The sector independence dimension is also related to some challenge characteristics. Consistent with Bennink (1982), high and coffee discipline articulation (FA) students show differences within the following two essential respects under cognitively demanding situations: (a) integrating a hard and fast of semantically associated sentences to answer inference questions and (b) remembering the real propositions themselves.

Holist-Analytic

In step with using and Cheema (1991), learning patterns have fundamental sorts of impartial dimensions. One is the holist-analytic measurement. The holists generally tend to view a scenario as an entire, whilst the analytics generally tend to view a situation as a collection of elements and frequently strain the simplest one or two aspects at a time. Intermediates can have the advantage of both patterns. The alternative is the verbal-imagery measurement, which has simple effects: (a) how records are represented, which includes verbally, imagery, or each, as well as (b) internal/outside, the focus of attention. Commonly, the imagers tend to be inner and passive, at the same time as the verbalizers tend to be external and stimulating. The latter kind is related to sensory choice described later on in this phase. The above findings were also supported using Sadler-Smith (1997).

The holist-analytical style develops even in younger children. Peters (1977) conducted a take a look at first language mastering among very younger children. Consistent with him, youngsters employed two basically distinctive strategies to study their first language. One is the analytic style, which proceeds from the parts to the whole. The other is the Gestalt fashion, which proceeds from the whole to the elements. Similarly, Peters speculated that those two one-of-a-kind languages gaining knowledge of strategies may also have neurological bases.

Holist-analytical patterns have relationships to the kind of instructional fabric and learning performance. consistent with using and Sadler-Smith (1992), amongst secondary schools or college students, kinds of academic fabric remedy, such as summary or pictorial presentation and cognitive styles, have very critical impacts on mastering performance. Especially, students on the analytic-imager measurement enhance maximum in studying due to the inclusion of greater pictorial shows approximately sure varieties of contents. Further, the findings inside the above take a look at were additionally said in different research.

Sensory desire

There is a big frame of studies approximately sensory modality preference. In keeping with Bissell, White, and Zivin (1971), a sensory modality is a device that interacts with the environment thru one of the simple senses. The most vital sensory modalities are visual, auditory, and kinesthetic. In line with Dunn and Dunn (1979), about 20% to 30% of Yankee students are auditory; approximately 40% are visual; the last 30% to forty% are both tactual/kinesthetic, visual/tactual, or some mixtures of the above most important senses.

The concept of sensory desire can be traced again to Galton (1883). In line with his research, visible imagery is infrequent amongst scientists and appears to be incompatible with scientists' summary thinking. Later, Bartlett (1932) located comparable results. To offer noticeably complete records approximately the distinguishing functions of verbal and visible thinkers, Smith (1964) published his Spatial potential. One of Smith's foremost findings is that verbal questioning is overemphasized in research and intelligence testing after overlooking spatial or visible wondering. Another most important locating is gender differences. Specifically, masculinity is related to visible wondering even as femininity is associated with verbal questioning. However, gender distinction isn't supported using Antonietti and Gioletta (1996).

Many studies have indicated that a visible style is useful for some duties. in step with Vicente, Hayes, and Williges (1987), psychometric assessments of vocabulary and spatial visualization are the predictors of task performance. Of those, spatial visualization is the most influential. This became supported with the aid of Sein and Bostrom (1989), in addition to Schofield and Kirby (1994).

Every other term just like verbalizer vs. visualizer is verbalizer vs. imager cognitive style, which become proposed by way of riding and Buckle (1990). This site was supported with the aid of driving and Cheema (1991), as well as using and Douglas (1993). Consistent with those researchers, the imagers are higher in overall performance than the verbalizers within the textual content-plus-image condition, even as the verbalizers are higher than the imagers within the text-plus-text conditions. Similarly, the imagers greater often use diagrams to illustrate their answers than the verbalizers.

Hemispheric choices

There is a massive frame of studies approximately hemispheric preferences. Researchers have conducted applicable studies from extraordinary views, together with mental, physiological, and neurological. According to Sonnier (1991), hemispheric possibilities are probably a prime contributing factor to individual differences. That is, left-hemispheric students are robust in analytical notion processing, whilst right-hemispheric college students are visual processors. In addition, O'Boyle (1986) proposed that the difference in cognitive processing between the two hemispheric asymmetries changed into more quantitative than qualitative in nature. In different phrases, it's far primarily a count of diploma rather than absolute capability.

Many studies have shown that hemispheric choices play a totally crucial position in cognition and success. In line with O'Boyle and Hellige (1989), hemispheric asymmetry, inclusive of the degree of dominance, the direction of dominance, characteristic arousal degree, and complementarity of functioning, play a vital role in person variations in cognition. In step with Gadzella and Kneipp (1990), proper-hemispheric students system facts nonlinearly and holistically, but left-hemispheric students' process records logically and sequentially. Similarly, consistent with Gadzella (1995), left-hemispheric college students acquire better grades than right-hemispheric ones, in particular, while the grades are based on the goal check.

However, a few researchers point out that the idea of cerebral choice has some limited realistic and theoretical implications. They warn that teaching models need to no longer be solely based on the students' cerebral options. Instructors have to use a couple of methods of coaching to improve students' learning in preference to the use of a single one.

Kolb's studying fashion model

Kolb's studying style stock is one of the dominant tactics for categorizing cognitive patterns. Kolb's version has been discovered to be effective in some language teaching sports. Consistent with Kolb, the 4 primaries' getting-to-know modes are defined as lively experimentation (AE), reflective statement (RO), concrete experience (CE), and abstract conceptualization (AC). In addition, getting to know the method isn't always only energetic and passive, but also concrete and summary. This version can also be taken into consideration as a four-level model: (a) concrete enjoy, (b) observation and mirrored image, (c) the formation of summary standards and generalizations, and (d) speculation tested by way of active experimentation main to new concrete experience.

Based on the four primaries getting to know modes, in step with Kolb (1984), there are 4 fundamental getting to know patterns: converger, diverger, assimilator, and accommodator. Their characteristics are described underneath respectively: (1) Converger. The convergent gaining knowledge of fashion depends especially on the dominant studying capacities of lively experimentation and summary conceptualization. This fashion has notable advantages in selection making, hassle solving, traditional smart assessments, and sensible packages of theories. Understanding is prepared in a way of hypothetical-deductive reasoning. Therefore, persons with this fashion are advanced in technical tasks and problems and inferior in social and interpersonal topics. They tend to pick out to concentrate on physical sciences. (2) Diverger. The divergent learning fashion has the alternative studying benefits over converger. This style relies mainly on concrete experience and reflective observation; it has brilliant blessings in inventive talents and attention of which means and values. therefore, men and women with this style tend to prepare concrete conditions from distinctive views and to shape their relationships into a significant complete; they recognition on adaptation with the aid of observation as opposed to through motion; they're advanced in generating opportunity hypothesis and thoughts, and tend to be ingenious, people- or feeling-oriented; they tend to pick to concentrate on liberal arts and arts. (3) Assimilator. The assimilative learning fashion relies upon in particular on summary conceptualization and reflective observation. This style has remarkable advantages in inductive reasoning, creating theoretical models, and assimilating exclusive observations into an integrative entity. Similar to converger, folks with this fashion tend to be more concerned about summary principles and thoughts, and less concerned about humans. However, people with this style tend to cognizance greater at the logical soundness and preciseness of the ideas, rather than their realistic values; they tend to pick to work in research and making plans gadgets. (4) Accommodator. The accommodative gaining knowledge of style has the opposite mastering advantages over assimilation. This fashion depends specifically on active experimentation and urban enjoyment; it has super blessings in doing matters, imposing plans, and tasty in new tasks. therefore, people with this fashion cognizance of chance-taking, opportunity in search of, and motion; tend to be superior in adapting themselves to changing on the spot conditions wherein the plan or principle does now not shape the records; additionally they have a tendency to intuitively solve problems in a tribulation-and-mistakes manner, relying in particular on different people for statistics instead of on their own thinking. Consequently, persons with this style tend to deal with people without difficulty; they tend to focus on motion-oriented jobs, including marketing and sales.

In step with Kolb (1984), the above patterns connected with these four fundamental getting to know patterns are exhibited continuously at various degrees of conduct, from character type to a few particular challenge-orientated talents and performance, such as professional profession and cutting-edge job function. Kolb's model changed into also empirically supported through other studies. In step with Trevino, Lengel, Bodensteiner, Gerloff, and Muir (1990), Kolb's above CE and AC are much like the perceptive vs. judging size measured by way of Myers Briggs Type Indicator (MBTI). The perceptive men and women are predicted to select wealthy media, along with the integrative use of photos, tables, and diagrams, at the same time as the judging people are predicted to choose lean media, including without the integrative use of photos, tables, and diagrams. This could have wide implications in distance schooling.

In addition, this model has proved to be of practical use. just as Tennant (1988) remarked, "frequently of thumb the model offers an incredible framework for making plans teaching and mastering sports and it can be usefully hired as a manual for understanding learning problems, vocational counseling, educational advising and so on". Although Newstead's (1992) take a look at indicated that the reliability of Kolb's mastering styles inventory became low and the underlying component shape became no longer in agreement with what become predicted, a correlation turned into determined between rankings at the energetic/passive (AE-RO) dimension and the scholars' academic overall performance. Therefore, it may be inferred that Kolb's model may be of some diagnostic use in higher education. Furthermore, in line with McCarthy (1980), the Kolb model, as well as the model of brain hemispheric dominance, is a completely vital foundation of the 4MAT curriculum design system applicable for syllabus development in a few establishments.

Wondering styles: constructive, Pessimistic, and Emotional

One of the key avenues of challenge in important and creative questioning is the popularity, acknowledgment, and appreciation of the effect of the human element on the thought process of each character. A broad spectrum of things, consequently, exists bearing a mark on how human beings think. Examples of such elements are lifestyle, emotion, strain, ego, among others. The subject of vital and creative thinking strives to direct the eye of every person at the worthwhile position played by way of these elements in making decisions. This paper analyses, and compares, and contrasts optimistic questioning, pessimistic wondering, and emotional wondering. Positive wondering is the sort of wondering in which someone chooses to align his/her mind at the advantageous aspect of existence irrespective of how gloomy matters appear. Human beings who have optimistic thoughts generally reassure themselves that all is properly in any condition they find themselves. This, of the path, has its benefits and disadvantages. Pessimistic questioning is the alternative to constructive questioning. It refers to a fashion of questioning wherein a character sees the poor side of situations. Inexact and bad conditions, such someone will continually have something to get him/her worried. This obviously has its advantages and drawbacks. One of the blessings is that such someone will be able to assume demanding situations, and plan on how to triumph over them. Emotional thinking is the style of thinking that is driven through what a person feels at a selected factor in time (Martin, 2010, p. 1). For instance, if a person is feeling depressed, this style of thinking will attract thoughts of hopelessness and different associated thoughts. The three thinking styles are largely comparable. One among their similarities is the reality that the three thinking patterns stem from the disposition of the unique person with whom they're associated. As an example, an emotional man or woman is possible to have an emotional questioning style; a pessimistic character is probably to have a pessimistic wondering style even as an optimistic man or woman is in all likelihood to have a positive thinking style. Further to this, emotional and pessimistic wondering styles are possible to have extra bad influences on a character than the positive wondering fashion. that is due to the fact the wondering fashion of someone is a key determinant of the appropriateness and achievement of movements that he/she takes as a way to make a situation higher. The way a person perceives and thinks after succeeding in a sure aspect is also a determinant aspect of destiny fulfillment. Someone with an emotional thinking fashion may as an instance over-rejoice an instance of achievement leading to destiny screw-ups. It's but vital to word that even though the positive questioning style is generally higher compared to the opposite two, it has its weaknesses. A person with an optimistic wondering fashion can also take things with no consideration even as assuming that all can be properly. This will fail a good way to make him/her by using surprise. After repeated screw-ups, such someone might also even increase a poor disposition like being emotional. This will make him/her an emotional philosopher. It's far, consequently, important to notice that tendencies are not static. Therefore, a person may also have greater than one of the 3 wonders styles throughout his/her lifetime.

Creativity

"Creativity is a shape of problem fixing that wishes to be applied in cases in which neither the shape of the solution nor the path to it is clear". Creativity surrounds ordinary life because it is innovation and the ability to learn the unknown. even though creativity and imagination are a need in society, no longer every person can be "creative". certain elements play a function in figuring out whether or not a pupil might be creative; however, those factors might be unpredictable and now not completely assure a baby's imagination. A psychologist has created checks which might be capable of recognizing creativity better and observe imagination. Even though results may be inconsistent, styles have arisen which have interested psychologist seeking to decide what factors into creativity. For instance, intelligence does seem to play a role in creativity; but, there's no clear ratio for someone's intelligence to their creativity, and best a certain amount of intelligence is needed to be innovative. Studies have verified that human beings with intellectual ailments have a better threat of being creative than a person who does not. Studies have also come to decide that scholars in a choose-free and diverse environment multiplied probabilities of having creativity and imagination. Even though creativity gives a tough project of pinning what contributes to the creativity in college students, styles have located that having a mental illness and being exposed to independent surroundings. One of the most mysterious traits of human beings, Creativity is difficult to understand. The common notion is that it belongs to few gifted individuals or the source of incredible portions of labor. The Dictionary defines it as 'the ability to transcend traditional ideas, guidelines, styles, relationships, or the like, and to create meaningful new ideas, paperwork, strategies, interpretations, and many others.; originality, progressiveness, or creativeness', and the phrase root is 'creative', which was first regarded in the 1670s that means "having the exceptional of creating". In this essay, I outline creativity as the "magical" procedure through which the abstract comes into manifestation in bodily form: something that produces the brand new (even though now not significant as per the above definition), inclusive of modifications or transformation to present lives, spheres, domains or nation-states, be them desired or undesired, can be considered an act of creativity. On the subject of psychological creativity, the 'opus' of the person is "the psyche itself", "the awakening of the soul" or, in Psychosynthesis terms, Self-attention: knowing our innovative potential. Creativity, therefore, has a relevant region for Psychosynthesis, for it awakes the relationship to self. on the private stage, this connection allows clients to better impact favored modifications of their lives; for counselors, it's far vital to enable therapists to apply bifocal imaginative and prescient, and regard customers' unmanifest potential.

It's been suggested that creativity has been an evolutionarily propagated part of the human psyche that has allowed them to live to tell the tale and thrive in the global. If that is the case, it'd advocate that creativity, on occasion thought of as a novelty, is simply a critical part of what it way to be human, and that creativity serves a completely vital characteristic in humans' lives. Evolution is in the end a creative undertaking. Darwin (2003) asserted that evolution happens via change, through new ways of being within the world. Creativity is nature's way of developing with original approaches to handling the problems of existence. Assuming that this argument is proper, it might no longer be a great deal of wonder to find out that human psychological health and psychotherapeutic change also are contingent on creativity. Thus, creativity would be a crucial part of the psychotherapeutic system. The following paper outlines a number of the triumphing studies the take a look at creativity and psychotherapy with the reason of suggesting that an exploratory take a look at creativity in psychotherapy could be vital take a look at for the sector of psychology. There had been many definitions of creativity, which shows that the revel in of creativity is subjective and various. Boden (2004) defined creativity as "the ability to give you thoughts or artifacts that are new, unexpected and valuable".

Method of Creativity

Creativity is popping new and inventive ideas into reality. It's the manner of seeing the world in new approaches, to locate hidden patterns. Creativity entails two tactics: thinking, then generating. If you have ideas, however, you don't act on them, you're ingenious however no longer innovative. It's far critical to outline creativity due to the fact it could imply a whole lot of one-of-a-kind approaches to one-of-a-kind human beings. Creativity is knowing the way to disguise your resources, Albert Einstein INNOVATION. Innovation is the utility of creativity to present birth to a brand new idea, product, provider, or technique delivering something new and higher to the arena. While we innovate, we work with the creative ideas we have developed and we exercise. Innovation is not pretty much making new gadgets. We may be progressive in lots of methods. We can make new designs, new ideas, how to lead and inspire people at their quality. "Innovation is creativity with a job to do." - John Emmerling what is the source of creativity and innovation? Innovation relies on creativity. You cannot build without first growing some thoughts. Creativity is the supply of innovation. If we do no longer use our creativity, we can't pick the fine thoughts and positioned them into practice. Every development starts with a concept. Consistent with theorists, the use of case studies has attempted to higher apprehend the sources of creativity and innovation.

The principle of Creativity

Creativity is something that exists and takes place each day but the cause or explanation of this phenomenon continues to be in question. Many psychological theories vicinity the foundation of creativity stemming from the character or through the 'innovative thoughts' they produce. other theories such as those proposed by using psychologist Mihalyi Csikszentmihalyi advise that creativity begins with the interplay of three shaping factors: individual, area, and domain. This essay will first discuss how the character has been visible as the center of the creative method. It'll then talk about how the three primary forces described in Csikszentmihalyi's structure's perspective of creativity present a less psychological method and man or woman-targeted model in change for a confluent system of equally contributing forces. The Ptolemaic view of seeing the person at the center of the innovative process has reduced the level that different factors make contributions to this phenomenon and separated it from the dependent system in which it operates. The problems with a person-centered approach are to locating wherein creativity starts are that people or human beings are constitutions of their surroundings. One should look externally from the individual, "if one wishes to explain why, whilst and in which new ideas or products stand up from and become mounted in a culture."

Creativity and creative questioning

CREATIVITY "Seeing what each person else has visible and wondering what no one else has notion" Einstein and Feynman introduction "creative thinking brings approximately new things; improvements. Creative humans are folks that produce such improvements and the creative procedure include the mental strategies concerned in bringing approximately innovations" (Weisberg, 2006.) Creativity/innovative wondering is an exception that each government/supervisor must own. However, creativity is not only an excellent that any creative man or woman possesses or is not only a concept that may be evolved by way of research. Creativity is innate however no longer all and sundry is blessed with it. A count number of true creativity is developed by using the need for it and those stories main to generate innovative thoughts by the method of getting worried into the one's situations or issues that require you to be innovative. the subsequent phrases via an extremely good innovator of the final century, Isadora Duncan (1930) who developed super dancing patterns simply primarily based on normal activities of going for walks, transferring, skipping and rightly so said- "I wonder what number of adults recognize that via the so-referred to as training- they're giving their children, they are only using them into the common and depriving them of any danger of doing something lovely or authentic" any problem both.

Chapter Nine

Cognitive Neuroscience

Cognitive neuroscience is the sphere of having a look at which specializes in the neural substrates of mental processes. It's at the intersection of psychology and neuroscience, however also overlaps with physiological psychology, cognitive psychology, and neuropsychology. It combines the theories of cognitive psychology and computational modeling with experimental facts about the brain. Cognitive neuroscience is one of the maximum dynamic regions of relevance for expertise in the way people assume, sense, act, and react in real existence. It's an interdisciplinary vicinity of research that mixes the dimension of brain interest (in most cases by neuroimaging) with the simultaneous performance of cognitive duties by using human topics. Those investigations had been a success within the challenge of connecting the sciences of the mind (Neurosciences) and the sciences of the mind (Cognitive Sciences). Advances in this type of study provide a map of the localization of cognitive functions within the human mind. Do those outcomes help us to understand how the mind pertains to the brain? In my view, the consequences obtained via the Cognitive Neurosciences result in new investigations in the domain of Molecular Neurobiology, aimed toward discovering biophysical mechanisms that generate the pastime measured through neuroimaging devices. In this context, I argue that the understanding of the way ionic/molecular processes aid cognition and awareness cannot be made by the usual reductionist factors. Information of ionic/molecular mechanisms can contribute our information of the human mind so long as we assume an opportunity shape of explanation, based on psycho-physical similarities, together with an ontological view of mentality and spirituality as embedded in bodily nature (and no longer outside nature, as regularly assumed in western culture).

Cognitive neuroscience investigates the emergence of cognitive features from the physical and chemical pastime of neurons inside the mind. Active representations in the mind include styles of neural hobby, processing takes vicinity through the propagation of interest thru excitatory and inhibitory connections, and mastering and reminiscence get up ordinarily through the change of connections. The organization of cognitive processing within the brain is an issue of a few debate, with some investigators arguing that particular brain areas perform wonderfully, encapsulated processing operations whilst others propose that every place contributes in a particular manner to a disbursed, interactive technique. numerous techniques contribute to the area, along with an examination of the outcomes of lesions on cognitive capabilities in human beings and animals, a study of neuronal activity throughout cognitive tactics through single- and multielectrode recordings, look at of human purposeful mind interest the usage of non-invasive methods together with fMRI and pet, and use of computational models to formalize specific hypotheses approximately the underlying mechanisms. Many of those strategies have emerged inside the Nineteen Eighties and 1990s, and they are in all likelihood to remain more desirable and extended inside the coming years. For that reason, in addition, breakthroughs in our knowledge of the neural foundation of cognition are probable. Cognitive neuroscience seeks to use observations from the have a look at the mind to assist unravel the mechanisms of the mind. How do the chemical and electric signals produced by using neurons within the brain provide upward thrust to cognitive processes, which include perception, reminiscence, expertise, insight, and reasoning? How is understanding—which includes an explicit understanding of items and activities in the global and in a single's very own personal history, as well as implicit know-how underlying acquired capabilities including professional overall performance and language—represented within the bodily structure of the mind, and how is it accessed and used in the concept, belief, and movement? Those are a number of the central questions addressed via the sphere of cognitive Neuroscience. It combines the experimental strategies of cognitive psychology with numerous strategies to clearly examine how brain function helps mental sports. Main this research in everyday people is the new strategies of useful mind imaging: positron emission tomography (pet) and magnetic resonance imaging (MRI). The roots of these techniques are traced to the century-long take a look at blood drift to the brain. For destiny, the hope is to mix the spatial size of responses captured with functional MRI with the temporal size provided by using encephalography (EEC) or magnetoencephalography (MEG).

Cognitive neuroscience strategies may be divided into two

important categories. Size techniques, as the call implies, degree modifications in mind function whilst a research player (human or animal) engages in some cognitive interest. a typical neuroeconomic experiment the use of a measurement technique might require the participant to make a chain of easy choices even as the researchers document changes in neuronal firing or metabolic hobby that could fluctuate between, say, better-value or decrease-cost selections. dimension techniques are frequently described (every so often derisively) as being "correlational" due to the fact they can show that indicators from a brain area co-occur with a feature of interest, but they can't display that a location is essential for that function. Manipulation strategies, in contrast, have a look at how perturbations of the brain's characteristic – either using transiently changing neuronal firing charges or neurotransmitter stages or by way of permanently unfavorable tissue – change cognitive features or conduct. As a consequence, manipulation techniques are on occasion known as causal processes. Neuroeconomics has used manipulation techniques to disrupt processing in precise areas, which in turn alters the alternatives people make (e.g., in interactive video games).

This chapter follows this basic department, first introducing strategies that degree modifications in brain characteristics which tune the variables inside selection fashions, then thinking about techniques that trade neural processing and also choice behaviors. It is important to apprehend that dimension and manipulation techniques provide distinct and complementary records about mind characteristics. Cognitive neuroscience studies progress faster when measurement techniques set up links among brain structure and cognitive characteristics after which manipulation strategies probe that dating to enhance inferences and models.

Unsupervised learning algorithms are used to organize cases based on similar attributes. These fashions are also called self-organizing maps. Unsupervised models encompass clustering techniques and neural networks. Distinct algorithms use exceptional strategies for dividing information into agencies. Some methods are rather honest, fast dividing the instances into companies based on common attributes or some different similarity. The two-Step clustering technique differs somewhat in that the most fulfilling number of clusters is determined in a preliminary skip via the facts, primarily based on certain statistical criteria. Institution undertaking is then made on a second bypass through the facts; hence the call "-Step." Neural networks are greater complex than a number of the opposite unsupervised studying algorithms and can yield results that can be tough to interpret.

For so long as I can remember, I have been interested in technological know-how and the wonders of the universe. From stargazing outdoor with the homemade telescope that my father and that I built to the absolute awe that I enjoy whilst taking into account the vastness of the cosmos and the subtle elegance of nature, I have been addicted to technology from the start.

For the duration of university, I started to awareness my hobby on neuroscience and the brain. What an excellent gadget! The certainly exceptional aspect about all of this, even though, is that every one of those recollections, such as their related attractions, smells, and sounds, reside in a mass of biological fabric sitting among my ears that essentially has settings: on and off. Some would possibly argue that neuromodulators and different similar entities complicate the state of affairs incredibly, but the backside line is that neurons, the primary additives of our brains, are both on or they're off. As a laptop, it is this aggregate of "on" and "off," the interconnectedness of those easy elements, and the associated parallel processing that offers us the complexity of what we recognize to be brain features.

Even as I do not necessarily maintain the conviction with Descartes that the seat of my soul is living someplace at the base of my brain, I do realize that everything from subconscious sports like respiration to my choice for the coloration green sits up there with rarely a conscious idea from me. More to the point, I understand that the individual variations that make the world so exciting, as well as the similarities both between and inside people and their behaviors that allow me to do my process as a behavioral scientist, also live in this neural computer.

Analysts spend a considerable amount of time looking to categorize and model the complexities of human behaviors. This practice is complex even in addition for crime analysts due to the fact the behaviors being modeled differ in a few ways from "regular" behaviors, if handiest for the cause that it's far unlawful. In extra, criminal behaviors tends to be relatively infrequent and are something that maximum oldsters have restricted experience with outdoor of the general public safety and security worlds. The potential to reduce these behaviors to styles and trends that may be now not most effectively defined however even predicted or expected in some situations still amazes me because it says a lot about human nature as it does about analysis. in lots of methods, predictive analytics and synthetic intelligence are charming in their strength and complexity, however possibly the real wonder is the reality that human behaviors can even be modeled and predicted in any respect. Cognitive neuroscience research largely implies that human mathematical skills are rooted in nonverbal mechanisms. It is accordingly particularly paradoxical that there seems to be a hyperlink between the development of arithmetic and studying capabilities in children. The aim of this bankruptcy become to offer an outline of two viable reasons for this hyperlink and confront those causes to available proof from developmental cognitive neuroscience.

First, the triple-code version indicates that solutions of the maximum acquainted mathematics statistics can be increasingly more retrieved from verbal-phonological codes as individuals turn out to be fluent. But, developmental cognitive neuroscience studies provide restrained proof for this assumption. One look shows that increases in pastime can be determined in the left temporal cortex as children become increasingly more gifted with single-digit multiplication problems, but this effect appears to be challenge-dependent. The contribution of verbal-phonological mechanisms to mathematics studying can also for this reason be restrained to facts that are explicitly discovered with the aid of rote in school.

Second, it has been proposed that gaining knowledge of arithmetic and learning to read might also each depend upon the automatization of policies and tactics. Procedural reminiscence systems can also hence be critical to the acquisition of both abilities, and impairments in procedural reminiscence can be at the source of each dyscalculia and dyslexia. not most effective does that hypothesis explain why one of the maximum regular results obtained in developmental neuroimaging studies is a boom of interest in the parietal cortex (as opposed to in the left temporoparietal cortex) however additionally it highlights the significance of procedural reminiscence for arithmetic learning. Due to the fact procedural reminiscence has long been hypothesized to also be vital to analyzing acquisition. This concept may additionally explain the link between mathematics and analyzing acquisition and the comorbidity among dyslexia and dyscalculia.

Overall, given the limited neurodevelopmental help for the concept that verbal-phonological processing underlies mathematics getting to know in children, the procedural speculation is an exciting reason behind the hyperlink among arithmetic and studying talents. Of course, this does not mean that other area-well-known factors can't additionally account for that link in a few children. As an instance, it's far clean that each mathematics and studying duties contain working memory, interest, or cognitive control. It's viable that disruptions in these area-trendy mechanisms can also cause each analyzing and mathematics impairments in kids (in addition to impairments in different abilities). That is normally constant with the idea that arithmetic getting to know includes an extensive variety of abilities and that dyscalculia can be a heterogeneous disease. Nevertheless, studying to examine and getting to know arithmetic might also both vicinity crucial needs on procedural reminiscence and automatization of capabilities, an element which can explain a huge part of the connection between arithmetic and studying overall performance in kids.

Cognitive neuroscience has made great development at the neural basis of perceptual selection making, see Gold and Shadlen (2007), in addition to cost-based totally choice-making, see Glimcher et al. (2005). fashions of selection making primarily based in large part on unmarried cell firing in monkeys assume that neurons encode a sequential chance ratio test, see Wald and Wolfowitz (1948), to statistically decide among competing hypotheses. Inside this framework, blended techniques can be defined at the extent of neuronal noise, Hayden et al. (2007), even though how noise biases chances toward gold standard strategies are much less understood. It's far even much less clean how those fashions of selection-making must be prolonged to games related to different humans.

While a person evaluates a sports tree they make selections which they expect will bring about a favored payoff aim. One approach to solving this problem is to depend on reinforcement getting to know, alone as calculated by way of the QRE of the sport. Such an approach is parsimonious and might most effective involve the goal-directed mastering parts of the brain, this is, the ventral and dorsal striatum, together with a technique for encoding strategies, most probably within the prefrontal cortex, and their payoff equivalents, for instance in pre-motor regions of the mind and the lateral intraparietal location, or other parietal areas encoding anticipated software maps see Montaguc et al. (2006). But, one problem with this method is the exceptionally long lengths of time it'd take humans to research the QRE of the sport. So necessary additions to a reinforcement mastering concept of sports playing would be numerous mechanisms for sharing intellectual states that could enhance the brain desire of an initial method and allow the mind to as should be weighed statistics and update desires to extra quickly study its pleasant strategic picks.

Preliminary techniques are probable to be selected primarily based on an examination of payoffs leading to a goal set.

Results of physical pastime at the Cerebral Networks

Cognitive neuroscience addresses age's effect on extraordinary cognitive features. Nowadays, the leap forward in this area is related to the purpose of organizing the extraordinarily complex network of mind areas implicated and the way they've changed with the aid of the growing older process, the kind of mission and pathologies like dementia. For this reason, integrity and deterioration of purposeful connectivity between brain areas associated with processes like language, attention, or memory are assessed. Numerous authors have studied structural connectivity in white count number pathways to check the integrity of anatomical connections, which underlies the verbal exchange among the nodes of these useful networks. It has been discovered that numerous networks guide exclusive capabilities such as sensory, motor, government, reminiscence, or language features. Neuroimaging techniques like practical magnetic resonance (fMRI) and magnetoencephalography allow the assessment of these cerebral networks in specific duties and the characterization of age-associated adjustments.

Recent research confirmed how episodic reminiscence is related to, besides areas from the medial temporal lobe

(MTL), an entire machine of mind regions associated with the default mode community. In an equal manner, interest research in the aged population showed that this cognitive function is broken, as they discovered a lower in visible precision and a better vulnerability to distraction from relevant records. Three distinct networks had been described in interest: alerting community, orienting network, and executive manages the network. The alerting community lets in to keep an alert nation and to express a particular response facing a specific stimulus. The underlying neurobiological substrates are parietal and frontal regions. The orienting community refers to the choice of facts from different sensory modalities, where parietal advanced lobe and frontal eyes fields are concerned. Subsequently, the government network includes the prefrontal cortex and the cingulate anterior cortex. Taking this complete functional connectivity into account, Zhou et al. (2011) display that there are great differences among young, center-elderly, and older Chinese adults, especially in the government manipulate the network. But, the age effect on alerting and orienting networks is subtle or nonexistent, respectively. it has been discovered that the prefrontal cortex, anterior cingulate cortex, and hippocampal areas are significantly damaged in getting older, so it seems that both government control and alerting networks are liable to the getting older procedure.

One of the mind networks that has acquired the most interest in the latest years is the so referred to as DMN defined as the group of brain regions which can be energetic at some point of resting states and inactive at some point of the execution of any aim-directed assignment. The resting nation occurs experimentally when the issue is asked to avoid falling asleep and reflect on consideration on something particularly. most of the instances, those studies of functional connectivity are based on neuroimaging techniques like fMRI, which have shown that the DMN consists of the medial prefrontal cortex, the posterior cingulate cortex, the retrosplenial cortex, and numerous hippocampal regions.

An expansion of adjustments has been found in aging-associated practical connectivity. The loss of contacts induces disconnection between DMN nodes, which is associated with cognitive decline, which in turn has been related to an impairment in purposeful connectivity in the course of the primary brain networks. However, Campbell et al. (2013) do not forget that, at some point of aging, there's the maintenance of the connectivity among the main DMN mind regions. No differences were found among older and younger topics on medial temporal lobe (MTL) areas, but aged topics confirmed weaker connectivity in subsystems which includes ventral posterior cingulate cortex and dorsomedial prefrontal cortex, however stronger connectivity inside the dorsal posterior cingulate cortex. Those authors maintain the idea that this better practical connectivity could be due to a larger influx of records from sensory regions to MTL areas, which could be generating greater problems to delete besides the point statistics in elderly people. This will favor interference and impair the memorization of the latest statistics. When appearing on a mission, elders display hyperactivation of prefrontal regions, associated with functional repayment responses that allow a successful venture execution.

Concerning statistics analysis, multivariate analysis strategies are one of the quality equipment in assessing and figuring out purposeful connectivity. Functional connectivity is established through the connection among exceptional brain areas participating in a selected moment facing a selected state of affairs. Thereby, whilst our pursuits are focused on detecting variations between groups submitted to specific remedies, ANOVA-derived strategies (evaluation of variance) in its distinct versions (intrafactor, interactor, blended) are a conventional useful device. on this context, and taking into consideration that we normally manage more than one measured variables, we can cross a touch in addition within the evaluation with the aid of the usage of a multivariate perspective and incorporating strategies which includes the multivariate analysis of variance (MANOVA) or the Discriminant analysis. most of the research about the brain growing older doesn't forget that we have to awareness not only in some precise brain areas, however in establishing practical networks by using searching out the regions of which pastime covariates during a specific undertaking. Correlation-primarily based techniques are the maximum generally used and, as we normally work with a high variety of brain regions implicated, the multivariate technique is optimal again. We can use applications of structural equation modeling, like most important aspect analysis, a couple of regression and canonical correlation (McIntosh and Gonzalez-Lima, 1994), or partial factor analysis. inside the closing many years, the utility of partial least squares (PLS) evaluation of neuroimaging data has received loads of reputation. PLS also form a part of structural equation modeling, but they avoid a number of the standard issues related to this area, consisting of collinearity, small pattern size, excessive variety of variables, or the presence of misplaced values. Due to that, they allow us to observe institutions among remedy companies and brain interest. Those evaluation strategies had been spreading currently to animal model-based studies, in which early-expression markers of neuronal activation inclusive of c-Fos or functional hobby mapping are used. Studies by Sampedro-Piquero et al. (2013) showed the benefits in neuronal metabolic activity of forced exercise in aged rats by the use of the Rotarod apparatus. Rats subjected to a 6-week exercising program confirmed less power intake in brain areas associated with spatial reference memory, which has been associated with higher overall performance in a spatial undertaking.

Gaining knowledge of and memory

The cognitive neuroscience of memory arguably started with Herbert Scoville and Brenda Milner's (1957) report of a reminiscence disease in HM after bilateral removal of his medial temporal lobes to manipulate excessive epileptic seizures. as a result of head harm from a bicycle collision whilst he became a younger boy, HM changed into beset with epileptic fits that multiplied in frequency and severity into his late 20s. As a remedy for the closing of the hotel, Scoville completed an operation in which he removed tissue in and around the hippocampus on each facet of HM's mind. Whilst the surgical procedure decreased HM's seizures, it had a profound and unexpected effect on his reminiscence. This result changed into the unknown at the time, and Scoville would absolutely have modified the system had he recognized this harmful result. The record of HM's case by way of Scoville and Brenda Milner (1957) became the primary to demonstrate immediately the significance of the hippocampus and surrounding systems for memory. Latest advances in cognitive neuroscience and progress in neuroimaging have noticeably changed our know-how of the neural mechanisms underlying human perceptual, cognitive, and motor functioning. Those findings are of tremendous significance for applied medical disciplines involved with the evaluation of human performance. for the reason that early 2000s, Neuroergonomics, the intersection of Neuroscience, Cognitive Engineering, and Human factors, proposes to observe the mind mechanisms and underlying human-technology interplay in increasingly more naturalistic settings representative of work and regular-lifestyles situations. The goal of merging these disciplines right into an unmarried discipline of research is to encourage move-fertilization and to offer new gear at the epistemological, methodological, and technical levels. This approach is called Neuroergonomics.

The difference between visual attention and cognizance: A Cognitive Neuroscience attitude

From the cognitive neuroscience perspective, a clear distinction may be made between attention and attention. Attentional selection is how sensorimotor processing is modified using the modern state of the neural network, shaped by using genetic elements, revel in, and current events (reminiscence). Phenomenal experience has a unique origin, that's the recurrent interplay among groups of neurons. Depending on the extent to which recurrent interactions between visible areas contain interactions with action- or memory-associated areas, awareness evolves from extraordinary to get admission to cognizance. Whether this takes place relies upon attentional selection mechanisms, through effects on both the feed-forward sweep and recurrent interactions. Different mechanisms, but, decide whether or not neurons will have interaction in recurrent interactions in any respect and, therefore, whether processing will cross from subconscious to an aware country.

Aware stimuli have reached a level of processing past preliminary function detection, where at the least an initial coherent perceptual interpretation of the scene is done. Whether or not at this degree the binding hassle, in all its range, has been solved isn't always clean but. The binding of a few features of an item, which include its color and shape, may additionally require interest, at the same time as different feature combos are detected attentively. So it can be that the conscious stage before interest has been allocated, includes tentatively certain features and surfaces, comparable to midlevel imaginative and prescient or the two.5D cartoon. There's a clear distinction, but, with subconscious tiers, wherein individual features, even capabilities that are never perceived, are represented.

The hypothesis forms the core know-how of the distinctive types of recognition, in the same spirit as we've middle understandings of sensorimotor modifications, memory, and attentional selection. Again, many stuff nevertheless wants to be labored out, the most vital being of the route to explain why recurrent interactions are essential for extra special revel in to stand up, and how we move from the sort of neural process to the phenomenon of intellectual enjoy. In that experience, the "tough trouble" stays as hard because it changed into. With this idea, however, we may also have a higher feel of what to look for.

Philosophy and Cognitive Neuroscience Psychology

Trends in psychological idea practice frequently parallel advances made in a generation. as an example, Robins et al. have documented the (successive) "virtual dying" of psychoanalysis, the upward thrust and severe decline of behaviorism, the emergence and huge ascent of cognitive psychology (the "cognitive revolution"), and the start of the upward thrust in neuroscience in the final century in the discipline of clinical psychology by myself – which can be seen to reflect technological advances. especially, as Tracy et al. (2003) well known, the cognitive revolution of the 1970s turned into pushed largely using the pc revolution – transferring its foundational theories of successive/linear statistics processing and practical modularity from system to mind. in step with Bechtel et al. (2001) the metaphor of the brain as information processor first came about within the Nineteen Fifties to subsequently grow to be cognitive science and then, with the emergence of neuroscience, and the appearance of neuro-imaging technology, came the expected move-cutting of the taxonomies of neuroscience and cognitive technology (Fodor, 1975) to sooner or later give upward push to cognitive neuroscience in the eighty's – worried with how cerebral approaches underlie cognitive programs. With the nineties came the "decade of the brain" and with the start of the 21st century, there could absolutely seem to be a preoccupation with neuroanatomy – wherein most of the people of cognition-primarily based studies emerge coupled with some form of neuroanatomical reference (Lake, 2007). Certainly, this could be seen to mirror the arrival of neuroimaging technology together with fMRI; arguably the maximum distinguished tool in cognitive neuroscience, invented in 1990. for the reason that then fMRI studies on my own have explosively multiplied, from simply 15 being published in 1991 to two, being posted in 2003 by myself; with there now being at the least 30-40 fMRI studies emerging weekly certainly, in which Kuhn (1970) has mentioned how clinical paradigms compete with one another till the constrained ability skills of 1 succumb to the riper possibilities of another, Rand & Ilardi (2005) have emphasized that technological advancements serve as fortifications for the boom and maturation of particular paradigms and their substitute of others. As an instance, Galileo's implementation of the telescope facilitated the arrival of a brand new technological know-how in an equal manner the improvement of the laptop functioned in cognitive science's overtaking of behaviorism as the most important paradigm in psychology. Likewise, the advent of neuroimaging and its coupling with cognitive technology may be visible as providing the pressure which inaugurated the cognitive neuroscience paradigm that's presently main. 'Cognitivism' arose in response to the insufficiencies of behaviorism. Behaviourism – itself a reaction to in advance colleges which employed introspectionist (deemed too unreliable because of its subjectivity), dealing with the mind as a 'black box'; handiest accounting for entering stimuli and output, observable behavior. The cognitive sciences as such emerged to address this 'black field' issue thru the implementation of a computational approach. The roots of this technique, says some authors lies within the eighteenth-century work through LaMettrie ('guy as device') from which the fundamental characterization of guy as being akin to a clockwork mechanism turned into drawingthe . no matter the several other metaphors LaMettrie used, it became this man-as-mechanism that caught; presenting impetus for the Enlightenment-era idea that underlying human behavior has been undying laws and rules. While taking metaphors rooted in technological advances can be beneficial; facilitating new insight, an inherent hazard lies in taking such metaphors actually. Mainly there is a twofold chance: reification (taking the summary to be a concrete reality) and assuming isomorphism among both referents of the metaphor (i.e. that all characteristics of every referent are the same e.g. man = gadget). Indeed with this is the concern that needs to we class computer as a questioning system (i.e. artificially wise) we in a roundabout way infer thinking-guy as a computer – as such, dehumanizing man while personifying device. As an alternative astoundingly, however, a few authors have without a doubt endorsed taking the computational metaphor actually (i.e. Plyshyn), claiming that treating it as an easy heuristic metaphor allows too many views and thereby obstructs progress. What Plyshyn here overlooks is that treating a metaphorical association actually can also impede progress – as being overly zealous in one precise paradigmatic method can near a one-off to new opportunities or avenues of investigation (MacCormack, 1984). Arguably, however, the laptop metaphor is taken literally in lots of practical time's i.e. biological psychiatry, precluding many intrinsically critical facets of what having a mind includes – i.e. subjectivity, intentionality, and many others.

As such, we can see that due to such inadequacies of the staunch cognitive clinical approach; and how it's branched into cognitive neuroscience and turn out to be more and more enmeshed with neuro-anatomical research, numerous authors are calling for a return to phenomenology (i.e. Shear, 1996) to deal with the problems the cognitive neurosciences have resurrected. certainly, as Mishara et al. (1998) have talked about, debates inside the philosophy of thoughts and cognitive sciences have begun to enchantment to theories of awareness as a way of highlighting the insufficiencies of the greater popular fashions of mind (i.e. mind as pc). 'Embodied' and/or 'enactive' cognition especially has grown to be a crucial angle on this reconciliation of attention and cognition. As such, we can outline 3 main procedures to cognition – symbolicism (or classical computationalism), connectionism, and dynamics (Eliasmith, 2005) which have been informing neuroscientific research. The rest of this essay aims to outline how numerous criticisms fueled through troubles inside the philosophy of thoughts & technology highlight the caution that ought to be taken whilst using the computational metaphor and further integrating experimental results from cognitive neuroscience into theories of thoughts. Inside the first instance, criticisms of the fundamental computational model of thoughts will be sampled. For issues of the area, dialogue concerning connectionism and dynamism-based totally methods will not be undertaken. The preferential remedy of computationalism is justified (I trust) insomuch that it is nevertheless one of the greater predominantly used models of cognition. Following this, the problematic problems regarding the implementation of neuroimaging 'evidence' to espouse paradigms inside the subject of technology could be highlighted. Consequently, it will be concluded that at the same time as cognitive neuroscience has excellent potential for unifying the field of psychology it could also be applied to propound specific viewpoints, jogging the hazard of undermining others and the lived experience of the human individual. The 'classical' computational approach involved the convergence of three main fields of research; artificial intelligence (AI), cognitive psychology, and linguistics. namely, the essential principles of AI research: claiming that intelligence changed into the managing/manipulation of symbol strings, cognitive psychology: modeling human cognitive methods at the operation of computer systems, and linguistics: which informed that units of regulations govern (semantic) operations within the mind, had been assimilated to broaden a "laptop among ears" or "representational-computational" view of the thoughts. This 'classical' view of the thoughts changed into summated by way of Fodor who provided the Language of idea hypothesis which claimed that we suppose in the language of the notion – a machine of symbols with semantic and syntactic properties, manifested by the structural layout of the brain. Such symbols are intrinsically representational neural occasions. whilst the computational technique isn't explicitly reductionistic, insomuch that questioning + mind feature integrates to instantiate computation, as hardware and software do; as I can presently allude to, this approach re-introduces a Cartesian dualism which itself reasons troubles. The computational gadget is characterized as constituted by sets of tokens for which units of guidelines govern association and/or transfiguration into other sets of tokens. Two of the primary criticisms leveled at the classical technique have been the symbol grounding trouble and the Chinese language Room argument. The essence of both these arguments refers back to the inherent hassle of particular degrees of reductionism in operation inside the computational paradigm which inherently throws away intentionality however resultantly re-introduces the Cartesian dichotomy and the 'difficult' trouble of consciousness. Explicitly, it's tough to envision how the computational gadget is familiar with and learns at an extrinsic stage. The input-procedure-output system, says Searle, surely cannot be "empirically aware". Other criticisms of computationalism are that its processing is primarily based on linear mechanisms – a dramatic obstacle considering the complexity of certain obligations- and that malfunction on the symbol-level includes entire abrupt disruption of strategies – in contrast to the "sleek degradation" that absolutely appears to arise inside the mind. Is also the inadequacy of advanced AI to acquire and preserve "common-experience" expertise (i.e. the frame trouble). In the end, is that its emphasis on rule-ruled symbol manipulation simply isn't biologically workable.

Therefore, while paradigmatic packages of computational standards often "in shape" with the mind (explaining their persisted popularity despite criticisms) they unavoidably push aside the ones additives of intellectual life which are "non-computable". It is these components that pose the largest task to (cognitive-) neuroscientific primarily based idea/research today. The "tough" problem of mind/attention plagues the rigid cognitive (neuro-) sciences insomuch that there exists a subjective element of awareness that is going beyond any materialist explanation of functions. Although this has been critically debated someplace else, it'd appear that any attempts to exclude subjectivity genuinely lead to its surreptitious re-front through the lower back door. For instance, the debts of the one which method thoughts and mind in basic terms reductionistic/eliminativist terms (i.e. in which subjective revel in is a trifling byproduct of mind mechanisms in action) in a feel customize cerebral components by way of granting them traits generally indicative of whole human competencies i.e. "studying" "perceiving" etc. Stapp (2008) comprehensively decomposes the problem insomuch that the difference between intrinsic and extrinsic description renders it inadequate. Particularly, should the brain be a machine of parallel computer processors (or the aggregate total of a variety of uniquely practical organic components), an intrinsic description details each processor as producing a selected unit of data (i.e. like a television set generating pixels)? The extrinsic description, conversely, is likened to that which an outside viewer of the TV set sees – i.e. now not individual pixels however a sum overall photograph. The laptop version cannot account for both intrinsic and extrinsic ranges of description without implicit attraction to meta-representational "ghosts within the machine" or homunculi and consequently implicitly re-introduce a Cartesian cut up. one of the most powerful re-interpretations (for my part) of this latter problem has been furnished by using Dennett (1978) who espouses a "navy of homunculi" method, in which a hierarchy of homunculi of lowering complexity/intelligence exist with the most basic strategies at the bottom. This is similar to a connectionist or 'Parallel distributed Processing' technique and suffices it to mention has been criticized itself. further to this charges of reductionism and/or dualism, with cognitive psychology's convergence with neuroscience to come to be cognitive neuroscience; a secondary supply of contention arises – specifically, inside cognitive neuroscience is the tendency to map cognitive strategies straight onto mind states or, even extra problematically, localize them to unique mind areas. The latter authors have attributed this "taking [of] phrenology within the head" to three particular actions inside psychology in the main: 1) the impetus evolutionary psychology and its concept of modular functioning provided for neurosciences to locate modules of a specific feature in the mind 2) renewed hobby in mechanistic explanations of thoughts and brain and 3) the emergence of cognitive neuroscience and the implementation of neuro-imaging strategies. the largest hassle with localization of tactics says the authors, is brain plasticity and the concordant multi-capability it offers neural components. Certainly attempting to find the function of 'anyone's cerebral area appears needless considering that the same vicinity would possibly perform several factors depending on what else is taking region within the mind. On a related point, the computational method has been criticized insomuch that it can perform only in phrases of static, discrete entities (i.e. symbols) that could simplest reliably to implemented to static, discrete realities and, by extent, static, discrete cerebral 'hardware'. Whilst it offers nicely with systematicity and productiveness, its 'crude' input-manner-output formulization belies trouble in accounting for the unendingly interactive and reciprocal nature of the connection between cognition, the body, and the environment. Further, as I referenced above, the mind is something however a static organ – as an alternative,, it's far dynamic, with multitudes of overlapping neural networks, and high levels of plasticity.

Notwithstanding the criticisms which have been leveled at these approaches to cognitive tactics, consequences from neuro-imaging technologies have the propensity to be used as a manner of aid for the reductionistic-computational money owed of free will, autonomy, self, and the whole thing such ideas entail (i.e. cognizance, lived to enjoy and so forth.). The use of neuroimaging technologies as evidence for localization, however, or reductionism, isn't as valid as might be the first concept.

Indeed, consequences from neuroimaging are often handled as though they are "photos of the mind", and are dealt with as objective sources of evidence regarding how the mind operates as regards overall performance in cognitive duties. McCabe and Castel (2008) have validated that mind pix have a considerably powerful effect on judgments of the validity of the scientific proof. Especially they determined that the presence of a mind photo (i.e. over a bar chart) extensively extended contributors' willingness to accept as true with the conclusions of the thing. on this experience we can get a hint of how such a way might be implicated, perhaps unintentionally, to propound objective validation of a particular paradigm, regularly undermining the totality of lived enjoy. To discover this factor further I'm able to now, in brief, define some of the criticisms of this belief of neuro-imaging as capable of presenting objective evidence.

Considering neuroimages as "snapshots of the brain" is an alternative inapt analogy as Roskies (2007) discusses. Particularly, treating neuro-pictures as an 'evidential medium' inside the way we deal with pics is an analogical misnomer in that they most effectively indirectly measure mind activity – they degree "the timescale of the de-phasing of water molecules inside the brain, [and no longer neural pastime]". The final pics which can be implemented in research and articles, which show elements of the mind as "lights-up"/activating, are in reality pc reconstructions of the actual information generated by way of the fMRI test and related null hypothesis importance checks (NHSTs) carried out on every region of the mind (voxels) – which facilitate the era of "statistical parametric maps" (SPM) splendid- imposed on the obtained photographs of the mind. Within the manner wherein the techniques are indirect measures, epistemic challenges may be posed.

At the sensible stage, as Bechtel & Stufflebeam (2001) define, a number of the epistemic challenges (i.e. are results artifacts of the method itself or genuine portions of freestanding, dependable records?) can be summated to consist of a lack of ecological validity and an assumption of religion in the cognitive decomposition-challenge. The former regards the novelty of the state of affairs – mendacity horizontal & closing motionless in a darkened, constrained space. This implies trouble in reliably judging the relevance of neuroimaging facts to real-life cognition – in which it's far noticeably fantastic that such regulations would exist.

The latter of Bechtel & Stufflebeam's challenges regards

the religion the experimenter places within the cognitive mission implemented within the experimental placing. Particularly it needs to be insured that the project genuinely draws upon the processes which one desires to research. Certainly, the modeling of many such processes and tasks comes from cognitive psychology and its primary computational model; which itself is extensively debated and contested (as formerly mentioned), in particular with the aid of the ones fashions of cognition which draw on dynamic structures principle and non-linear processing paradigms. As such, as the authors contend, any imaging study is simplest as right as those assumptions which it is primarily based upon.

While questions have additionally been raised regarding the terrible reliability of neuroimaging throughout research, extra problematically are those theoretical and conceptual problems that lie at the center of the generation itself and not just merely in its realistic software. Klein's (2009) exegesis of the underpinnings of how fMRI technology operates is a clear expression of how inherently difficult the usage of neuroimages as evidential statistics is. Especially, the fact that fMRIs do not show with no trouble interpretable photos of sign variations within the mind but alternatively they display an amalgamation of the areas for which there was found to be a statistically massive difference in signal among challenge situations illustrates a source of contention. Especially, since neuroimaging facts are the result of heaps of simultaneous null speculation assessments they inherit the many conceptual troubles inherent in the NHST method.

Indeed, one of the essential problems with neuroimaging consequences is the result of the 'causal density of the brain. Any and each mission could have considerable consequences at the mind – however, fMRI will no longer display those as, for a large part, those consequences may be small and functionally insignificant (in the statistical experience). Though, the reality that they arise is a crucial point – they might be vital for the cognitive process' instantiation. That is relatively similar to the problems of arbitrary thresholds and vague alternatives Klein (2009) similarly describes. especially, concerning the former factor, the "activation" of cerebral places that we see in neuroimages are based on the choice of an alpha level of significance however this choice is alternatively arbitrary; should we be conservative in our choice. Then only a few regions will seem to "prompt". in the meantime a more liberal desire of alpha degree will result in much more activation apparent across the mind. a far cited study using Haxby et al. (2001) as an example has proven that prediction of object magnificence being perceived i.e. a house or a face, can be reliably ascertained thru analysis of styles of activation that arise underneath the edge for significance with the exclusion of those regions displaying tremendous activation (i.e. the Fusiform Face area in face belief). As such, many areas now not found out by neuroimages may be gambling an essential purposeful position in the methods beneath investigation.

in addition, so far is that excessive activation in an area does not equate to an essential practical position; it would truly be a derivative of the cognitive manner and not particularly indicative of a vital and sufficient circumstance for stated specific cognitive system. for instance, research has shown that while enormous hippocampal activation happens at some stage in delay classical conditioning strategies, hippocampal lesions do no longer disrupt this function. Furthermore, one of the maximum simple points is that imaging studies aren't based on causal connections – alternatively, they will simplest reveal probabilistic covariance, an elicitation of the properly-worn adage "correlation does no longer imply causation".

As such, even as cognitive neuroscience has first-rate potential to reconcile the many factions of disjointed psychology – linking biology to the concept, it conversely can be used to propound certain paradigms over others, inappropriately so. The strategies of neuroimaging aren't infallible resources of objective finalists proof; as a substitute, they inhere a diploma of interpretation and feature several practical and conceptual limitations.

Therefore, in end, where the computational version drives cognitive neuroscientific studies, we ought to be cautious in our use of the metaphor of mind-as-laptop lest it is reified and constrain progress (a type of "prison house of perspective"). further, whilst reductionism is a necessity for development (Brendel, 2003) i.e. a bottom-up method, we need to stay wary of eliminativism in the sense that just due to the fact records from cognitive neuroscience (i.e. neuroimages) cannot account for the likes of the totality of lived experience (i.e. intentionality, subjectivity) does now not necessarily infer that they're mere, insubstantial via-merchandise of neural pastime. Most significantly is that warning is exerted within the interpretation and assimilation of results, specifically when it comes to applying them nearly (i.e. inside the medical remedy of psychopathology). In this way, as Rand & Ilandi (2005) attest, while cognitive neuroscience can reconcile the technology of psychology and decrease-order natural technology domain names; its different programs have to be approached prudently.

Chapter Ten

Learning and Developmental Disabilities

Cognition refers, quite honestly, to questioning. There are the obvious programs of conscious reasoning doing taxes, playing chess, deconstructing Macbeth—however concept takes much subtler bureaucracies, inclusive of interpreting sensory enter, guiding physical movements, and empathizing with others. The vintage metaphor for human cognition became the pc a logical records-processing gadget. You may spell cognition without the "cog." yet even as some of our minds can be binary, there is a lot greater to our "wetware" than zeros and ones. Research on cognition focuses now not simply on thinking, however additionally on attention, and the introduction and storage of reminiscences, expertise acquisition and retention, language learning, and logical reasoning. As humans advantage new experiences, their cognition can alternate in subtle however effective approaches. The greatest divide among people and all different animals resides in our better-order intellectual techniques. Studies in cognition have of past due been in particular focused on how humans make selections—including through rapid or gradual questioning. Speedy thinking is intuitive, computerized, and nearly impossible to exchange off, relying on heuristic methods to return to a "right enough" choice. By way of contrast, slow questioning takes an exceptional deal of time and strength to study all available information before accomplishing a conclusion. Cognitive biases consisting of stereotyping and self-serving biases, which include the perception that one is above average on many a trait, have also been isolated and explored by behavioral scientists in an try to help humans assume extra objectively.

Memories aren't impartial and accurate recordings of what happened in the past. They can be formed using present experiences, desires, and fears. It's additionally viable to unintentionally create a fake reminiscence to fulfill a mental want. Extraordinary styles of memory can consist of the sensory, short time period, and long time, and the manner that reminiscence is stored will have a profound effect on how we analyze and observe know-how.

Metacognition is the act of considering one's very own intellectual strategies. Metacognitive focus permits humans to perceive, display, and uproot negative self-communicate and self-proscribing beliefs, and to be efficient in intention-placing and task execution. Thinking about and difficult one's own thinking is at the heart of many sorts of remedy, which includes CBT.

Neuroscience is the technological know-how of neurons that's the lively factor, or the aspect answerable for questioning, performing, and perceiving in our brains. For greater than a century people had been analyzing neurons and running out the biology of neurons and the way they work, and grow, and engage with each other. Frequently searching at experiments with slices of mind in a dish, operating at how neurons work on the microscopic stage. In parallel, additionally, for extra than a century, there's been the study of psychology and behaviors, so how we behave, understand, and recollect matters, and how we act in our each day existence. At a sure point, neuroscience and the examination of cognition started to become interrelated in which humans started to recognize that our brains are what generates our behaviors and that it's the neurons that are the key elements in our brains that do this.

Professor of Neurology, Neurosurgery, and Biomedical Engineering at McGill university Sylvain Baillet on mind "software program", mind mapping, and neuronal interactions.

Basically, the sphere of cognitive neuroscience slowly came into being where people started to examine the premise in the behaviors of person neurons and structures of neurons in the brain, of our personal actual behaviors, mind, and cognition. There's an intersection among the form of molecular, biological neuroscience, and cognitive psychology, the observance of behaviors, which was called cognitive neuroscience. Early experiments with the aid of human beings recording from person neurons in animals, or possibly analyzing how the harm to parts of the brain in human neurological sufferers is related to behaviors. For instance, what you can and couldn't do once you damaged a selected part of the brain or what unique neuron is regarded to be represented within the mind – animal models, for example. This was the start of the area of cognitive neuroscience.

Perhaps in the overdue sixties – early seventies this became a real topic and slowly started to amplify. By using the nineteen nineties it became a large subject matter; it became clear that almost all psychology departments would want to have some information of the connection to the mind of the cognitive things they studied. And almost all structures neuroscience departments that have been inquisitive about the biology of neurons could want to recognize something approximately what they definitely do, how they generate brains and behaviors, and perception.

Inside the mid-nineties, the university college London determined to set up an institute of cognitive neuroscience, in which we are now. In this US, it was the first institute of cognitive neuroscience to carry collectively human beings from psychology, neurology, and neuroscience. They may all be inside the identical construction to attempt to apprehend what they had in commonplace about their expertise of how the brain labored and how it helped us to behave, understand, don't forget, and think. Now there are many subfields within cognitive neuroscience. Human beings are inquisitive about how we understand the arena around us, inquisitive about vision, hearing, contact, and additionally, of course, in movement, how we move, and motor neuroscience. In the center, human beings are interested in better cognitive notions, for example, reminiscence, planning, and choice-making. The conventional psychology department could have an interest in all of these unique regions. Now human beings are inquisitive about how the brain generates those different components of cognition. We see cognitive neuroscience as a hobby in these kinds of one-of-a-kind areas, too. We see a mainly thrilling era of latest thoughts coming all of the manners from know-how how neurons in the visual cortex constitute what we're seeing, pioneered by Hubel and Wiesel's work in the 60s.

Going all the manner via to motor neuroscience and

understanding how the hobby of neurons inside the motor cortex, for example, through the backbone sincerely controls muscle contractions and lets us transport. Then within the center, there's the huge vicinity of cognition among perception and action which includes how we don't forget things which have befell to us earlier than and how which could inform what we're going to do subsequent, and how we can think about the future, plan we're going to do. And I haven't even noted language which for people is a very important area, even though it's a bit more difficult to look at it in animals.

These days we see folks that they have come into the sector of cognitive neuroscience, neither from a widespread psychology historical past nor from neurology, or, possibly, biology. We do see human beings from all of these regions coming into cognitive neuroscience, however additionally folks who studied physics or engineering. Make it easy for them to layout experiments or use new technology which can be coming online. So, one of the drivers of the growth in cognitive neuroscience, in addition to the realization that the brain was the key to understanding many aspects of behaviors and cognition, is the improvement of the era. We see that during many one-of-a-kind regions.

For instance, in simple neuroscience, we see molecular biology and ontogenetic strategies that permit us to affect the activity of styles of various styles of neurons within the brain and we will see how that performs out in behaviors, and we can file from that sort of activity. And in human cognitive neuroscience, purposeful mind imaging has given us a window into looking at the metabolic activity and how it varies throughout the mind whilst humans are considering different things, or perceiving different things, or maybe acting, so long as they don't move their head an excessive amount of. So given this technological enhance there is additionally a role for laptop scientists and engineers and physicists and so forth to come into this area to make the most of the new generation that's permitting new experiments and consequently enabling the whole subject to continue to increase and make discoveries.

The massive advances in cognitive neuroscience have come via people from exceptional disciplines running together. Definitely, initially, there weren't definitely many departments of cognitive neuroscience and there weren't students who were educated in cognitive neuroscience. manifestly, cognitive scientists and neurologists, people who knew the way to do purposeful neuroimaging, neuroscientists had to come together to have interaction, to discover new motives that might be manufactured from cognition and behaviors are given what we recognize about what's taking place inside the mind. However, that would type of characterizing the kingdom of the field within the Nineties.

Now there are many cognitive neuroscience applications and there are students who have executed stages, or masters' guides, or PhDs in cognitive neuroscience. So many sorts of current researchers perhaps would nevertheless keep in mind themselves to be a psychologist, or a neuroscientist, or a physiologist. But now they're able to use several techniques that permit them to study behaviors and cognition at the equal time as factors of what's occurring within the mind. in recent times, the modern-day cognitive neuroscientist is an interdisciplinary employee, however, it's becoming more of a mature subject so that you could say which you're just a cognitive neuroscientist and that is your field.

There are several exciting traits in cognitive neuroscience in the meanwhile that clearly exemplify the contemporary path of the sphere of know-how the brain and behaviors. This kind of is widely mental health. For the long term, human beings understood psychiatry and medical psychology in terms of remedies and drugs that show up to work and there's a protracted record of experience with them. However the real mechanism of the way that remedies certainly modifications the behaviors or the elements of cognition which might be dysfunctional isn't nicely understood, what that mechanism isn't always simply recognized. Lately, there's been a trend in the direction of trying to recognize what these mechanisms are both healthful, typically processing humans and how they've gone incorrect in certain psychiatric or neurological conditions. So that we can try to apprehend behavioral interventions and pharmacological interventions in phrases of the neural mechanisms which you need to restore or that you want to alternate back to how they must be. This region of mental fitness is becoming more of technological know-how, greater like neuroscience than a sensible enjoy based field like medicine.

Neurobiologist Sophie Scott on human speech, exaggerating gender variations, and the perception of voice information and the truth that we can now document and manipulate the interest of neurons and synapses within the mind with extraordinary specificity, regularly in animal models, means that we can genuinely look at the neural mechanisms of cognition in a manner that we could not earlier than. So it's possible to, as an instance, reactivate the neurons that have been active in a specific scenario and display that the mouse, in this situation, thinks that it is returned in that state of affairs again. So the molecular biology has technological advances has also made a huge improvement on the form of the microscopic stage that informs cognition. Similarly on the macroscopic stage what goes incorrect with international cognition is starting to be understood in phrases of the mechanisms that appear within the mind concerning actual neurons and synapses.

The destiny for cognitive neuroscience is to make an actual practical effect on treatment in psychiatry, intellectual health, and neurology. Preferably, beginning to apprehend what the neural mechanisms are behind everyday cognition and how components of cognition can go wrong need to truly begin to impact on treatment and remedy. In the next ten years hopefully,,,,,, we'll see a mixture of intellectual health practices, psychiatry, and cognitive neuroscience, as we saw among psychology, cognitive technology, and neuroscience in cognitive neuroscience. It will optimistically begin to put this form of mental fitness medicine firm mechanistic heritage in preference to having to depend basically on treatments that we recognize work, but we don't clearly recognize why they work.

Types of Cognitive approaches

- Attention: attention is a cognitive method that lets human beings focus on a particular stimulus inside the environment.
- Language: Language and language improvement are cognitive procedures that involve the capacity to

understand and express the mind thru spoken and written phrases. It allows us to talk with others and plays a vital role in ideas.

• Getting to know: getting to know requires cognitive tactics worried in taking in new things, synthesizing information, and integrating it with prior understanding.

• Reminiscence: memory is a crucial cognitive technique that permits people to encode, store, and retrieve records. It's an important element inside the getting-to-know procedure and lets human beings maintain understanding approximately the world and their private histories.

• Perception: perception is a cognitive process that permits humans to take in statistics thru their senses (sensation) after which make use of these statistics to reply and engage with the sector.

• Thought: thought is an important part of each cognitive method. It lets human beings engage in choice-making, problem-solving, and higher reasoning.

Cognitive procedures affect everything of lifestyles, from school to work to relationships. Some precise uses for those cognitive processes include the following. gaining knowledge of calls for being capable of absorbing new facts, form new memories, and make connections with different things that you already know. Researchers and educators use their expertise in those cognitive methods to assist create instructive substances to help humans analyze new principles. Memory is a primary subject matter of interest within the area of cognitive psychology. How we keep in mind, what we recall, and what we overlook display a terrific deal about how the cognitive approaches function. while humans frequently consider reminiscence as being much like a video digicam, cautiously recording and cataloging lifestyles activities, and storing them away for later don't forget, research has located that memory is plenty greater complicated. Whenever human beings make any sort of decision, it involves making judgments about things they've processed. It would involve evaluating new facts to earlier knowledge, integrating new facts into present thoughts, or even replacing antique understanding with new knowledge before creating a preference. The cognitive procedures have an extensive-ranging effect that affects the entirety from daily existence to standard fitness. As you're taking in sensations from the sector around you, the facts which you see, hear, taste, touch, and odor should first be transformed into signals that your brain can recognize. The perceptual process permits you to absorb sensory information and convert it right into a signal that your mind can recognize and act upon. The arena is complete with an infinite quantity of sensory stories. To make that means out of all this incoming data, it's far critical on your mind to reduce your enjoyment of the world all the way down to the fundamentals. You take into account the entirety, so events are reduced all the way down to the vital concepts and ideas which you need. Similar to reducing statistics to make it extra memorable and understandable, humans additionally complex on those reminiscences as they reconstruct them. In a few cases, this elaboration takes place whilst people are suffering to keep in mind something. Whilst the facts cannot be recalled, the mind sometimes fills inside the lacking statistics with whatever seems to match.

Cognition includes now not only the things that move on interior our heads but also how these thoughts and intellectual processes influence our actions. Our attention to the arena around us, memories of beyond activities, know-how of language, judgments approximately how the world works, and abilities to remedy problems all make contributions to how we behave and engage with our surrounding surroundings. Cognitive procedures are encouraged with the aid of a range of things including genetics and studies. At the same time as you can't trade your genetics, there are matters that you can do to shield and maximize your cognitive talents:

- Live healthfully. Lifestyle factors which include eating wholesome and getting ordinary exercise could have an impact on your cognitive functioning.
- Suppose significantly. Question your assumptions and ask questions on your mind, beliefs, and conclusions.
- Live curiously and hold mastering. One superb way to flex your cognitive capabilities is to preserve difficult yourself to analyze extra approximately the world.
- Bypass multitasking. While it would appear to be doing several things right now could help you get finished quicker, research has proven it surely decreases each productivity and work ability Pitfalls

it is vital to take into account that those cognitive approaches are complex and frequently imperfect. A number of the feasible pitfalls which could affect cognition consist of:

- Issues with attention: Selective attention is a restricted resource, so there is a range of factors that can make it tough to focus on the whole lot in your environment. Attentional blink, for example, happens while you are so focused on one thing that you completely pass over something else happening right in front of you.
- Memory troubles and limitations: quick-time period

reminiscence is fairly short, normally lasting just twenty to thirty seconds. Lengthy-time period reminiscence may be enormously solid and enduring, however, with memories lasting years or even many years. Reminiscence can also be tremendously fragile and fallible. Occasionally we forget about it, and other times we're a problem with incorrect information effects that could even lead to the formation of fake memories.

• Cognitive biases: Cognitive biases are systematic errors in questions related to how people procedure and interpret facts about the arena. The affirmation bias is one commonplace example that entails most effectively being attentive to information that aligns along with your existing beliefs at the same time as ignoring evidence that does not support your views.

Studying issues are considered a type of neurodevelopmental ailment. Neurodevelopmental issues are neurologically based totally situations that seem early in adolescence, usually before college entry. These problems impair the development of private, social, educational, and/or occupational functioning and typically involve problems with the purchase, retention, or application of particular capabilities or sets of data. The disorders may additionally contain disorder in interest, memory, notion, language, hassle-solving, or social interaction. Other common neurodevelopmental issues consist of attention-deficit/hyperactivity ailment, autism spectrum problems, and highbrow disability.

Unique gaining knowledge of issues affect the capacity to

- Understand or use spoken language
- Recognize or use written language
- Recognize and use numbers and cause using mathematical standards
- Coordinate actions
- Focus attention on a challenge

Accordingly, those disorders contain problems in studying, mathematics, spelling, written expression or handwriting, and knowledge or the usage of verbal and nonverbal language. Maximum mastering issues are complex or mixed, with deficits in a couple of devices.

Among students receiving special schooling offerings, 34% (or about 5% of all students) had specific getting-to-know disabilities (1). Boys with learning issues outnumber ladies even though formal diagnoses can also assist a few children to get assistance, characterizing one-of-a-kind capabilities as disorders dangers musicalizing them as in some way pathological. The important element is to identify folks who need distinctive or extra assist mastering and offer access to the assistance they want.

Getting to know problems may be congenital or obtained. No unmarried cause has been defined, however, neurologic deficits are presumed to be worried whether or now not different neurologic manifestations (ie, aside from the studying disease) are present. Genetic influences are regularly implicated. Other feasible causes include

- Maternal contamination or use of poisonous drugs throughout pregnancy
- Complications during being pregnant or shipping (eg, recognizing, toxemia, prolonged labor, precipitous shipping)
- Neonatal troubles (eg, prematurity, low beginning

weight, excessive jaundice, perinatal asphyxia, publish maturity, breathing distress)

Capability postnatal factors consist of exposure to environmental pollution (eg, lead), vital worried device infections, cancers and their remedies, trauma, undernutrition, and severe social isolation or deprivation.

Signs and symptoms

Children with getting to know issues typically have at the least common intelligence, even though such problems can occur in children with decrease cognitive characteristics properly.

signs and signs and symptoms of excessive learning issues can also occur at an early age, however most moderate to moderate gaining knowledge of issues are not diagnosed until faculty age, whilst the trials of educational studying are encountered.

Educational impairments

Affected children can also have problems getting to know the alphabet and can be behind schedule in paired associative mastering (eg, shade naming, labeling, counting, letter naming). Speech notion can be limited, language can be discovered at a slower rate, and vocabulary can be decreased. Affected children might not understand what's examine, have very messy handwriting or keep a pencil awkwardly, have trouble organizing or beginning obligations or retelling a story in sequential order, or confuse math symbols and misinterpret numbers.

Government feature impairments

Disturbances or delays in expressive language or listening comprehension are predictors of academic problems beyond the preschool years. Memory can be faulty, inclusive of brief-time period and long-time period memory, reminiscence use (eg, rehearsal), and verbal take into account or retrieval.

Problems might also arise in conceptualizing, abstracting, generalizing, reasoning, and organizing and making plans information for hassle solving. People with executive function problems often have issues organizing and finishing assignments.

Visible notion and auditory processing troubles might also arise; they encompass problems in spatial cognition and orientation (eg, object localization, spatial reminiscence, cognizance of position and area), visible interest and memory, and sound discrimination and evaluation.

Behavior issues

A few children with learning disabilities have difficulty following social conventions (eg, taking turns, standing too close to the listener, not understanding jokes); those problems are frequently components of slight autism spectrum issues as properly.

Brief interest span, motor restlessness, first-rate motor problems (eg, negative printing and copying), and variability in performance and behaviors over the years are different early signs and symptoms.

Problems with impulse control, non–aim-directed behaviors and over interest, field problems, aggressiveness, withdrawal and avoidance behaviors, excessive shyness, and excessive fear might also occur. Mastering disabilities and attention-deficit/hyperactivity sickness (ADHD) frequently occur collectively.

Prognosis

- Cognitive, instructional, scientific, and psychological critiques
- Scientific standards

Kids with learning issues are usually identified while a discrepancy is identified among academic potential and educational overall performance. Speech and language, cognitive, instructional, scientific, and psychologic reviews are important for determining deficiencies in talents and cognitive techniques. Social and emotional-behavioral reviews also are vital for making plans to remedy and tracking the development.

Assessment

The cognitive assessment generally includes verbal and nonverbal intelligence trying out and is typically completed by way of a faculty psychologist. Psychoeducational testing may help describe the kid's desired manner of processing information (eg, holistically or analytically, visually or aurally). Neuropsychologic assessment is especially beneficial in kids with recognized critical frightened device injury or contamination to map the regions of the mind that correspond to particular functional strengths and weaknesses. Speech and language opinions establish the integrity of comprehension and language use, phonologic processing, and verbal reminiscence and can also examine pragmatic (social) language.

Academic assessment and overall performance assessment using teachers' observations of lecture room behaviors and resolution of academic overall performance are important. Reading evaluations degree competencies in word interpreting and recognition, comprehension, and fluency. Writing samples ought to be acquired to assess the spelling, syntax, and fluency of ideas. Mathematical capability needs to be assessed in phrases of computation capabilities, the expertise of operations, the know-how of ideas, and interpretation of "word problems."

Clinical assessment includes detailed own family history, the child's scientific history, a physical exam, and a neurologic or neurodevelopmental examination to search for underlying disorders. Although rare, physical abnormalities and neurologic symptoms may also imply medically treatable reasons for gaining knowledge of disabilities. Gross motor coordination troubles may also indicate neurologic deficits or neurodevelopmental delays. The developmental degree is evaluated in line with standardized criteria.

The psychologic assessment facilitates perceive ADHD, behavior disorder, anxiety issues, despair, and poor self-esteem, which frequently accompany and should be differentiated from gaining knowledge of disabilities. Mindset towards faculty, motivation, peer relationships, and self-assurance are assessed.

Clinical standards

Diagnosis of getting to know disorders is made clinically based on criteria inside the Diagnostic and Statistical Manual of mental issues, fifth version (DSM-5), and calls for proof that at the least one of the following has been present for six months notwithstanding centered intervention:

- Faulty, gradual, and/or effortful word analyzing
- Issue know-how the meaning of written material
- Difficulty spelling
- Problem writing (eg, more than one grammar and punctuation mistakes; ideas no longer expressed simply)
- Problem mastering variety feel (eg, know-how the

relative magnitude and relationship of numbers; in older youngsters, issue doing simple calculations)
• Difficulty with mathematical reasoning (eg, using mathematical ideas to solve problems).
Talents must be extensively below the level predicted for the kid's age and additionally substantially impair overall performance at faculty or in everyday activities. Also, the difficulties ought to now not to be better accounted for with the aid of highbrow incapacity or other neurodevelopmental issues.

Treatment
• Academic management
• Medical, behavioral, and psychologic therapy
• On occasion drug remedy

Remedy of mastering issues centers on academic management however may also involve clinical, behavioral, and psychologic remedy. Effective teaching programs may additionally take a remedial, compensatory, or strategic (ie, coaching the kid the way to examine) technique. A mismatch of instructional methods and a child's mastering sickness and gaining knowledge of choice aggravates the disability.

A few kids require specialized preparation in the simplest region while they keep wai forting ordinary training. Different kids need separate and intense educational programs. Optimally and as required using US regulation, affected children ought to take part as plenty as possible in inclusive instructions with peers who do now not have got to know disabilities.

Pills minimally affect educational success, intelligence, and widespread mastering ability, even though certain pills (eg, psychostimulants, along with methylphenidate and numerous amphetamine preparations) can also decorate attention and attention, permitting youngsters to respond more effectively to education.

Many popular treatments and therapies (eg, casting off food components, the usage of antioxidants or megadoses of nutrients, patterning by sensory stimulation and passive movement, sensory integrative therapy through postural sports, auditory nerve training, and optometric education to remedy visible-perceptual and sensorimotor coordination strategies) are unproved.

Forms of gaining knowledge of and Developmental Disabilities

Are you concerned about how your infant functions both at home and in school? Is he or she lagging in the back of his friends or older siblings at a comparable age? Are ordinary developmental milestones related to on foot, language, or exceptional motor abilities ignored or delayed? Then talk over with your pediatrician in Las Vegas, NV, Dr. Nasreen Majid, or Dr. Susan Hirata. Their know-how in diagnosing and treating chronic and acute infection and in tracking your children's intellectual, bodily, and emotional improvement assist you to care for your teen as he or she navigates the challenges of early life.

Kinds of mastering disabilities

Researchers at the countrywide Institute of fitness nation that in reality due to the fact a baby struggles with a mastering challenge or area of observing, this always does now not suggest a studying disability. however, if the problem continues over time, your pediatrician in Las Vegas, NV, may additionally suggest extra testing from the school psychologist or an unbiased professional, including an audiologist or neuropsychologist.

Common mastering disabilities affect how a teen speaks, listens, movements pays attention, calculates,,,,,, and examines. You may have heard of a number of the following disabilities:

• Dyslexia affects handwriting, math computation, telling time, sequential reminiscence, and analyzing comprehension.

• Dyscalculia expresses in handwriting this is illegible for the child's age.

• Dysgraphia is a math/arithmetic incapacity.

• Dyspraxia entails noise and contact sensitivity, negative coordination, and venture company and balance issues.

A few lesser-known disabilities are imperative Auditory Processing sickness, in which a toddler struggles to interpret the sounds, and ideas he or she hears, and add and ADHD which combines behavioral abnormalities with gaining knowledge of issues. Trouble concentrating and finishing obligations at the side of hyperactivity are commonplace to both interest Deficit ailment and attention Deficit Hyperactivity disorder in varying degrees.

Kinds of developmental disabilities

Down syndrome, Cerebral Palsy, autism, and hearing/vision loss rank high in incidence amongst American children. Crossing socioeconomic, ethnic, and racial obstacles, these disabilities vary from moderate to profound and affect a full fifteen percentage of younger individuals, say the facilities for ailment manipulate in Atlanta.

Just like learning disabilities, developmental problems may

additionally change how an infant learns, speaks, and methods the sector around him, but additionally, those problems impact mobility, impartial functioning, and the ability to earn a living. Many experts in academia, remedy, and psychology link those disabilities to birth defects, prenatal strain, dietary deficits, and environmental toxins (along with lead).

Developmental disabilities are a collection of conditions due to an impairment in physical, getting to know, language, or behaviors areas. Those situations start at some stage in the developmental duration, can also impact everyday functioning, and generally final during a person's lifetime. Abilities along with taking the first step, smiling for the primary time, and waving "bye-bye" are referred to as developmental milestones. Children attain milestones in how they play, learn, talk, behave, and flow (for example, crawling and taking walks).

Children develop at their own tempo, so it's impossible to tell exactly whilst a child will study a given talent. However, the developmental milestones give a trendy concept of the adjustments to count on as a baby gets older.

As a discernment, you know your child satisfactory. if your toddler isn't assembly the milestones for his or her age, or in case you think there can be a hassle with the manner your toddler performs, learns, speaks, acts, and moves communicate to your baby's medical doctor and share your concerns. Don't wait. Performing early could make an actual difference!

A baby's increase and improvement are accompanied via a partnership among mother and father and health care professionals. At each properly-baby visit, the physician appears for developmental delays or issues and talks with the dad and mom about any issues the parents might have. This is referred to as developmental monitoring.

Any problems observed at some point of developmental monitoring ought to be observed up with developmental screening. Developmental screening is a brief check to inform if a toddler is studying basic abilities when she or he needs to, or if there are delays.

If a baby has a developmental postpone, it's miles critical to get assistance as quickly as feasible. Early identity and intervention will have a giant impact on a toddler's capacity to research new abilities, in addition, to reducing the want for high-priced interventions over time.

Causes and hazard elements

Developmental disabilities begin anytime at some point of the developmental period and usually close at some point in someone's lifetime. Most developmental disabilities start before a child is born, but some can show up after beginning due to harm, infection, or different elements.

Most developmental disabilities are thought to be due to a complicated blend of things. these elements consist of genetics; parental fitness and behaviors (along with smoking and ingesting) at some stage in pregnancy; headaches at some stage in birth; infections the mom would possibly have during pregnancy or the child may have very early in existence; and publicity of the mother or toddler to high stages of environmental pollutants, which include lead. For some developmental disabilities, consisting of fetal alcohol syndrome, which is caused by consuming alcohol during being pregnant, we recognize the motive. However, for maximum, we don't.

Following are a few examples of what we recognize

approximately unique developmental disabilities:

• At least 25% of listening to loss amongst infants is due to maternal infections at some point of pregnancy, along with cytomegalovirus (CMV) infection; headaches after beginning; and head trauma.

• A number of the most not unusual acknowledged causes of highbrow incapacity consist of fetal alcohol syndrome; genetic and chromosomal situations, inclusive of Down syndrome and fragile X syndrome; and certain infections at some point of being pregnant.

• Children who have a sibling with autism are at a better risk of additionally having autism spectrum disorder.

• Low birth weight, premature birth, multiple starts, and infections throughout being pregnant are related to an extended chance for lots of developmental disabilities.

• Untreated newborn jaundice (high levels of bilirubin inside the blood throughout the first few days after delivery) can cause a form of brain damage referred to as kernicterus. Children with kernicterus are more likely to have cerebral palsy, listening to and vision issues, and problems with their enamel. Early detection and remedy of latest-born jaundice can prevent kernicterus.

The study to discover early development (SEED) is a multi-year look funded by CDC. It's far currently the largest examination inside the USA to assist identify elements that may put youngsters at risk for autism spectrum issues and other developmental disabilities.

Developmental disabilities occur among all racial, ethnic, and socioeconomic organizations. Recent estimates within the United States display that approximately one in six, or approximately 17%, of kids elderly via seventeen years,, have one or more developmental disabilities, which

include:
- ADHD,
- Autism spectrum sickness,
- Cerebral palsy,
- Listening to loss,
- Highbrow incapacity pdf icon,
- Getting to know disability,
- Imaginative and prescient impairment pdf icon, and
- Different developmental delays.2

For over a decade, CDC's Autism and Developmental Disabilities Monitoring (ADDM) network has been tracking the wide variety and characteristics of youngsters with autism spectrum disorder, cerebral palsy, and highbrow incapacity in several numerous communities at some stage in America.

Living with a developmental incapacity

children and adults with disabilities need fitness care and health packages for the same motives absolutely everyone else does—to live properly, active, and a part of the network. Having an incapacity does now not imply a person is not healthful or that he or she cannot be healthy. Being healthful approach the equal factor for each person—getting and staying well so we can lead full, active lives. That consists of having the equipment and data to make wholesome picks and knowing how to prevent contamination. some health situations, consisting of allergies, gastrointestinal symptoms, eczema,, and skin hypersensitive reactions, and migraine complications, have been determined to be extra not unusual among kids with developmental disabilities. Consequently, children with developmental disabilities need to see a health care company frequently. Even though there may be more records than ever earlier than regarding formative years developmental and mastering disorders there are nevertheless so many things we don't quite apprehend and there's also a lot of misinformation available. The purpose of your pediatrician is to offer you all of the information you and your infant want to apprehend their gaining knowledge of or developmental disorder and the handiest treatments and interventions available.